Achieving Against the Odds

In the series

The New Academy,

edited by Elizabeth Kamarck Minnich

Achieving Against the Odds

How Academics Become Teachers of Diverse Students

Edited by

ESTHER KINGSTON-MANN
AND TIM SIEBER

TEMPLE UNIVERSITY PRESS
Philadelphia

Temple University Press, Philadelphia 19122
Copyright © 2001 by Temple University
All rights reserved
Published 2001
Printed in the United States of America

Library of Congress Cataloging-in-Publication Data

Achieving against the odds : how academics become teachers of diverse students / edited by Esther Kingston-Mann and Tim Sieber.
    p. cm. — (The new academy)
  Includes bibliographical references and index.
  ISBN 1-56639-850-9 (cloth : alk. paper) — ISBN 1-56639-851-7 (pbk. : alk. paper)
  1. Minority college students—Massachusetts—Boston—Case studies. 2. Multicultural education—Massachusetts—Boston—Case studies. 3. College environment—Massa-chusetts—Boston. 4. Pluralism (Social sciences). 5. University of Massachusetts at Boston. I. Title: How academics become teachers of diverse students. II. Kingston-Mann, Esther. III. Sieber, R. Timothy. IV. Series.

LC3727.A34 2001
378.1'9829—dc21   00-060754

*Dedicated to all of our students,
past, present, and future*

Contents

Foreword

ACHIEVING AGAINST THE ODDS takes us into some of today's classrooms, the heartlands of higher education, where we encounter vividly
some of the inherited and contemporary purposes of higher education as
they tangle with each other—among them, conserving a dominant culture; developing critical consciousness; producing new scholarship,
including some that critiques, challenges, and reconfigures prevailing
fields and "canons"; training a future professoriate; effectively teaching a
highly diverse citizenry; preparing people for jobs, professions, *and* "the
examined life"; nurturing the development of students of many ages and
backgrounds; engaging scholars with the pressing issues of the day;
working cooperatively with government and business; providing a space
for learning free of other pressures; and more. A brew of purposes such
as these creates a high tension today that can lead to extraordinary, transformative learning, but it can also lead to a collapse into the kinds of divisions and silences that are as tragic as they are familiar.

The authors gathered in this book write as scholar-teachers who have
accepted the confusing challenges of our times, first of all by opening
themselves to the calling of welcoming fully every student who comes
to them. This centering on the classroom, where educational purposes
must move from the level of abstraction and rhetoric to that of particular practices (often on the level of, What do I do *now?*), gives the book
its special purchase and intense liveliness. Practicing teaching as an art
predicated on the respectful welcoming of all students is no small feat,
not even for professors who have long since recognized that education
in and for a would-be democracy requires that this feat be attempted. It
never was easy, not even when most students and almost all faculty
members came from more similar backgrounds because "others"—the
majority of the populace, women from all groups alone comprising 51
percent—were excluded or marginalized and silenced. It is most
assuredly not an easy matter today, as the demographics of the United
States change rapidly in a transfiguring world, and curricular changes

supported by an extraordinary outpouring of boundary-crossing scholarship are both called for and strongly resisted.

A teacher who would welcome students into the creation of a fully shareable class culture and experience needs special skills today (as always, but also in ways that differ significantly). This teacher needs to be open personally and intellectually; to be gifted and practiced in the art of asking good questions that may not have suggested themselves before; to be able to hear through each student's words to their intended meanings, however startling and, sometimes, initially troubling; and to be skilled in the arts of translation essential to holding strikingly different students and texts and issues together in one multivoiced discussion. Hard enough, but even more so when, increasingly, the individuals in the classroom community-in-the-making bring with them—as intimate aspects of who they are—what the world has defined them to be, so that with them, the schisms that most painfully divide and differentiate our still radically unjust world also enter the classroom. Teaching then becomes challenging in ways still often seen as public and political, and thus as not "properly" academic.

Hence the storms of controversy and intense eddies of concern that characterize discussions of teaching, learning, curricula, and assessment today, when so much more of the world is entering our classrooms. In *Achieving Against the Odds*, however, what we find is that "politicized" learning situations can provide opportunities to overcome many kinds of old divisions and the tangling of purposes they create. When we recognize that public life, in all its diversities and with all its struggles, is already in our classrooms and can be denied only by shutting our eyes, ears, hearts, and minds, we are, it turns out, forced out of old ruts of many kinds. Among them are complaints about students that were never apt but that managed to persist anyway. Not so long ago, faculty members used to fuss endlessly about "apathetic students" while discussing how to arouse their interest without degenerating into mere entertainment mode (which used to make me wonder if being unable to interest students was not being protectively conflated with being A Serious Professor). Well, apathy is *not* a problem for teachers who recognize both the reality of and the need to respond to changes in the populations of students walking into their classes. Apathy is also not a problem in the classes taught today by teachers who have kept up with the burgeoning literatures in virtually all fields that critique, challenge, and transform what once passed as the best and soundest scholarship. It is not even a problem in some courses taught in the same old ways using the same old materials as if nothing had changed, because today's students are very likely to challenge such teaching and materials.

As a result of the world being in our classrooms in all its rich messiness now, faculty anxieties and endless shop talk are far more likely to concern how to deal with identity issues, confrontations between students, and searing confessions of painful lives that are met sometimes, terrifyingly, by raw prejudice and sometimes by hurtful ignorance. The teachers who have spoken so honestly about their classroom experiences in this gathering of reflective practitioners' stories focus on those hard, morally fraught, politically pressing, and therefore profoundly intellectually challenging issues. In their classes, the sparks caused by connecting across differences that until recently were both determinedly suppressed and maintained jolt both students and teachers into wide-awake thinking. This, one would think, is what should happen in good classes, but while we thought we wanted nonapathetic, engaged students, we weren't imagining students who would confront each other and argue with "the classics" as well as with newer scholarship and even with The Professor. It is as if the dominant culture, which long virtually deified Socrates, has finally realized what he meant by saying that thinking begins when we are stung awake by a biting fly or jolted by an electric eel.

Similarly, we are being jolted into the realization that genuine connections between theory and practice are not all easy to live with and think through. As several of these authors tell us, their students do fine with, say, sociological theories about socioeconomic stratification—until personal experiences voiced by classmates of persistent racialized and gendered class barriers, fear of sexual differences, hard immigrant experiences, and more are connected with those theories. This kind of immediacy can produce protective, even hostile, reactions, particularly when the professor her- or himself evidently embodies a nonprivileged "kind" or has in some way self-identified with a "kind" not yet familiar to some students as allowably authoritative or even properly visible in public at all. When connections between "them" and "us," theoretical constructs and lived experiences, are made, as today they are in such classrooms of teachers and students as we meet in this volume, sparks fly—lives, identities, meanings, beliefs, values are suddenly on the line.

This happens when diverse students speak truly and are heard; it also happens when a great deal of contemporary scholarship is taught. Theories, studies, stories, and artworks that no longer perpetuate the old partial, hence faulty, generalizations and universals that used to conflate all of humankind with a very small group (taken to be and represent Man, Who is Rational) touch on the realities of human lives. When they do so, intense, passionate intellectual inquiry results, and it bursts out of classrooms. These teachers tell story after story of late-night calls from students still engaged by what came up in class, of letters and calls and visits that continue sometimes for years. No apathy here; these students are examining their lives and can no longer be stopped.

Professors have long said that this is just what we wanted to happen, but nevertheless we have found ourselves ill prepared for it. It is not just that we were not taught how to teach in graduate school, another common plaint. It is that we did not learn democratic arts, mores, ethics, and, crucially, ways of thinking that bridge these skills with scholarship. And when we begin to learn those essential ways of being among and thinking with diverse people in the miniature publics of today's classrooms, we bump into the systematic and attitudinal barriers of our fields and institutions. The heroic teachers in this volume who, like figures such as Socrates, do not stay within bounds but talk and think with whomever comes, going wherever the thinking goes, are without doubt loved by some of their students and colleagues, but they are also without doubt suspect to many others. Remarkably, this has not stopped them; their intellectual and political skills have helped them negotiate in larger publics as well. And through it all, because of it all, they never cease questioning. They tell us here of the times they have failed to act in a difficult class as they would like to have acted, just as they also tell us what they have sometimes painfully learned and what they are trying now. They neither pose as experts nor dwell on their successes. Their interest, clearly, is in reflective analysis of what they are trying to do, how it goes or doesn't go, what it means, how they could do better. Their Socratic wisdom, we could say—remembering that Plato called Socrates the best citizen Athens ever had, just as the oracle called him the wisest—lies, like his, in knowing that they do not know and in finding that quite wonderful.

Truly active, lifelong learners, these scholar-teachers. And this, finally, is one of the lessons they most want to share with us—that scholarship is practiced in the classroom and in campus life as well as in the library, at the desk, at conferences, online with peers and research sources, in the field, and in the laboratory. In this volume, we are reminded of just how much there is to learn with and from diverse students actively engaged with scholarship. These scholar-teachers' questions, reactions, analyses, storytelling, challenges, and confirmations take scholarship out into the world where the students are and thereby provide crucial tests of that world as well as contributory, even transformative, perspectives on it. Good teachers have long said that they learn from their students. What we need now to realize is that they don't say so merely out of a kind of (too often slightly condescending) kindliness and generosity. Scholarship enclosed within professional discourses is not the only kind; teachers learning with, from, and for publics of learners of many sorts are also doing scholarship, challenging and enriching both the store and the practice of meaningful human knowledge.

Like cities and settlements located at crossroads where many lives, languages, and traditions meet, some of today's classrooms have become vibrant centers of complex learning. Those who have had such invigorating experiences do not miss the old walls, the old divisions, which they now know to be barriers to full and free thinking that no aspiring democracy should allow.

ELIZABETH KAMARCK MINNICH

Acknowledgments

WE THANK Jackie Cornog for her able administrative assistance in helping to bring the book to final form. We also gratefully acknowledge the permission of the National Education Association to reprint portions of Peter Kiang's "Crossing Boundaries, Building Community," *Thought & Action* 15 (1): 48–60 (1999).

We owe special gratitude to our students and, with the exception of Chapter 6, always use pseudonyms when referring to them as individuals.

Achieving Against the Odds

ESTHER KINGSTON-MANN AND TIM SIEBER

Introduction

Achieving Against the Odds

LIKE STRANGERS in a strange land, today's increasingly diverse and financially burdened students enter the world of higher education intent on succeeding at academic institutions that were originally designed for culturally homogenous, middle-class populations. Throughout their college careers, they are expected to learn from faculty trained primarily as researchers rather than as teachers. Student dropout rates and levels of faculty burnout are high—a phenomenon leading some conservative educators and politicians to demand that higher education be saved by eliminating "unqualified" students or their professors. However, once we consider the possibility that neither students nor faculty have exhausted their potential for significant growth and development by the time they meet in the college classroom, new and better solutions emerge.

In the essays that follow, scholar-teachers from a wide range of disciplines address their encounters with today's students and document a complex and challenging process of pedagogical transformation. Like most faculty, we are veterans of graduate schools that failed to emphasize or value the acquisition of teaching skills. Academically trained as researchers in history, anthropology, language and literature, psychology, theology, sociology, and political science, we had no choice—if we took seriously our work as teachers—but to become autodidacts in the field of pedagogy.

But we were autodidacts of a particular sort. Many of us were ourselves the untraditional students that sociologist Patricia Hill Collins has described as "outsiders within" the academy.[1] Diverse in our cultural backgrounds, we could not disentangle our teaching priorities from our own life experiences as people of color, women, gays, working-class people, and "foreigners" of one sort or another. Veterans of an academic socialization process that promoted replication of the very pedagogies that frustrated us as students, we attempted to balance

1

home cultures dear to us with the culture of the academy. In this ongoing process, the voices of our diverse students reminded us that they too are engaged in similar struggles to be who they are, even as they learn to use education in a meaningful and rewarding manner.[2]

In addition to the scholarly training that most faculty bring to the practice of teaching, we bring as well some hard-won understandings of "the rules of the game" that operate in academic life. Having ourselves successfully decoded the university's culture, we are in a position to help students understand how to survive and overcome academic practices that devalue and marginalize them. Eventually, efforts to improve our own teaching have led us to engage with colleagues in initiatives for curriculum change and in challenges to the usual (and artificial) divisions that universities traditionally maintain between teaching, scholarship, and service. In our experience, these boundaries may function more as a constraint on intellectual and pedagogical innovation than as a guarantee of consistency and high standards.

We are aware, for example, that despite many years of experience, teaching nonetheless somehow remains "not our field" because it is not the area in which we obtained our Ph.D.s. Yet writing about teaching is an activity that profoundly challenges both intellect and imagination. It leads us to draw on a wide range of theoretical sources and cultural discourses within and outside "our fields" for guidance and inspiration, to engage in more systematic critical reflection on our work,[3] and to generate insights and suggestions of value to on- and off-campus colleagues. Although writing about teaching traditionally occupies a kind of borderland between "teaching," "scholarship," and "professional and institutional service"—as Gloria Anzaldúa has suggested,[4] borderlands are a place where illuminating critical insights are particularly likely to emerge.

Such insights seldom emerge in isolation. The pedagogical experiments and discoveries made by contributors to this volume were fostered and deepened by the support and assistance that we received from one another as scholar-teachers at the University of Massachusetts Boston (hereafter referred to as UMass/Boston) and from yet other colleagues whose voices are not represented here. It is not only private reflection and attention to student voices that promote better teaching; our individual initiatives were often the product of sustained opportunities to learn from colleagues. As we see it, the individual and collective struggles and achievements of our diverse contributors sharply illuminate significant issues in U.S. higher education.

WHAT IS GOOD TEACHING?

Like most faculty, we began teaching after spending many years in classrooms where professors were not only the center of attention, but also the exclusive source of authoritative information and ideas. On becoming junior faculty, we generally became conventional good teachers who received positive course evaluations from students familiar with lecture formats and appreciative—or at least tolerant—of our youth and enthusiasm. But, although we began by reproducing the educational environments over which we had triumphed, for most of us, schooling had been not only a source of credentialed knowledge, but also often an experience of pain—and sometimes of assault upon our values, cultures, and identities. As a consequence, when UMass/Boston students expressed anger, dismay, and frustration at the difficult trade-offs that higher education seemed to require, their voices resonated with our own experiences. Instead of keeping the spotlight on ourselves and our specialized knowledge, we began to consider it more important to pay attention to the factors that affect student learning.

New pedagogical opportunities emerged as we attempted to facilitate the process by which course content becomes a part of the cognitive and affective apparatus with which students make their way in the world.[5] In the political science course described by Winston Langley, students at differing levels of skill and academic preparation were invited to engage with complex ideas and materials in a classroom environment that fostered honest reflection, open curiosity, and critical questioning; language professor Reyes Coll-Tellechea reports on the important discoveries about self and subject matter that students made in her Spanish classes when she situated herself as a Spaniard teaching Latino students their own language.

Intent on creating a challenging and supportive environment for learning, historian Esther Kingston-Mann set out to promote student achievement—not by "lowering standards," but by valuing student potentials for understanding, empathy, and analysis. Like other contributors to this book, she asks students to consider data in its cultural context, to reflect on the ways that it can be understood (and misunderstood) and on what

counts as understanding in a particular discipline. Her efforts to grapple
with such issues are rooted in the belief that students are in fact capable
of engaging in serious and significant intellectual discourse.[6] According
to Kingston-Mann, proponents of the most rigorous academic standards
might well delight in the intellectual achievement of undergraduate student Eva Taino, who writes:

> The most important thing I learned during this semester is that every-
> thing I read has already been filtered through the mind of another human
> being. With this in mind I began to look more closely at what I read, but
> also to keep an open mind about the information given to me. I tried to
> get as many sides to a story as I could so when I came to a conclusion it
> would be a fair, thought-out and educated one.

However, despite our best efforts to help students realize a measure
of their potential, there are no guarantees against classroom disaster,
unresolved and bitter misunderstandings, and persistent challenges to
our most deeply held assumptions and preconceptions. These negatives
cannot be ignored or relegated to a distant past when we were inexperienced teachers. The accounts by theologian Kathleen Sands and
sociologist Estelle Disch indicate that, when teachers face racist or
homophobic comments by students, explore volatile subjects like gender and sexuality, or attempt to include the voices of students fearful or
unaccustomed to speaking out, students may react with rage, resentment, or withdrawal, even when the teacher does "the right thing."

Trained as scholars to work with intellectual rather than emotional
content, we have found that valuing diversity in the classroom challenges us not only to consider our students, but to reflect as well on our
own priorities as teachers—and on our knowledge about the many cultures represented in our classes and the degree of comfort we have with
these cultures. Aware that there are dimensions of difference with
which we are not yet knowledgeable or comfortable, we have committed ourselves—as individuals and as colleagues—to continue to confront our uncertainties.[7]

In this challenging process, there is no way to ensure that students
will be open or tolerant. They may respond with hostility to the gender,
racial, class, or sexual identities of their teachers. Estelle Disch reports
that it is not unusual for male students to question her impartiality as a
woman teaching about gender. Kathleen Sands describes the complex
impact on gay and straight students of her decision to refer to her own

sexual identity in the classroom. Psychologist Castellano Turner and English professor-poet Pancho Savery note that when as African Americans they teach about race, white students question their "objectivity." Classroom conflicts and silences that "buzz loudly" (Sands) may on occasion undermine teacher efforts to foster civility, compassion, and tolerance for differing views. At the same time, difficult interactions among students or between students and professors may also become crucibles for deeper critical reflection and more complex and grounded learning for all parties.

It is also worth considering the possibility that "problems" in teaching may be compared usefully with the dilemmas that emerge in our scholarly work. In the fields of anthropology or psychology, for example, recognition of a "problem" would be not a reason for self-reproach or for punitive measures by one's department but a source of generative questions and creative intellectual activity.[8] As a number of leading educators have recently suggested, once we situate "teaching problems" in a framework that emphasizes the deepening of our understanding, problems are no longer an embarrassment but something to be shared with colleagues and used as a basis for the exploration of new strategies and practices.[9]

It is revealing, for example, that when classroom interactions and assignments indicated to historian Esther Kingston-Mann and anthropologist Tim Sieber that students weren't learning what they thought they were teaching, they attempted a multiyear Diversity Research Initiative that invited students to learn research skills through participation in collaborative, student-faculty research teams.[10] A variety of classroom challenges led ESL specialist Vivian Zamel and Asian American studies scholar Peter Kiang to research and analyze the learning trajectories of students in their classes.[11] All of our contributors have engaged in the intellectual work of reframing the academic subjects they teach[12] and are involved in ongoing efforts to understand who our students really are (as opposed to resting on our assumptions about who they should be).

As American studies professor Lois Rudnick observes, we as faculty cannot expect that students will be blessed (or burdened) with the same motivations and interests that inspired our own learning. There is no reason to assume that students wish to be our intellectual clones, nor should that be the goal of a university education. As a student presenter at a recent UMass/Boston conference pointed out: "What if I want to work in my community as a nurse instead of going on to graduate school? Does my choice mean that I am not as intelligent as other students, or that I am a failure?"

Questions of this sort, raised by students attempting to construct their own definitions of academic success, have placed important constraints upon the impulse to claim the status of role model in any simplistic sense of the term. Instead, we have turned our attention to the design of activities that recognize the realities of student diversity in cultural and linguistic background, learning styles, levels of academic skill and preparation, and academic and life goals. As we see it, efforts to develop more sophisticated and inclusive notions of teaching and learning benefit all students, *including* those at more elite, privileged, and—on the surface—culturally homogeneous institutions. It seems likely that we can do better if we become more realistic in recognizing the diverse realities of the college classroom and begin to revise and transform the traditional institutional standards for assessing teacher and student successes and failures that have for so long dominated U.S. higher education.[13] It can be argued in fact that, if diversity is defined broadly to include race, class, gender, age, disability, sexual orientation, and ethnic and national culture, significant diversity issues exist at every college and university in the country.[14] Everywhere in higher education today—whether in suburban or urban institutions and even in the traditional "college town"—students present similar challenges and a new degree of diversity to their professors.

CONTEXTS FOR CHANGE: THE UNIVERSITY OF MASSACHUSETTS BOSTON

The site of our efforts at pedagogical, curricular, and institutional transformation is UMass/Boston, a complex of red brick buildings built in 1964 on a landfill overlooking the Boston Harbor. In a city that saw its racial, ethnic, and class conflicts erupt into violence in the 1970s struggle over school desegregation and busing, UMass/Boston symbolized unprecedented opportunity to the majority of our first-generation college students. The university's urban mission—to provide low-cost, high-quality education to a primarily urban and low-income population of varied backgrounds—placed it in the forefront of efforts to deal with the racial crisis that racked the city and its public school system. At a defining historical moment in Boston and the nation, UMass/Boston offered to all of Boston's troubled constituencies (and to many of its new faculty) what may have been the first diverse and multicultural community that many of them had ever experienced.

A chronically underfunded, nonresidential campus within the University of Massachusetts system, the university's primary commitment is to Boston, a city of rich but unevenly distributed educational opportunities. Although there are more than sixty local colleges and universities in the Boston metropolitan area, before UMass/Boston was established in 1965, the rate of college attendance among Boston high-school graduates was lower than the statewide level of college attendance in Mississippi. The university students omnipresent in the streets and cafes of Boston and Cambridge were seldom of local origin. Even today, in the Cambridge cafes frequented by area academics and students at elite institutions, UMass/Boston students are likely to be the ones serving the coffee rather than the ones drinking it.

Students

In contrast to most area colleges, UMass/Boston was graced from the outset with students more varied in their backgrounds than any other institution of higher learning in New England. Efforts to reinforce and increase the diversity of the student population have accelerated in recent decades. In 1987, 16 percent of the student body of thirteen thousand were people of color and over 50 percent was female. By 1998, the percentage of undergraduate students of color stood at 30 percent; 53 percent were women. In 1998, 50 percent of the entering class were students of color. Sixty percent of the undergraduate student body were the first in their families to attend college, over four hundred are students with disabilities, and the mean age of a UMass/Boston student is now twenty-nine. Today, the hallways, classrooms, and cafeterias of UMass/Boston are thronged by a diverse student population that makes it one of the most inclusive and truly public institutions in our city.

UMass/Boston's demographics and urban mission have ensured that it would never be an isolated "ivory tower" where students prepare for a wider life of social encounters after graduation. Our students are already linked to a wide range of cultures and communities, and they possess experiences that profoundly complicate and enrich traditional classroom discourse. UMass/Boston classrooms might include a father who brings to an education course his perspective as a member of his town's school committee, a welfare mother who shares her experiences with fellow economics majors, a disabled Vietnam veteran (the university enjoys the largest percentage of veterans of any university in the country) who tells of wartime encounters in a course on the Sixties, a Haitian immigrant who speaks of growing up as a nonminority person in a sociology course on race and ethnicity, and an Italian American student who shares her experience of work on an assembly line in a classroom discussion of the Industrial Revolution.

The products of schools where they were frequently undervalued, underestimated, unchallenged, and sometimes excluded, they balance a hope that UMass/Boston will be different—a place where they will acquire empowering and transformative knowledge—against the impulses toward cynicism and skepticism produced by earlier encounters with schools. UMass/Boston faculty are frequently challenged by the low expectations of first-year students who are tired of working at dead-end jobs but skeptical about institutionalized learning. To a student like Amy, "High school was like a penance imposed for some unknown sin. Everything I ever learned that was important to me was learned outside of school. So I never thought to associate schools with learning." In her pre-college experience, Amy thought that teachers "lived in a world of their own."

Faculty

UMass/Boston's faculty is relatively diverse, though far less so than the student body. From the outset, many were graduates of major research universities. (Local newspapers occasionally remark with surprise that UMass/Boston—at the bottom of the local academic totem pole as the only accessible, public university in town—possesses the highest percentage of Harvard Ph.D.s of any university in the United States.) A number of senior faculty deliberately chose UMass/Boston because they wanted to teach diverse students in an urban setting. In 1990, a national survey of faculty members at 328 four-year institutions revealed that 88 percent of our university's faculty approved of programmatic efforts to focus on cultural diversity and ranked the hiring of more minority faculty as a priority second only to the goal of promoting intellectual development. In contrast, faculty members at all four-year institutions ranked minority recruitment as their twelfth priority.[15] As of late 1998, university recruitment efforts have resulted in a faculty that includes 20 percent people of color and 40.1 percent female (the total number of full-time faculty is 456).

A UMass/Boston Model of Faculty Development

In the 1980s and 1990s, UMass/Boston was unusual in the level of institutional support it offered for pedagogical innovation and for a successful effort by a diverse student-faculty-staff coalition to win widespread acceptance for a university-wide diversity curriculum requirement. One of the nation's first university-level teaching centers was created by UMass/Boston faculty in 1983 with funding support from the Ford Foundation.[16] From the outset, UMass/Boston's Center for the Improvement of Teaching (CIT) sought to provide organizational support for colleagues attempting to bridge the gulf between their specialized graduate training and the pedagogical challenges they faced as new and inexperienced college teachers. Relying on a grass-roots strategy for faculty development, CIT drew on the hard-won wisdom of discipline-trained faculty colleagues instead of depending on faculty or outside experts with advanced degrees in education.[17] With support from UMass/Boston's chancellor and from provosts who came to value CIT as a key component of the university's commitment to an urban mission, the center invited faculty from a wide range of disciplines to improve their pedagogical skills, claim ownership of campus efforts at pedagogical transformation, and become active participants in an expanding constituency for change.

In semester-long faculty development seminars that met regularly throughout the 1980s and 1990s, faculty participated in what many described as their *first* conversations about teaching and their first experiences of collaboration with colleagues from other departments and colleges. Seminar discussions were kept confidential (under rules prohibiting their use in any personnel process), and participants were free to share problems, implement innovations, and reflect—together with colleagues—on student responses to the changes they attempted. According to one seminar participant:

> I used to avoid students in my class by lecturing the entire class and lecturing above their heads. I knew they were bored and disconnected from the class and their exams showed that. Maybe I was afraid of my students because I didn't know who they were. I went to the seminar looking for

help and support. I came away being able to take risks, to know students in my class, to let go of my Ivy League notion of higher education—and feel that it was okay to teach differently.[18]

For faculty from departments whose evaluation and reward systems focused on scholarship rather than teaching, CIT seminars were sometimes an occasion for the poignant discovery by a faculty member that, despite the indifference of her department, she had long been a gifted teacher (and that this was a valuable achievement)!

Seminar participants played a leading role in the passage of the university-wide diversity curriculum initiative adopted in 1991. The product of a Diversity Working Group of students, faculty, and staff coordinated by CIT, the requirement defined diversity broadly to include race, class, gender, age, disability, sexual orientation, and culture. The success of this initiative meant that henceforward, the university's curriculum—the most powerful statement of the university's academic priorities—would communicate the message that an educated person needed to study issues of diversity. Faculty previously challenged by students demanding to know why they had to learn about gays, working-class people, or members of nonmajority racial and ethnic backgrounds could now respond that the university as an institution mandated the study of diversity as a prerequisite for graduation, because an understanding of diversity was indispensable to life in the modern world.[19] Currently, more than a hundred diversity courses are offered at UMass/Boston; they are taught at every level, in many disciplines, and in every college in the university.[20]

A FACULTY COMMUNITY
DEDICATED TO STUDENT LEARNING

Although the CIT seminars were created to improve teaching, one of their most significant consequences was to foster the emergence of a community of sophisticated and action-oriented faculty. In the words of English composition specialist Ellie Kutz,

> Providing faculty with the opportunity to engage in shared and extended inquiry into their work as teachers in an urban university helps to strengthen our institution, not only by helping us to improve the teaching that is the central focus of our work, but by enabling us to identify and strengthen other aspects of our work that contribute to the university's

mission. . . . I've found myself returning to the very questions and issues raised by my colleagues in the Ford seminar. The seminar allowed me to see more clearly a fundamental coherence to the many elements of our common enterprise.

By 2000, 206 professors, almost 45 percent of the full-time faculty, had participated in semester-long faculty development seminars; three hundred had attended one or more teaching-related workshops or an annual campus conference, Teaching and Transformation.

For junior faculty, and for all faculty who belong to historically marginalized social groups, CIT seminars became a particular source of support and encouragement and an entrée into a network of supportive colleagues. In the anguished words of one junior faculty member, "How in the world did my scientific research prepare me to teach any students, let alone those that differ so much in levels of skill and academic preparation?" Kathleen Sands refers to the encouragement from seminar colleagues that sustained her effort to initiate more open classroom discussions of sexual orientation. Other veterans of the seminar experience have written about it as "the first time I came to believe in the good will of my white colleagues" and a "reason for hope that UMass/Boston is changing, becoming more inclusive."

As teachers, we are aware that we understand our intellectual work better as we teach about it. When the issue is teaching itself, as distinct from the subject matter of our disciplines, we have found that mentoring/teaching relationships—both with colleagues and with teachers at other levels of education—have been indispensable for gaining a critical perspective on our own pedagogical practices. All of our contributors have been participants and/or coordinators of the CIT faculty development seminars mentioned above. Those of us who have taught in teacher preparation programs for elementary, secondary, and adult education teachers credit our dialogues with our teacher-students as an important source of critical reflections on effective teaching. From this perspective, a commitment to public education by university-level faculty is not simply an altruistic endeavor, but also a contribution to the pedagogical renewal of those who engage in it.

In the course of our collaborations, many of the contributors to this volume have emerged as campus-level "experts" who present workshops to colleagues on such topics as "Anguish as a Second Language: ESL Student Challenges" (Vivian Zamel), "Teaching Students with

Disabilities" (Estelle Disch), "Managing Classroom Diversity" (Castellano Turner and Tim Sieber), and "Redefining Academic Disciplines" (Esther Kingston-Mann and Winston Langley). As faculty members trained to be specialists in our fields, we now share questions, methods, and strategies related to teaching and learning with a widening circle of colleagues from other disciplines and institutions at the National Conference on Race and Ethnicity in Higher Education, at Association of American Colleges and Universities/Ford Foundation conferences called Diversity, Democracy, and Liberal Learning, and as participants in the Ford National Campus Diversity Network.

In this process, we began to view both our struggles and our innovations in the context of similar efforts by colleagues across the country. Although our efforts are not unique, initiatives like ours are rarely discussed in national debates on innovation in higher education. In general, faculty efforts at non-elite academic institutions like UMass/ Boston are documented almost as rarely as the experiences of our non-elite students.[21] We hope that our collection of essays will invite a broader exploration of the possibility that, at all kinds of institutions, faculty trained as scholars can engage with today's students, grow as teachers and as human beings, and transform their teaching practices in more effective directions.

INSTITUTIONAL TRANSFORMATION, ACADEMIC STANDARDS, AND GOOD TEACHING

At UMass/Boston, the mutual support and encouragement we have given one another as colleagues and our emergent sense of community has provided critical support for what each of us has been able to accomplish—and reinforces our efforts to build community in our own classrooms. The familiar story of the individual faculty member struggling alone against a hostile environment can be a tragic tale ending in defeat— but this can be avoided if faculty are supported by a network or community that fosters collaboration among colleagues. Our experience suggests that faculty cannot hope to enjoy support or even to gain much critical purchase on their efforts unless they share, compare, and interweave their stories with others, as we ourselves have done in this volume. We strongly encourage other faculty to join local colleagues—in supportive, nonhierarchical settings—in collaborative dialogues on teaching.

In many respects, UMass/Boston exemplifies a widespread, current shift in higher education away from an exclusive allegiance to the "research university" ideal and toward what Rubén Martinez has called "the responsive university"—a place where the teaching and mentoring of increasingly diverse student populations achieves greater parity with traditional research as an institutional priority.[22] Our volume documents this important but rarely noted shift at the grass roots of today's academic culture. It may be that so-called "nontraditional" institutions like UMass/Boston should be considered *mainstream* American universities, because they welcome a truer cross section of young adults studying in today's United States and require a more thoughtful, multifaceted model of achievement and success in higher education.

It should be emphasized that the commitment to student learning reflected in the work of our contributors does not mean that classrooms become encounter groups or that academic course content is devalued. It is precisely our fidelity to the material we teach—with its multiple human valences in the experiences of everyone in the classroom—that complicates our task.[23] As Tim Sieber observes, most of us began our professional journeys confident that our job was to present significant information with intelligence, enthusiasm, and good will. Gradually, we came to discover that, in order to teach challenging curricular material, it was necessary to reflect on how to handle its affective, personal, and political implications, to consider the kinds of dialogue we are willing to encourage, and to review the traditional methods by which we assess and measure learning. In today's higher education, the pursuit of excellence must be extended to include high standards for pedagogy as well as content, along with regular critical examination of our pedagogical performance. With such an approach to excellence, we need no longer aspire to be "bouncers at the gates of knowledge." Instead, we can begin to consider how to link media and political demands for "accountability" in higher education with the implementation of practices that genuinely expand student opportunities for learning.

In contrast to conventional stereotypes that pit "energetic and open" junior faculty against their "stodgy" elders, the experience of our contributors demonstrates that midcareer faculty can continue to learn and develop (and that junior faculty may be burdened by inexperience and by fears about tenure that place constraints on risk-taking). Our experience suggests that the challenges of higher education today—however stressful—do not inevitably lead to defeatism, retreat, burnout, indifference, or the introduction of impersonal, assembly-line modes of instruction frequently emphasized in media accounts of today's professoriate. Our contributors demonstrate that faculty can benefit from collaboration with colleagues and can learn to construct classroom environments that encourage students to share ideas and insights and to take responsibility for their own learning. As Peter Kiang suggests in his chapter below, it is through "sharing voices, crossing boundaries, and building communities" that we and our students move forward.

At the same time, it is important to recall that our pedagogical powers and expertise, while real, are not infinite. We can never be sure that we will understand, predict, or deal effectively with every problem that arises. This is not as depressing an admission as it might seem. As in other areas of learning, pedagogical advances are seldom linear. If faculty—like students—recognize that difficulties are not a sign of incompetence, it may become easier for them to learn. Faculty socialized to see themselves as all-purpose authorities frequently find the challenge of learning through mistakes and misjudgments more difficult than do our students, who are inescapably aware that they are *supposed to be learners.* It is ironic that an academy whose raison d'être is education has traditionally defined teaching as something either mysterious (with some individuals gifted and others incurably mediocre) or mechanical (with a set of cut-and-dried techniques that apply to every classroom)—rather than as an enterprise that benefits from careful reflection, collaboration with others, creativity, and the investment of time and energy.

Our narratives suggest that dedicated teachers would do well to abandon fantasies of omniscience and omnipotence, that is, the notion that they should be able to foresee all difficulties and resolve them quickly and happily. By becoming more realistic, faculty see more clearly and find themselves more attuned to the potentials for change in unexpected situations. What are referred to in the literature as "teachable moments" teach us (the faculty) as much as they teach our students. It is in this complex and realistic spirit that we acknowledge, honor, and encourage colleagues at UMass/Boston and elsewhere who are committed to changing the existing distributions of knowledge in U.S. society.

NOTES

Acknowledgments: Our book's title first came from Esther Kingston-Mann's interview for the 1995 filming of an orientation video, released in 1996 under the title *Achieving Against the Odds,* that was produced by Jean Humez of the Women's Studies Program and designed to support new students at UMass/Boston.

1. See Patricia Hill Collins, "Learning from the Outside Within: The Sociological Significance of Black Feminist Thought," *Social Problems* 33 (6): 14–32 (1986), and the valuable perspectives set out in Paula Rothenberg, ed., *Race, Class and Gender in the United States: An Integrated Study* (New York: St. Martin's Press, 1998).

2. A significant discussion of the relationship between academic culture and cultural identities in the schooling of minorities is John Ogbu's "Frameworks: Variability in Minority School Performance," in Evelyn Jacobs and Cathy Jordan, eds., *Minority Education: Anthropological Perspectives* (Norwood, N.J.: Ablex, 1993).

3. At UMass/Boston, examples of such writing by scholar-teachers include James H. Broderick, ed., *Teaching at an Urban University: Papers from the Ford Seminars in Teaching at UMass/Boston, 1983–1987* (Boston: Center for the Improvement of Teaching, University of Massachusetts/Boston, 1987); Tim Sieber, ed., *What We Have Learned: Meeting the Challenge of Inclusive Teaching at UMass/Boston* (Boston: Center for the Improvement of Teaching, University of Massachusetts/Boston, 1995); and Esther Kingston-Mann, ed., *A Diversity Research Initiative: How Diverse Undergraduate Students Become Researchers, Change Agents, and Members of a Research Community* (Boston: Center for the Improvement of Teaching, University of Massachusetts Boston, 1999).

4. Gloria Anzaldúa, *Borderlands/La Frontera: The New Mestiza* (San Francisco: Spinsters/Aunt Lute, 1987).

5. Jane Fried, "Bridging Emotion and Intellect: Classroom Diversity in Process," *College Teaching* 41, no. 4 (1993).

6. Among the many explorations of the link between academic challenge and student achievement are Claude Steele, "Race and the Schooling of African Americans," *Atlantic Monthly,* April 1992, 68–78; Jerome Dancis, "Alternative Learning Environment Helps Minority Students Excel in Calculus: A Pedagogical Analysis," <http://www.math.umd.edu/~jnd/Treisman.txt>; James P. Comer et al., *Rallying the Whole Village: The Comer Process for Reforming Education* (New York: Teachers College Press, 1996); Deborah Meier, *The Power of Their Ideas: Lessons for American from a Small School in Harlem* (Boston: Beacon Press, 1995).

7. See Donna Duffy, *Teaching Within the Rhythms of the Semester* (San Francisco: Jossey-Bass, 1995), p. 137.

8. Randy Bass, "The Scholarship of Teaching: What's the Problem?" *Inventio: Creative Thinking about Learning and Teaching* 1, no. 1 (1999).

9. See the useful discussion of conventional notions of success and failure in Frederick Erickson, "Transformation and School Success: The Politics and Culture of Educational Achievement," and Perry Gilmore, Shelley Goldman, et al., "Failure's Failure," in Evelyn Jacobs and Cathy Jordan, eds., *Minority Education: Anthropological Perspectives* (Norwood, N.J.: Ablex, 1993).

10. Funded by the Ford Foundation between 1996 and 1999, this project brought together three to four student-faculty research teams per semester that made use of the university as the site of inquiry into issues of diversity. See Esther Kingston-Mann, "Building a Diversity Research Initiative: An Introduction," and Tim Sieber, "Research and Research Methods in the Diversity Research Initiative," in Kingston-Mann, ed., *A Diversity Research Initiative*.

11. See, for example, Eleanor Kutz, Suzy Q. Groden, and Vivian Zamel, *The Discovery of Competence: Teaching and Learning with Diverse Student Writers* (Portsmouth, N.H.: Greenwood-Heinemann, 1993), and Peter Kiang, "Crossing Boundaries, Building Community," *Thought & Action* 15 (1): 49–60 (1999).

12. See, for example, Estelle Disch, ed., *Reconstructing Gender: A Multicultural Anthology*, 2d ed. (Mountain View, Calif.: Mayfield, 2000).

13. Perry Gilmore et al., "Failure's Failure."

14. The foregoing definition constitutes the core of UMass/Boston's diversity curriculum requirement. See page 10 in this volume and notes 20 and 21 below.

15. See Higher Education Research Institute (HERI), "National Survey of Academic Personnel" (Research Brief 2.90, University of California at Los Angeles, summer 1990, photocopy).

16. The Center for the Improvement of Teaching was the creation of literature professors Francis Hart and James Broderick. After the initial Ford grant expired, the university supported a modest range of center activities. In 1991, under CIT director Esther Kingston-Mann, UMass/Boston received a second, urban-commuter university grant that supported diversity-focused faculty development seminars for ten faculty per semester. By 1996, when the latter grant expired, assessment of the impact of the seminars on UMass/Boston faculty had become so favorable that the provost's office and the deans of UMass/Boston's five colleges agreed to fund the seminars out of their own budgets.

17. As other educational innovators have noted, grass-roots strategies may be the most effective basis for sustained institutional change. However valuable the insights of visiting experts, it is difficult to sustain the momentum created by new ideas after the speaker leaves. See Duffy, *Teaching Within the Rhythms*, p. xiii.

18. Quoted in Suzanne Benally, "External Assessment: The University of Massachusetts at Boston: A Public, Urban, Non-Residential Campus Responds to the Challenge of Diversity" (Report to the Ford Foundation, 11 March 1997, photocopy), p. 5.

19. Before the diversity requirement was passed, Esther Kingston-Mann reported on students who found the study of African history "not really history, but appreciation," and asked why—if such topics were so important—they didn't hear about them in other classes. See Chris Reardon, "An Urban Commuter College Responds to Diversity," *Ford Foundation Report* 23: 4 (winter 1992): 10–15.

20. See Esther Kingston-Mann, "Multiculturalism Without Political Correctness: The UMass/Boston Model," *Boston Review*, May–June 1992, and Estelle Disch, "The Politics of Curricular Change: Establishing a Diversity Requirement at the University of Massachusetts Boston," in Becky W. Thompson et al., eds.,

Beyond a Dream Deferred: Multicultural Education and the Politics of Excellence (Minneapolis: University of Minnesota Press, 1993), pp. 195–213.

21. To some extent, this state of affairs reflects the priorities of publishers. Although the majority of America's college students attend urban commuter institutions, Jossey-Bass—one of the leading educational publishers in the United States—declared to us in a June 1998 letter that it was their policy *not* to consider for publication any manuscripts that focused primarily on the experience of urban commuter institutions. According to Jossey-Bass, the study of teaching, learning, and curriculum change at urban commuter institutions is too narrow a topic for readers concerned with changing U.S. higher education. Such arguments also deny that there are broader lessons for higher education that emerge from the experience of urban commuter universities.

22. Rubén Martinez, foreword to Raymond V. Padilla and Miguel Montiel, *Debatable Diversity: Critical Dialogues on Change in American Universities* (New York: Rowman & Littlefield, 1998)

23. See Esther Kingston-Mann, "Diversity and Academic Standards: Reflections in a Different Mirror," *Diversity Digest*, summer 1998.

KATHLEEN M. SANDS

1   Coming Out and Leading Out
Pedagogy Beyond the Closet

THE BIBLE is based on a coming-out story; it's called the Exodus. The people who came out on that occasion were a motley crew, unified less by blood than by a common, miserable social status. To say that they were chosen for this journey is to admit that they would not have wandered in the wilderness had not circumstance compelled them. But their commitment to freedom was to become a foundational myth of Western culture, a feature of the horizon of every subsequent movement for liberation.

As a lesbian teacher and scholar of religious studies, I take comfort in this story because I also find myself in a motley group, one unified not by who its members actually are but by the laws and discourse of others. In the classroom, I would never choose to foreground my sexual preference were it possible simply to speak what I know and present who I am without making the splash called coming out. On reflection, though, I see that my teaching is threaded through with issues that I wish were not there, such as racism, economic exploitation, misogyny, and the decline of the biosphere. The beauty, coherence, and community that I actually want to teach are generally wrought from such crude, unwanted materials. In my own case, what is crude and unwanted is the intensive scrutiny to which gay, lesbian, bisexual, and transgendered lives are subjected by the strictures of sexual normality. Discussed and judged, we can either retreat into a doubled silence or take charge of our self-presentation and turn the inquisition into a conversation. Educators are people who lead out, and to lead an exodus, you have to be willing to go on one. So I have moved, rather slowly and with as much company as I could muster, not in the heroic tradition of Moses and other lone rangers, but more like Miriam, who preferred to sing in a group.

That this journey would pull me between a rock and a hard place became evident during my very first semester teaching at UMass/Boston seven years ago. I was teaching an introductory course dealing with several religious traditions, and I was trying to lead a discussion on "Song of Bear," a piece of old lore attributed by Ann Cameron to the Nootka women of Vancouver Island. Long ago, the story told, a young woman had left the menstrual hut to bathe in the stream. While she was bathing, she saw a bear watching her from the bank and trembling with desire. She invited the bear to join her for a swim, and afterwards, as they lay in the sun to dry, the bear tearfully confessed, "I love you." "I love you, too," the woman replied, but this only made the bear cry harder, because the situation was even worse than it seemed. "I am a female bear," she finally choked out. The young woman took this in for a minute and then said, "If I can love a creature that looks as different from me as you do, why should I care if you are a male bear or a female bear?" And so, the story concludes, they went up to the bear's mountain cave, and they loved one another.[1]

Since this story was one of about twenty in the collection in which it appeared, and since the collection itself was only one book of several in the course, it did not consume much class time. In fact, it consumed almost no time at all, because after a half hour of free-ranging discussion, not one student in our class of forty had made reference to it. Clearly, I thought, this is a hot potato. Finally, so that the piece would not be overlooked entirely, I asked casually whether anyone had noticed the story about the bear and the woman. Some nodding heads, but no comments. I floated a couple of broad questions. "How did you react when you read this story?" No response. "Did it surprise you? Did you find it funny or sad or weird or what?" Still no takers, so I became more directive. "What do you think it suggests about how homoerotic love is seen in this culture? Is it a different attitude than we find in mainstream American culture?" The silence in the room began to buzz loudly. "Have you ever heard the term *berdache?* That's a word Europeans used for a type of person they were surprised to find in most Native American groups—people we might call gay or lesbian or transgendered. Native Americans themselves often call these people 'two-spirited.' They are considered to be special, gifted; traditionally, they played special roles in group rituals or decisions. Interesting, huh?" I forced myself to tolerate the silence for another long minute, while in my mind a thin limb creaked ominously. Finally, I retreated and moved on to a different story.

Later that afternoon, a student from that class showed up at my office to express his disappointment that I had "backed away" from the topic of homosexuality.[2] I was new at the university, and coming out was not yet routine for me. So I simply said, "David, I am on your side" and then to his quizzical look, "I am *really* on your side." But I went on to explain that I could not do this all on my own. If no student picks up on the topic, some students might see me as perseverating on a sexual issue that nobody else wants to talk about. David was gracious enough to accept this, but the fear I expressed to him proved prescient. For later in the semester, when I asked for some informal evaluations, someone bitterly complained that the teacher was "working out her lesbianism in the classroom."

Needless to say, I was deeply embarrassed and disconcerted upon reading this. I tried to run back over my every word in the course. Had I ever said, either directly or indirectly, that I am a lesbian? No, I was certain I had not; in my hypervigilance about this topic, that would never have slipped out. Had I raised the topic of minority sexuality often? No, only in the single, uncomfortable instance of the bear story. Feminist analysis, however, had been among the critical threads of the course. Could it be that, for this student, feminism and lesbianism were the same thing? Were other students likely to think the same way? What if such comments appeared on my formal evaluations? Would a personnel committee ask for my side, or would they simply make up their own story about this lesbian junior professor? And what if several such evaluations had accumulated by the time I got to tenure review?

My dilemma was rendered thornier still by the fact that I am a scholar of religion. On the bright side, this places me close to the heart of the issue; unfortunately this is also the site where the conflict seems least negotiable. After all, long before (and long since) homosexuals were diagnosed as psychologically sick, we have been condemned on moral and religious grounds as against God and nature, scriptures and synods, hadith and halakah. There have been countervailing realities and traditions as well, but, as three decades of feminist scholarship have made painfully clear, the patriarchal bias that undergirds heterosexism has been a main function of world religions. Of course, most religious feminists also believe that, besides sacralizing the status quo, religions afford means for social critique and change. Still, almost by definition, the most critical uses of religion are usually its minority uses. Moreover, many religious students today are social conservatives, while socially critical students are often antireligious. How was I to promote discussion between those for whom I couldn't say too little about sexual difference and those for whom I couldn't say too much? How could there be communication between people who explain their positions by adverting to irreconcilable sources and assumptions? How could I present religion to gay or lesbian students as even worth studying? And to religious conservatives, who often confuse my role with that of clergy person, how could I present myself, a lesbian theologian, as something other than a walking blasphemy?

Daunted by all this, I adopted for several years a kind of "don't say, don't deny" policy, the first principle of which was that I would never be vulnerable to the accusation of pushing homoeroticism as a personal agenda. On the other hand, I would work to include materials by and about sexual minorities wherever heteronormativity would otherwise be operative—for example, in Christian history, in sexual ethics, in coming-of-age stories. As for myself, I decided that I should come out only in those classes or settings where the salience of personal experience and of sexuality would be obvious to everyone. My course called Feminist Theology and Spirituality clearly fit the bill: it is explicitly concerned with integrating experience and reflection, it always includes at least a few lesbians or bisexuals, and the connection (or disconnection) of sexuality and spirituality is a recurrent theme. Besides, in this one course, I had figured out how and when to come out, always a large part of the struggle. In the first class, we would always introduce ourselves (at my suggestion) by sharing something that we wanted the group to know. By way of breaking the ice, I would start by saying three or four things about myself, among them the fact that I am lesbian. Inevitably, several students would then also mention something about their sexualities, and the topic would get integrated seamlessly into the rest of the course.

My coming-out strategy worked so well in the feminist theology course as to provide, over time, a basis for noticing how anxious I was in those situations (most) where I was not out. I would be striding into my classroom or walking across campus crossing the catwalk to the building I teach in and I would recall, say, the lovely sensation of my last night's sleep, spooned against my lover. And while the inside of me would be filled with that warmth, I would feel the visible surface of me being observed and, usually, presumed heterosexual. And I would wonder: what if they knew? Would there still be a smile or a meeting of eyes? Would there be shock or disgust, even an impulse to violence? These fears

were with me all the time, like a low-grade fever, as they are for all lesbians and gay men, all bisexuals and transgendered people. It is something like what W.E.B. Du Bois called "double consciousness." We learn
to bear up under it, to compose ourselves with a modicum of serenity
while poised at each moment to duck a psychic or physical blow. In my
case, that stress had a special inflection, knowing the venom reserved by
the righteous for perverts who pretend to some kind of religious or moral
authority. I am enough of a religious person to have a slightly inflated
sense of honor and dignity, such that I am wounded by the self-image I
see in the ugly mirror of other people's condemnation. The loneliness of
this took a certain toll on me and, I am sure, depleted the relationships I
might have had with students and colleagues.

And I wasn't the only one who was anxious. In my classes, there was
no denying the palpable nervousness that students exhibited whenever
issues of sexual difference came up, dramatically more so than when we
dealt with other hot topics. I recognized this as an indicator of how
unanalyzed was the knotted riddle of sexuality and how suffocating
was the fear of ostracism felt by sexual minorities and sometimes even
by straight students who would want to support us. No doubt, my own
half-in, half-out position exacerbated the tension for some. Bisexual,
gay, and lesbian students, who usually knew of my involvement with
their student center, were placed in the strange situation of needing to
discern whether they could show that they knew I was a lesbian—in
other words, the situation of having to protect me. Unsurprisingly, they
themselves very rarely came out in my classes during this period. If I
couldn't even make the classroom safe for myself, they must have wondered, how was I going to make it safe for them? So I effectively con-
fined them, like myself, to the patterns of dissimulation that are the
survival strategies of the closet: leave out the pronouns when you mention your partner, talk about sexuality or prejudice in only the most gen-
eralized terms, test the waters, don't go deep.

The other side of my strategy in these years also had limited success.
I did manage to include some gay and lesbian materials in my classes,
but they were usually optional because I felt so awkward addressing
them directly. The net result was that, in contrast to my constant attention to other social issues, I was avoiding this one precisely because it
so involved me. And *that*, I came to see, was truly perverse. One example that comes to mind is my handling of Dorothy Allison's autobio-

graphical novel *Bastard out of Carolina,* which I teach as a spiritual coming-of-age story. Allison is famous as a lesbian writer, and I would mention that in introducing the book. But her story leaves off before her full sexual awakening, which is foreshadowed only by her closeness with a lesbian aunt. Dwelling on her lesbianism would therefore have violated my first defensive principle: don't appear to be making an issue of it unless it plainly is an issue. The theme of physical and sexual abuse, on the other hand, is central to the book. I would therefore lead them in examining the abuse the character Bone suffers at the hands of her stepfather, while avoiding the subtextual question that, I suspect, preoccupied many students: does she become a lesbian because a man abused her? Certainly there is a popular cultural predisposition to look for what went wrong in the psychohistories of gay and lesbian people, but students were unlikely to surface these unspoken assumptions when the classroom itself was thick with secrets. Since my sexuality was among those secrets, there was no way for me to debunk this myth from my own experience or that of other lesbians I know. So we would leave the story with the myth unchallenged.

Living in the closet, in short, was significantly limiting my integrity and effectiveness as a teacher. For me, this conclusion was as difficult to accept as it was inevitable, because the emotional hurdle of coming out had only grown higher during the years when I had contemplated jumping it. To be out in all contexts became my goal, although, in kindness to myself, I did not take this on as a standard to be met at every moment. I am mindful, too, that gay and lesbian professionals, including some of my colleagues, do not take this on even as a goal. While I miss their companionship, I fully understand why they might refuse to make this "their issue," particularly when their subject matter is not so obviously tied as mine with moral and social questions. And it would trouble me if the university community were to perceive sexuality as the special issue of those of us who are out. The fact that we cannot abide the closet does not make heterosexism our problem to solve, any more than racism is a problem to be solved by people of color. In both cases, the contrary is nearer the truth.

Indeed, the more I have come out in the intervening years, the more I have come to understand that it is chiefly straight people who build and rebuild the closet. This has been especially obvious in how straight colleagues have responded when I come out of it. Prior to my tenure

year, for example, I lunched with a senior colleague to get her suggestions about how best to survive the process. Toward the end of the conversation, I asked her whether she thought my being an out lesbian
would place me at any risk. Though I had assumed she knew this about
me, her speechlessness clued me in that this was not the case. When
finally she collected herself, her first comment was, "I prefer to believe
that students are not thinking about my sexuality at all." Now it was my
turn to be speechless, for despite the wedding ring on her hand and
countless other signals, the public character of her sexuality was not
really evident to her. I knew this colleague meant me no harm; her purpose in speaking with me was wholly supportive. But that, in a way,
was what was most scary. If someone who knew me a little and meant
well could be so unnerved by my unclosetedness, what might happen
to my career in the hands of those who did not know me and whose
roles would be to judge rather than to support?

That experience was multiplied on another occasion when, in a faculty discussion group, I raised the question of how (not whether) to
come out in the classroom. One or two colleagues immediately took this
as a question about how personal—that is, self-disclosing—teachers
should be. Now I do think that maintaining appropriate boundaries,
especially where sexuality is concerned, is something about which we
ought to be vigilant. But what startled and then angered me was that the
simple statement of my sexual preference seemed to step over those
boundaries in a way that the exhibition of heterosexuality did not. After
listening to these good colleagues for only an hour, I knew quite a lot
about their sexual and family lives—tidbits about kids and spouses,
even mention of an in-law or two, and again the nearly omnipresent
wedding band. They, on the other hand, did not know whether I even
have a lover (or no lover or a whole gaggle of them), what kind of sexual commitments I have made, whether I have kids, or any details of my
sexual practice. When I come out, I am not baring my soul; it is no more
personal a disclosure than are the routine self-presentations of straight
people. Yet, some colleagues were concerned that simply naming
myself as a lesbian might constitute an impropriety. And if coming out
is an impropriety, then what propriety demands is the dissimulation
known as the closet.

Again, I know that these colleagues meant me well; their intention
was only to protect me from any negative consequences, whether fair

or unfair, that my coming out might entrain. Nonetheless, to be judged inappropriate or unprofessional for coming out would damage my reputation and therefore endanger my livelihood. The threat of that judgment was therefore a form of ostracism, and it had operated as such in my life through the fear and anxiety I had carried for years. As I learned from my colleagues, the judgment was encoded in a notion of the private or personal, which, like the notion of the natural, presented itself as a criterion for judgment while actually legitimating a pre-existing taboo. I am not being facetious, then, when I propose a merciless campaign of outing heterosexuals! As it is, straight people rarely reflect on their sexuality as a personal choice or preference because they tacitly assume it as the norm. This heteronormativity then becomes ubiquitous and, in that sense, invisible. It does not appear as a rule that is enforced through coercion and intimidation; it disappears the way water disappears for fish. This is how the closet functions as a social institution. Sexual variety, complexity, and malleability cannot be seen as such; they can only appear momentarily, here and there, as an anomaly of society, a monstrosity of nature, or most benignly, a minority identity.

The question of identity also arises in connection with coming out, and interactions with other faculty have clarified this for me as well. What exactly is it that emerges from the closet? What does it mean to say "I am lesbian," "I am gay," "I am bisexual," or, most bewilderingly, "I am transgendered"? What does it mean, for that matter, to say "I am heterosexual"? Some faculty, straight and not, hesitate to make such claims lest they be taken to mean that their sexual behaviors are set in concrete, that their views or feelings can be predicted from this single affiliation, or that sexuality is the most determinative factor in their lives. These questions represent the recession in recent years of "identity politics," the kind of activism based on the assumption of a fixed and univocal group identity.

In many ways, I count myself among the critics of identity politics. Coming out as I understand it need not be interpreted as a loyalty oath to being gay or lesbian; it is simply an affirmation of the lives we are living. And progressive religious ethicists need not argue (though unfortunately they often do) that the reason homoeroticism can be moral is that God created some people with gay or lesbian natures. Defining the moral as fidelity to the natural is a circular and thus unilluminating procedure, as is defending rights in terms of identities. Those who already support the rights of sexual minorities may find this procedure compelling, but for our opponents it is not, because what the closet denies is less our *existence* than our *legitimacy*. Belief in gay natures does not entail belief in gay rights, because these minority life forms can by the same logic be judged intrinsically inferior. That is the danger of the absurd and potentially eugenicist search for the "gay gene." Nature, as a political/ethical concept, is wholly ideological; its power rarely exceeds that of the group that defines it. So, for example, if those who are most powerful ever decide to lock up all the queers, nobody will save herself by saying, "Oh, no, you don't mean me; I have homoerotic sex, but it's not my *nature*."

The moral argument against such a scenario must be more robust than "Please accept me this way, because I can't help it." Nor will the libertarian argument that the sexual expression of consenting adults is nobody else's business suffice, since the range and content of society's investment in sexual behavior is exactly what is at issue. Ethically, what is most persuasive is the same as what is most politically efficacious: to show the world what concrete social goods are promoted when we embrace sexual diversity—for example, what new kinds of love and family, insight and delight are thereby opened. People raised under the regime of heteronormativity cannot recognize these as good until and unless they experience them as such, and that takes prolonged, humane contact with people who are not straight. This contact is exactly what having an openly gay or lesbian teacher provides, which explains why many straight people who otherwise purport to endorse gay civil rights nonetheless insist that we should not teach or, if we do teach, that we should remain scrupulously closeted. Young people who have had uncloseted teachers will know from experience that communities actually do include people who are not straight. They will know that when you welcome these people, the atmosphere—far from exploding— becomes more comfortable, more interesting, and more honest. That is the really explosive information, and students will not easily forget it.

All these questions and conversations, even when there was disagreement, have moved me along in this exodus. I have also benefited from the climate of support that is created by the gay rights law of the Commonwealth of Massachusetts and the diversity policies of the university. Indeed, my own turning point in this journey owed something to the university's support for teachers—specifically to the seminars sponsored by the Center for the Improvement of Teaching. When I participated in the seminar of spring 1995, I made coming out in the classroom my particular objective. Week by week, I could clarify out loud how this had become a moral and pedagogical commitment for me, and I could share the classroom outcomes with friendly colleagues. Since then, I have managed to come out in all my classes; the question is only when and how.

Coming out right at the start of the course seems to have the richest and most integral effects, and I wish I could do that in all classes where the closet would otherwise exist—that is to say, in all classes. Most students, however, do not understand the dynamic of the closet, and I do not want to shock them more than is necessary. For that reason, I usually come out at the beginning of a course only if that course has a clear relationship to sexuality. And whether I come out sooner or later, I avoid a bombshell style of self-disclosure (à la "I'm here, I'm queer, get used to it"). I may refer to gay and lesbian people as "we" rather than "they" or, more explicitly, may note that I am among those our fundamentalist authors condemn when they write of homosexuals. Or, where the discussion warrants some personal reference, I might refer to my "partner," and I do not avoid the pronoun "she."

The closet, however, is amazingly resilient. A striking example of this took place in a class in which a well-meaning student, ardently defending gay rights laws, sealed his case by concluding, "If it weren't for our law in Massachusetts, people like you could lose your teaching jobs!" This would have been "outing" me, had I not already come out on my own only a couple of classes earlier. Nonetheless, the start that went through the room after Alan said this was as undeniable as a fire alarm. Without my effort and indeed despite it, the closet had sprung up again. The only difference was that now, my sexual preference had been shifted into the category of *open* secret; it was no longer a matter of simple ignorance but of active denial. The reason for the denial, it seemed, was to protect me from the very kinds of punishment (such as losing my job) that Alan had so indelicately named. Conceiving of the closet as something that protects me, this class could not recognize it as a punishment, and certainly not as a punishment that they themselves were helping to execute. And so, as meticulously as a cat in a litter box, they covered over my impropriety. That is why it is so important that students like Alan keep the conversation going, even if their comments occasionally fall like the proverbial lead balloon.

The initial response of a class to my coming out is usually a momentary silence. Once or twice, there has been an audible gasp or some nervous giggling. Gay and lesbian students watch me with tense, eager faces and sometimes spring out the closet immediately afterward. Supportive straight students seem to square their shoulders, as if to be a buffer between me and whatever might get hurled back. There is also a palpable shifting of classroom power. Students know that in this moment, I am socially vulnerable, and they have to decide how to handle the power they are now conscious of possessing. I *feel* vulnerable, too. My heart beats too fast; I blush and then, if I notice it, blush still more. Since as a teacher I am cautious about boundaries, the fact that some students may respond as if I had stood on the desk and stripped will always be extremely hard for me. However, as time goes on, I become smoother at this, and the worst of the physiological panic begins to recede. More than anything, what I feel immediately is the increased equanimity that comes from doing what I believe to be right, along with a deepened security from knowing that, liked or not, I am met as who I am.

So far, the responses I have encountered are largely positive, and the effects of that on me go as deep as the cumulative pain of all the destructive stereotypes: for example, that gays and lesbians are sexual predators of hapless straights (bizarre since, *unlike straight people*, gays and lesbians cannot survive unless we know where we are not wanted), or that lesbians hate men (why would whom you love depend upon whom you hate?). Women colleagues and students rarely drew away from me, as I had feared they would. The many warm relationships I now enjoy with male colleagues and students not only belie the myth of the man-hating dyke, but also assuage my fear of hostility from straight males. And so far not a single negative comment about my being out has appeared on my evaluations, though a couple of positive comments have been made.

The broadest change in my relationships with students is that I now hear many more stories about their struggles to make moral sense of sexual complexity. It is as if the opening created by my coming out allows their unmetabolized suffering and unspoken confusion to find light and air. I think of Luke, who adored his lesbian mother but did not yet know how to be as proud of her in public as he was in private. Or I think of Amy, a straight woman who, in her journal, gradually told me that she discovered her father's sexuality only after he was killed by a serial murderer who preyed on gay men. Students have all kinds of experiences that blur the boundaries supposedly dividing the sexually normal from the abnormal—Derrick dates a woman who turns out to be lesbian, Julie falls in love with her best woman friend, and so on. When that happens, they need to redraw those boundaries and re-envision a sexual world that feels both good and true. Because the questions are personal rather than just theoretical, they need to do that in a way that admits sexual experience as material for moral and social reflection, and that is just what I admit in being out.

My self-understanding as a teacher also has had to grow in the movement out of the closet. I have never much liked the idea of teacher as role model because, like teacher as authority, it seems to give me more responsibility and students less power than either side deserves. But I have come to accept that who I am and how I comport myself as a person does exert some influence in the lives of students. That is most obviously so for gay and lesbian students, who, like me, exist as partial strangers in a straight land. I am one of the handful of people at the university they can claim as their own, and that, they tell me, makes a dangerous world feel a little safer. On good days, when I sound smart or look sharp, I also offer them an image of someone like themselves as a passable adult and professional. I need not wax messianic in order to be the package for that gift.

Individual gay and lesbian students sometimes need me to fill more specific role deficits. One example was Stacey, an Italian American from a large, working-class family, who took two or three of my courses before she came out to me in her written assignments. She was Catholic in a traditional, uncomplicated way; this meant mostly that she wanted to feel like a good person and a part of her family and heritage. She had been sexually active as a lesbian for almost a decade and very much wanted to be accepted in this by her family, most of all by her mother. But whenever she raised the topic, her mother would leave the room, literally in Stacey's mid-sentence. Stacey's tours with me through Christian history and religious thought could not have left her thinking her road would be easy. But it gave her plenty of opportunity, especially in papers, to define her own path, as well as reminders that she was in ancient and honorable company. Probably my own steady presence also gave some assurance that she too might survive and flourish. In her last semester, she came once to talk about her fear that God would think she was bad for being gay, and once more to tell me that this fear had subsided. In retrospect, I see that I stood in a bit for the walking-away mother, at least enough to keep Stacey from rejecting herself.

I could name many similar instances in which my being available as an out teacher made a constructive impact on the lives of lesbian and gay students—Judy, a Jewish lesbian who studied with me for years, who sought a spiritual path different than but respectful of that of her Hassidic father (who in the end was able to celebrate at Judy's wedding, which I also attended); John, a closeted gay man, who hated straight people because of the antigay slurs he was never spared from hearing; Meg, a lesbian who was trying to reclaim her sexuality and live with her rage after a gang rape; Billy, an openly gay man with AIDs who, in addition to facing his own physical decline, had to decide whether to assist with the suicide of a dying friend. These dilemmas of the soul were integrally related to religious studies, making vividly real the themes of our courses: spiritual maturation, historical reflection, moral delibera- tion and choice. Our methods were the regular ones—reading, dis- cussion, analysis, writing, community service and activism. But this learning might not have happened, surely not at the depth that it did, without the support of a teacher they could know as an ally, one who would not find their self-disclosure inappropriate.

For my straight students as well, my coming out enriches not only their social sensibilities, but also their study of religion. Most of them want to cast off negative stereotypes of sexual minorities, but to do so they need to come to grips with inherited traditions of moral and reli- gious condemnation. It takes person-to-person contact to unravel those stereotypes, and it takes training in religion and ethics to counter con- demnations that have been proffered in the name of God without one- self becoming cynical. At the least, after my class these students will have met a person who was a lesbian yet respected religion and seemed fairly normal. At the most, they will have moved dramatically forward in a direction they already wanted to go, becoming more judicious citi- zens and wiser moral agents in the process.

My greatest pedagogical challenge, of course, is to work well with students who are actively opposed to sexual difference or who hold onto an unreflective repulsion. Here it is most important to discern what kinds of change are and are not within my direct purview as a teacher.

Politically, I would like to see the complete dismantling of heterosexual privilege, but pedagogically my aims are substantially more modest. Whether fairly or not, heterosexism still possesses, for many, a kind of moral credibility that has begun to atrophy for prejudices such as racism or sexism. Insofar as heteronormativity is a *pre*-judgment, I have to push my students forward toward judgments that are more authentic, conscious, and deliberate. I do this partly by making them contend with some critical angles on sexuality, either through course materials or simply through the questions I raise and my unapologetic self-presentation. But that is as much as I can or will insist upon. If students want to sustain a moral judgment against gay people, transgendered people, or homoerotic sex, their freedom to do so must be respected.

Within those parameters, there is still plenty for a teacher of religious studies to do, because one of the functions of religions is to encode cultural absolutes, and I am training people to think about religion. In other words, I am training them to retool their reflective and communicative capabilities at precisely the point where those capabilities ordinarily stall out and disagreement becomes intractable. Whether framed in religious or moral language, we are clearly up against absolutes when debate begins on the ethics and politics of sexual difference. Why do some people think that gays shouldn't raise kids? I might ask in a classroom. *Because the kids might turn out gay,* comes the reply. Well, that doesn't usually happen, but if it did, why would that be bad? *Because they would be abnormal!* Or I might ask, Why do people object to out gays in the military? *Because they will upset the other soldiers!* Why will the straight soldiers be upset? *Because they don't like gay people!* Or I might query, Why is it wrong to have sex with someone of the same sex? *Because it's unnatural!* Why is it unnatural? *Because a penis fits into a vagina!* Well, can't a penis go into an anus or a mouth or a hand? (And let's not even get into all the ways a clitoris might be excited!) *But that wouldn't be natural!*

While the circularity of such arguments might make one reach for a dose of Dramamine, to dismiss them is a major pedagogical mistake. That is a problem with the pathologizing term *homophobia*, which neither conveys the hatefulness nor takes seriously the moral judgments that may be involved. When students defend those antigay judgments with reference to moral or religious absolutes, I try to remember that we all work with premises that cannot be reduced to unequivocal proof. The modern academy has tended to forget this, since it was founded on the notions of objectivity and universality—notions, moreover, that entailed a special animus toward religion. That has often resulted in the exclusion of religious claims from public, rational inquiry and, correlatively, the impairment of religious people's ability to be rational about what they believe. If students who oppose homosexuality know they will not be able to explain their viewpoint in a way that the teacher will respect, they have little psychological choice but to remove themselves from the reflective processes of the classroom. Indeed, it could well become a matter of faith or principle to do so, because they will feel that their teachers are belittling what is most sacred to them. And, in the case of their teachers who are knee-jerk secularists, they will be right. That is by no means my situation, but I too must take care to welcome the voices of these students, regardless of whether their views are initially presented in a way that seems ill founded. I also need to protect them from impatient treatment by students on the other side, who may be emboldened by my openness to display more bravado than is possible for them in other settings.

On all sides of this issue, however, there is plenty of cognitive blockage. People often do not wish to understand what they adjudge as bad, and if a student is tacitly committed to misunderstanding something, odds are that he or she will succeed. More often than not, students enter the issue of sexual difference more equipped with judgments than with reasoned, communicable understanding. My first task, then, is to free up the faculty of understanding until students can represent others' views on their own terms, in a way that those others would recognize. The pedagogical principle here is no different than that which applies to grasping an unfamiliar religious tradition or a different historical era, and the gains in intellectual maturation are the same. In courses that directly involve sexuality, I present students with sources that condemn homosexuality or homosexual acts as well as sources that provide critical analyses of heterosexism. There are no surprises as to which student groups will best comprehend which materials, but the patterns of intellectual sclerosis are a little different: progay students tend to deal with the antigay materials in an sheerly polemical way, while the moral opponents of homosexuality may politely ignore every source and argument other than their foreordained authorities. In both cases, I have to keep sending them back to the drawing board until deeper insight is attained.

Understanding the person next to you, who can talk back, is more rewarding but may also be more frustrating than trying to understand a text. In classroom discussion, the primary difficulty is that positions are so frequently explicated with conversation-stoppers such as appeals to divine revelation on one side and contemporary trends on the other. In unmixed company, people may communicate in such cognitive shorthand, but in the mixed company of the public sphere, this does not take us very far. Like claims about the origins of homosexuality, appeals to authority do not so much show how one's positive or negative judgment came about as they legitimate a judgment that has already been made on other grounds. Appeals to contemporary practice do not resolve much either, since many people across the political spectrum think that something may be radically wrong with the contemporary world. The goal, then, is to get students to avail each other of the grounds on which their judgments actually rest, when they are inclined simply to fly their familiar flags and expect everyone else to salute.

This is hard learning, because people do not ordinarily notice their assumptive worlds. "It is hard to describe someone you know so well," a favorite literary character of mine says about her deceased sister. The same can be said of the contents of one's own mind and heart. In practice, as the histories of science and ideas teach, what goes as knowledge is always a tangled nest of facts and values, observation and judgment, assumption and inquiry. And sexuality, as I have argued, is as tangled and obscure a nest as any. My task, then, is to help students explicate their views in this richer, less reductive way—more horizontally than vertically, as it were. What is it you question about sexuality, I might ask, and what do you assume? If you ask what causes homosexuality, do you also ask what causes heterosexuality, and why or why not? How many kinds of sexuality are there, and how well do they fit into the categories we use? What kinds of relational patterns have you seen between women and men, men and men, women and women? What kinds of relational patterns would you like in your own life or community? What do you mean by "man" and "woman," and how well do your working definitions cover your experience of people? Of the many things that sex can do (such as give pleasure, enact violence, express love, make babies, explore fantasies, spread diseases, or seal a commitment), which if any do you think it must do in order to be moral and why? Which do you think it must not or need not do and why? On reflection, what are your sexual values, and what would the world look like if people lived by them? Who would feel most free and secure in such a world? Would anyone be missing?

We often speak of creating civility in public discourse, and this is no small accomplishment when the topic is sexuality, where judgments are often taken for granted or rendered by edict or insult. In my classes, I can at least ensure that students will be listened to with interest and respect, whatever their social and sexual ethic, and that religion will not be dismissed or derided. In this setting, the religious opponents of homosexuality are free to be less defensive. I recall an evangelical student named Louisa who, for a small group discussion, deliberately chose a group including a gay man and a lesbian so that she could hear their points of view. I think of devout Sunni Moslems I have taught—Seyla, Omar, Yvonne—whose astonishingly deep reflections on sexuality and other existential matters in their written work were clearly not inhibited by the fact that a lesbian teacher was reading them. Or I think of Roger, a sexually innocent Christian fundamentalist, who wanted my guidance on how to find a love relationship suitable to his own values, and of Tina, a Dominican Pentecostal who gently and consistently expressed the view that sex belongs only in heterosexual marriage; I remember her rushing up after class and startling me with a hug after reading my positive response to her paper. The opposition to homosexuality on principle usually remains, but it is tempered with the less moralistic and more socially critical proclivities of religion: the sense that ultimate judgments should be left to God, that violence and cruelty are never acceptable, or that love may surpass understanding. Seeing this, students who are sexual minorities learn to meet their opposition with less terror and hostility and to discern more points at which good will might be advanced and gains negotiated.

It may happen that people's views change quite dramatically when they engage in this kind of inquiry and communication. But even if their conclusions remain the same, there will be a distinct increment in understanding and a stronger sense of community. Beyond civility, teaching as I see it is a practice of compassion. In religious contexts, compassion is exercised especially in regard to what we find repulsive—in other words, especially when we face the most profound disagreement and make the most negative judgments. A memory of shared humanness may bleed through at such moments, such that to

judge ill of another tastes of defeat, and to foster this memory is to practice compassion. Living with many such defeats, the bitterness may
seem as natural as, for many, my way of loving seems unnatural. But if
people like me are unnatural, I like to reply, maybe that is because we
are miracles, flowers too extravagant for convention but blooming
everywhere nonetheless. In truth, however, I think that passion and
community partake of the miraculous wherever they spring up, as does
change, as does learning. For to lead out is to pass through the margins
where the forgotten and defeated live, where relations strain and rules
are contested. And on the margins, as the Exodus story recalls, may be
found the moving edge of history.

NOTES

1. Ann Cameron, *Daughters of Copperwoman* (Vancouver, B.C.: Press Gang
Publishers, 1981).

2. Since the term *homosexuality* has usually implied a pathology, I employ it
only when repeating someone else's usage.

2   Three Steps Forward, One Step Back
Dilemmas of Upward Mobility

INITIATION

HAVING LEARNED from my unschooled parents that the world of academe was a Promised Land of wisdom and rational discourse, I arrived at my first scholarly conference in 1973 with high expectations. A fast-talking, dark-haired, working-class woman of Eastern European Jewish background, I hoped against hope that there was nothing about my style or manner that would signal to this predominantly male and middle-class gathering in a luxury hotel that I did not belong.[1]

At my first conference session, I sat in the back of the room, awed by the camaraderie of men in dark suits and ties, who nodded casually to people they knew as if standing in a position of authority before an audience of scholars was nothing special. I listened intently and was surprised to find the presentations easy to follow and not very challenging.

The moderator then opened the discussion by calling on the men he knew by their first names. The spirited repartee that followed was exclusively male. We [the women] did not meet each other's eyes; a few raised their hands and eventually lowered them. But I, enraged at such injustice in my newfound world of Reason, continued to wave my hand in the air. The moderator looked at me blankly and proceeded to call on several more men. Then, glancing to the right and left and seeing no other hands raised, he slowly nodded in my direction. By this time, I was incoherent with anger and could not even manage to formulate my question.

Not an auspicious debut. My contribution to the conference session was to reinforce whatever stereotypes those present may have already had about the irrational and unsocialized lower-class females in their midst.

36

I doubt if anyone saw a connection between my incoherence and the structure of that workshop session.

It was three years before I was willing to try again—much better defended this time and accompanied by a supportive colleague. But this painful and embarrassing initiation into the world of scholars turned out to be one of the most illuminating sources of insight into the teaching/learning process at UMass/Boston. Like many of my students, I had failed in an encounter with powerful structures established to value and reward individuals who most resembled those already in authority. Although I had always been praised for my verbal skills, it had taken less than an hour for a conference workshop to teach me how to become incoherent and inarticulate. My deficiencies were not inborn; they were site specific.

In my graduate training at Johns Hopkins University, silence was a learned response to what were to me puzzling academic hierarchies and intellectual exclusions. As a historian-to-be in the late 1960s, I was exposed to intellectually stimulating but narrow conceptions of historical knowledge—a background text entitled *History of the Modern World* turned out to be a history of Europe, women and working-class people were absent from the assigned readings, and none of my professors seemed to notice these omissions. As Ronald Takaki has suggested in another context, studying history was for me like looking in a mirror and seeing nothing. Aware of my graduate student status, I did not question the professors who chose these exclusionary texts, lectured about their universal significance and applicability, and delighted most in students who invited them to explore more deeply the narrow track of understanding they had laid out. Better, I thought, to remain silent and bide my time until I could find a place to speak more freely—at my first scholarly conference, for example. Or at least so I thought then.

As a junior faculty member at UMass/Boston, it seemed to me that if my students were to learn to respect and develop their intellectual powers and to claim their places in a wider world without inordinate pain and suffering, their learning experiences would have to differ pretty dramatically from my own. It was clear to me that I needed to learn how to teach in a manner that differed from those who had taught me. What follows is a story of my search for such knowledge in the lessons of outsider experience and in the challenges, support, and insight I received from students and faculty colleagues.

FACULTY DEVELOPMENT: FIRST ENCOUNTERS, INTELLECTUAL CHALLENGES

When I joined UMass/Boston's Department of History, I soon became a traditional good teacher. I worked hard to prepare informative lectures that would engage students in questions and discussion at the end of the hour, and received very positive feedback from students and from my department. Believing in the importance of social issues and popular culture, I devised reading packets that contrasted with the required textbooks' focus on politics and high culture. My choices were not always popular. Some students—especially history majors—wanted me to emphasize the kings and wars that had been the focus of their high-school history courses.

As a young woman with a soft voice, my authority was frequently tested by students like Henry, who always sat in the front row with legs stretched out so that they reached under the table behind which I sat. (Each morning, I would come to class early to push the first row of desks a bit further back from the table.) I still remember how the innocuous statement that the Emancipation of the Russian serfs occurred in 1861 drew from him the sarcastic response, "Well, I know that's your *opinion!*" I tried not to laugh at Henry. But then I looked around the room, registering the intensity with which the whole class—particularly the female students—were watching to see how I would react. "Sorry, Henry," I replied. "Many things I say may be debatable, but the date of the emancipation isn't one of them. You might want to check the textbook and come talk to me if you still have any questions." Students seemed relieved that I had claimed my authority as teacher and could produce a snappy verbal comeback.

I met with students at least once and sometimes twice in the course of the semester, ostensibly to talk about exams or research projects but in fact to learn more about their interests and concerns. Certain that our meetings were a personal favor from me that required a special reward, they frequently brought me cups of coffee and donuts. Many students found it hard to believe that holding office hours was a part of my job, or that I might actually want to meet with them. A number of working-class students in their twenties and thirties, as well as older students who viewed themselves as radicals, strongly identified with me, and some became lasting friends. I am not sure what drew them—my lengthy office hours, my enthusiasm, or the "alternative" content of my courses. In those years, it could not have been my innovative teaching methods. And while I enjoyed the positive feedback I received, I wasn't satisfied. I was in search of a pedagogy that was more informed by understandings of inclusion and exclusion and by my involvement in contemporary struggles for social and political change.

LEARNING TO LEARN FROM STUDENTS

My discomfort with some of the more conventional features of my own teaching was linked with issues of content as well as pedagogy. Reacting against the Western European orientation of the History Department, I proposed a first-year course called Modern World History and took advantage of the high percentage of Vietnam veterans on campus in the decade following the Vietnam War to devise a research project that focused on their experience. As a social historian, I knew that veterans—particularly those of working-class origin—had important and as yet untold stories to share. As a teacher, I was intrigued by the possibility that students might best learn history by becoming producers as well as consumers of historical data and knowledge. At that time, my students differed widely in age (eighteen to fifty-six) and in their levels of skill and academic preparation. Few were students of color, but their European ethnic backgrounds were quite diverse. Males and females were almost equal in number. About one third of the students in the class came from the nearby working-class neighborhoods of Dorchester and South Boston, which had contributed and lost so many recruits to the war.

Their assignment was to interview a Vietnam veteran—either an acquaintance or someone connected with the campus Veterans' Center. I began by dividing the class into small groups whose task was to propose five questions they considered worth asking a Vietnam veteran. After I distributed a master list of all the groups' questions to the class as a whole, we proceeded to discuss what constituted a "good" and a "bad" question. Although I guided the discussion, students themselves quickly decided to eliminate questions that were really accusations and were unlikely to elicit useful responses (for example, How did you feel about killing innocent people?). While recognizing the need for basic biographical data about age, rank, social background, and time spent in Vietnam, they also decided to create a special category of "sensitive questions" to be asked only with the subject's explicit permission. At my suggestion, they agreed that it was important to explain to the subject why the information was being collected, to ask permission to use the interview, and to promise anonymity.

Once students had approved the questionnaire they had constructed, the interview process began, and the structure and organization of the course started to change. Instead of waiting for me to begin class, some students began arriving early to brainstorm about how to make sense out of the stories they were hearing. Others joined in, excited about gathering data from people who were "part of history." The classroom began to become a place where both inspiring and difficult encounters could be shared. One student asked for advice about how to respond when an uncle confided that he had never before spoken to anyone about his Vietnam experience. Two Vietnam veterans who were students in the class confessed that they could not yet face researching the histories of other Vietnam veterans.[2] Mary, who had lost a son in Vietnam, wept in class as she reported on her subject's insistence that the war's violence was pointless.

At the same time, students became more confident as they assumed the role of "expert" on an important and original body of evidence instead of being empty vessels into which I was obliged to pour large quantities of knowledge. In other areas of the course, students began to raise more questions and to challenge my generalizations and judgments. These shifts in traditional student/faculty power relationships moved us onto uncertain—for me, sometimes uncomfortable—but exhilarating terrain. Students were increasingly engaged as critical learners, but I was distressed that I was unable to cover as much material as I had planned. Questions of "coverage" became a permanent concern, as I began to lecture less and allow more time for class discussion. As a way of recognizing and respecting the changes taking place, I instituted a twice-a-week, student-run "check-in" time of ten to fifteen minutes for the sharing of questions, troubling or interesting answers, and words of encouragement for those who were finding the research process difficult or painful.

While I could have predicted that student interview data might challenge my own assumptions about U.S. Vietnam veterans, I did not foresee how much this assignment would teach me about student abilities and potential. Skills and talents that are invisible in conventional classroom settings began to emerge into the open. In researching a topic that deeply interested them, students usually categorized as "unprepared" revealed strengths that are seldom utilized in the world of academe. In contrast to many professional scholars of the day, their desire to learn about Vietnam veterans was informed by a far greater sensitivity to how their research subjects might be misunderstood, misled, or otherwise hurt by the data-gathering process.

Following the example of my own teachers, I warned students against the danger of romanticizing their subjects, but students in turn reminded me that cynicism and objectification could also be obstacles to good scholarship. Having themselves experienced a variety of situations in which options were narrow, students of working-class background empathized with the feelings of veterans compelled—in their words—to carry out society's "grunt work." Because they treated their subjects as fully realized, heavily burdened human beings—not unlike themselves—these undergraduates were entrusted with information that might not have been given to others.

In their research papers, I asked each student to consider her/his subject's testimony in the light of the total body of collected interviews and to answer the following questions:

1. What stood out for you in these interviews, and what did they teach you about the war in Vietnam?
2. What important issues were you *unable* to explore on the basis of the interviews? In other words, what were the limitations imposed by the evidence you examined?
3. What issues would you like to pursue further?

Although their sophisticated data gathering and their reflections on the research process produced first-rate questionnaires and a valuable body of evidence, the final student papers were not as impressive as the process by which they were created. My first-year students remained inexperienced writers who found it difficult to produce a focused description or analysis. At the same time, the majority of their papers reflected a marked improvement over earlier efforts and contained a wealth of complex and unexpected insights. Even more important from an academic point of view was the clear evidence that they had begun to see themselves—and to act—as *researchers*. Their efforts over the course of the semester had placed these beginning students not in the same location but on the same research continuum where I worked as a professional historian. How was this sort of achievement to be "counted" in the academic scheme of things? What was the relationship between grades and student learning?

During the three-year period that the Vietnam veteran project continued, students questioned me more closely than ever before about my own scholarly work. How, they asked, did I organize data, decide what was most significant, tell the story, and document my findings? Did I study ordinary people as well as the famous and powerful? Students were intensely curious about my own struggle to legitimize the study of social history in the politics- and ideology-oriented field of Russian and Soviet studies (my area of specialization). So when I was invited to speak about my research at Harvard, I invited students in my classes to attend. Although Cambridge is only minutes away from UMass/Boston's Harbor Campus, they were markedly unenthusiastic about setting foot in Harvard Yard. But Ahmed wanted to come. An Iranian-born émigré involved in political activity that on occasion took him to Cambridge, he was less intimidated by Harvard's forbidding aura.

The hierarchy and demographics of my Harvard presentation recalled my first, demoralizing conference experience (with the important exception that this time I was the presenter). Counting myself and a woman UMass/Boston colleague, there were four females present in an audience of thirty-five; the only person of color was my student Ahmed. Faculty members sat at a large, rectangular table; graduate students sat against the wall at the back of the room or on the floor. Ahmed—not knowing the protocol—had arrived early and made the mistake of sitting at the table. He smiled with relief when I arrived, while I noticed with dismay the presence of a historian who disliked my work and looked as if he were present under protest. As I began speaking, some of the graduate students took notes, but everyone else seemed frozen in expressions of mild indifference or boredom. My "critic's" attention was riveted at a place six inches or so above my head. The longer I spoke, the harder it was to resist the temptation to turn around to see what he was looking at. When I finished, several graduate students and my UMass/Boston colleague asked questions.

As the audience filed out, I noticed Ahmed following closely after my scholarly critic. When he returned, seething with anger, he said,

All through your talk, that man was trying to break you down. He kept staring over your head and then he took his pens—four of them, very expensive fountain pens—out of his pocket and laid them one by one on the table in front of him. He picked up each pen and looked at it carefully, permitting five minutes for each pen, and then he replaced them all in his pocket! He wanted to show everybody that nothing you said was worth writing down.

I smiled uncertainly, and Ahmed went on:

Well, I decided to teach him a lesson. When I followed him out of the room, I put in his pocket a piece of paper on which was written the word "Pig!" I would like to see his face when he finds that in his pocket!

Somewhere between laughter and tears, I hugged Ahmed and hurried him out the door. On the one hand, I was clearly no longer in the initiation stage of my professional life, no longer likely to be rendered inarticulate by rituals of exclusion. But on the other, my instinct—which I did not question at the time—was to protect Ahmed against any unforeseen reprisal for bad behavior in the Promised Land.[3]

THE MOUNTING ODDS

In the 1990s, my students became far more diverse than before in racial, ethnic, and linguistic backgrounds and seemed to me financially and emotionally much closer to the edge. They were also more likely to be working forty hours a week and raising children while attending college on a full-time basis. In a political climate that increasingly scapegoated the poor, I noticed greater harshness in the judgments that students imposed upon themselves. Rejecting my efforts at reassurance, they argued that the obstacles and difficulties they faced were proof that they were not really "college material." As material and psychological struggles for survival took an increasing toll on student academic work, I was forced to re-examine the more traditional expectations and assumptions about students that I still possessed.

Lateness

Anita is always late for our appointments. She eventually appears, looking exhausted and embarrassed. Her husband is disabled, and she worries that he won't be able to care for their two children while she is on campus or at her evening job. When Anita tells me that she is distracted by a recent doctor's report that she has a heart problem, I wonder to myself how long she will remain in school. I urge her to put her name on the waiting list for the campus child-care center and to consider withdrawing from a class or two. But Anita explains that the university's financial aid and scholarship regulations require her to remain a full-time student. Convinced by Anita that I can only play a minor role in her struggle for academic survival, I am left to reflect on my annoyance about her "lateness." Somehow, she manages to survive the academic year with a B− average.

Tetteh has also missed several classes and several appointments. He is taking Modern World History for the second time, works six nights a week at a mental health center, goes to school full time during the day, and has a fourteen-month-old baby. I remember how little English he understood when he enrolled two years ago, only six months away from his home village in Cameroon. He is enjoying class and looks forward to reading the English version of Achebe's *Things Fall Apart* (having already read it in French translation). According to Tetteh, the only thing he needs now is the time to read and study. I agree; he would have to be superhuman to succeed academically when his nonacademic burdens are so heavy. For Tetteh, course withdrawal is not an option. In an angry voice (angry with whom, I asked myself), he declares: "I can't fail again, not for a second time!"

During the last four weeks of the semester, Tetteh is absent from six classes and cancels several appointments—his child has been hospitalized. When we finally meet, he apologizes for "insulting me" by missing our meetings and falling behind. I am dismayed at the depth of his feeling of shame—it's almost as if he feels dishonored by the burdens he is carrying. With the help of a tutor, we draw up a study plan that Tetteh considers moderately realistic. But he doesn't show up for the final exam. I telephone him, and we make an appointment to meet. On the next day, Tetteh leaves a message telling me that he deserves a failing grade and wants me to give him an F. He doesn't return my phone call.

Grades

Delores appears in my office to talk about a grade of D on a recent take-home essay exam in which she answered half of two questions and did not respond at all to the third. Explaining that she had repeatedly reread the assigned material and rewritten the exam, Delores points angrily at my marginal comment: "This was not written with a great deal of care." I apologize. With a felt-tip pen, I draw a thick line through it. The tension between us subsides a bit, and we are able to talk about strategies for answering exam questions. I still think she was careless. But if the improvement of her academic work was indeed my top priority, my judgmental statements seemed to be a distraction.

For more than twelve years, Joe, a Vietnam veteran, has carried in his wallet a silver bullet and a piece of paper with harsh comments from a teacher on his "clumsy" writing and "superficial" ideas. After receiving a grade of B on one assignment in a Russian history course, he wrote me the following letter:

> I want to express how inadequate, limited, and poorly thought out and exe-cuted my paper was. I think that my paper should be dismissed and given no credit for the course. I think that an incomplete grade should be given me until such time that I finish a proper paper, appropriate to the course's requirements. I want you to know that I value the education that I am receiving here at UMass/Boston. I would like to be able to meet my pro-fessor's expectations, but I do not feel that I have done so. I'm ashamed of some of the material I have presented to you and other professors. I believe that I am capable of doing better. I am aware that we live in a time-oriented society, but that should not be an excuse for shoddy or superficial work. I would appreciate it if you would respond favorably to my request.

We meet, and I try to convince Joe to let me be the judge of his work. He relents and receives a B+ in the course.

I meet with Patrick, a student fascinated by historical issues and a questioner who sends our class discussions in wonderfully unexpected directions. I especially like the way that he thinks aloud, serving as a role model for many students who may never before have considered taking themselves seriously as thinkers. But Pat's midterm exam contained too much abstract discussion and not enough concrete data for a history course, and I returned it with a grade of C. Pat then notified me that he plans to withdraw from the course but would like to speak with me beforehand.

Pat describes himself to me as a man burdened by a heavy sack of rocks that includes fear about his own abilities, a wish not to disappoint me, and the precariousness of the 4.0 average he seeks to maintain in order to gain entrance to graduate school at the age of forty-three. According to Pat,

> I need every advantage I can get. And although I really like your class, I'm
> not sure I can *afford* to be in it. I've read your comments over and over,
> and I really see what you mean—but I probably would have seen just as
> well if you had given me a B. Do you really think that I can do any better
> in this course?

In Patrick's case, the grade of C was not only hurtful; it also distracted
him from solving the quite manageable problems I had identified in his
paper. I put all of my persuasive powers into convincing him that he
should not withdraw. Unlike Tetteh, Pat allows himself to be reassured
and finishes the course with a well-deserved grade of A. In his case,
grades did not seem to promote either learning or achievement. While
I wanted Delores and Pat to pay attention to the problems I saw in their
exams, it seemed to me that that grades were positioning me as a sort of
"bouncer" at the gates of knowledge.[4]

Building Connections: Learning from Colleagues

In the 1990s, the lessons of the Vietnam veteran project were reinforced
by ideas and perspectives gained as director of UMass/Boston's fac-
ulty-based Center for the Improvement of Teaching (CIT). I was invited
to take this position because I was viewed as an already successful
teacher. But CIT became an opportunity for me to move toward deeper
understandings, to join with colleagues to build a more inclusive curriculum,[5] and to learn more about alternative teaching strategies that provide students with challenging work in a supportive setting. Although I
was already accustomed to investing time and energy into the creation
of course materials with intellectually engaging and provocative content, CIT workshops and forums linked me with diverse colleagues—
many of whom are contributors to this book—who helped me learn
more about how to encourage students to engage with each other and
with me in a more cooperative learning process.

Names

Although I always tried to learn the names of students in my classes, my
colleagues taught me that students might be more engaged and better
supported in their uphill academic efforts if they knew the names of
their peers in addition to the name of a professor. I introduced a "name
game" strategy to which we devoted the first five to ten minutes of each

fifty-minute class. At first, students good-humoredly tolerated this exercise as one of the many incomprehensible tasks that teachers routinely require. But they soon wanted to succeed in the game by learning each other's names. Somewhat puzzled but open to my participation in the circle, they spontaneously—and often with a great deal of tact—helped classmates who forgot particular names.

In the course of this exercise, I observed a number of "majority" students becoming aware of how very difficult the name game was for non-native speakers. More than most other students, the ESL students took the exercise very seriously—by making lists, repeating each name as it was spoken, and even practicing with each other outside the classroom door. On the other hand, native English speakers frequently reported that our class was the first time they had ever been expected to pronounce Vietnamese, African, or Spanish names. At the end of the semester, one non-native speaker declared that the university seemed less "scary" because she now knew twenty-five people by name (these were, she said, the only first names she knew at UMass/Boston). A biology major named Chris commented, "I like this class, but it's really not like a college course . . . because I know everyone's name."

Journals

In order to engage students in reflection and writing about their reading assignments, I learned to use ungraded but required in-class journals. Unsurprisingly, some students were skeptical about my claim that required writing would not in fact be graded. Circumspectly but persistently, they tried to find out if my written comments on their journals constituted a covert sort of grading system. Would I really accept journals that expressed dislike for the assigned readings or disagreement with my interpretations or judgments? I always responded with words of positive reassurance. But it was of course a continual struggle to avoid the impulse—born of years as a member of the professoriate—to respond as the universal expert and judge to student writing.

On occasion, student journals revealed that assignments or texts that I considered transparent were in fact ambiguous and open to interpretations I had not foreseen. For example, in journal responses to the character of Okonkwo in Achebe's *Things Fall Apart*, most of the males in one class (both Euro-Americans and students of color) commented approvingly on Okonkwo's physical strength and courage and sympathized with his hatred for an unambitious father. In contrast, female students were more impressed by Okonkwo's violence and cruelty to his wives and daughters. Males and females were equally astounded at each other's responses. Richard described Okonkwo as a typical "American-style" male; Anita argued that he was not even typical of the African males portrayed in the Achebe novel. A quite sophisticated discussion ensued, in which students questioned their beliefs about what constituted "typical" behavior and proceeded to consider the similarities between the traditional, patriarchal Ibo society portrayed by Achebe and the traditional societies with which they were familiar in the local neighborhoods of South Boston, Dorchester, and Brighton.

Frequently, journals encouraged participation in classroom discussions. Since each student prepared a journal entry, I could ask even the shyest person, or the people most nervous about speaking in English, to participate by reading their journals aloud. On occasion, positive feedback from me and from classmates served as a bridge to greater involvement. But not always. I remember Dong's fear that her "bad English" kept her from finishing in-class journals during the time allotted. I sympathized, but assured Dong that her journals to date were in fact perfectly acceptable. When I suggested that she come to my office to look at some other student journals, Dong responded with a smile: "I don't want to bother you." I tell her that my office hours are for her to use. She smiles again and shakes my hand.

But Dong soon withdrew from the class. The encouragement I gave to her was evidently not as compelling as her fears or the weight of her previous schooling. Her disappearance from class did not lead me to question the value of journal writing, but it reminded me that panaceas were in short supply. Students at UMass/Boston were always balancing new experiences against the lessons of their personal history, and they drew different conclusions at different points in their own evolution as learners.

INCLUSION AS A CLASSROOM STRATEGY AND AN INTELLECTUAL SKILL

In recent years, as I have tried harder to link course content and structure, questions of historical method and epistemology have begun to take center stage in all of my classes. I ask students from historically marginalized groups—whose experience of studying history is often like looking in a mirror and seeing nothing—to analyze the process by which historical "mirrors" are constructed. In first-year and upper-level courses, I ask students to collaborate in small group efforts with four goals: (1) to identify the voices deployed to tell the story of a particular event, movement, or intellectual development, (2) to become aware of how many voices are presented, (3) to notice which voices are missing, and (4) to consider how the story might be better and more fairly told.

For example, in Modern World History, we examine England's Industrial Revolution as viewed by a Chartist factory worker, a factory owner, and the author of the required textbook. Groups of students are assigned the task of deciding what kinds of evidence and values are presented in each historical account they read. They are asked to try to characterize the voice of each text as a source of information, and they present their group's judgment to the class. Adam finds the discussion of multiple voices unsettling. "If you really believe that no source is neutral—you couldn't believe anyone!" John is even more put off by the implications of these methodological inquiries. After one class, he tells me,

> I expected the university to be like a supermarket. You shop around, decide on different courses, and then get the information that goes with each course. But it feels like the real agenda in our class is to open everything to question. That's not why I came to school.

But Abby asks, "Why was the textbook so obsessed with economics and technology? Couldn't he have told us something about women, or about the Poor Laws? In the packets we learned that many of the radical Chartist factory workers were Irish, but the textbook didn't mention either the Chartists or the Irish." According to Meghan, "I had never thought of questioning the objectivity of textbooks. I can see now that they are written by human beings and not by robots." Eva concludes,

> Everything I read has already been filtered through the mind of another human being. With this in mind I began to look more closely at what I read, but also keep an open mind about the information given to me. I now try to get as many sides to a story as I can so when I come to a conclusion it would be a fair, thought-out, and educated one.

For a number of students, the African voice is the most painful and transformative to hear. Gina angrily comments, "I grew up with so many stereotypes about African jungles filled with lions. Now I come to find out that most of Africa is desert, and lions don't live in jungles!

If I could be so dumb about something so basic, then what I think I know about Africa must be worse than nothing." Some students use the history of their own ethnic group to try to understand the history of others. Eric tries to imagine being in a situation where a lack of understanding could threaten his survival:

> I hated the cartoons we saw which showed the Irish as animals. I had never seen racist judgments on my heritage before. Maybe I at least have a small understanding of the feeling of anger, but nowhere near the magnitude that other groups must have. I never knew before how many Africans were killed in the slave trade or how Europeans tried to justify the killing.

Paul links the historical experience of the Irish with his current attitudes toward Southeast Asians. In his words,

> When I read about how Bostonians of the 1850s viewed my Irish ancestors and how they were ridiculed for being noisy, unlawful, dirty people, I was appalled. It was then I realized, to my chagrin, that my friends and I are doing the same thing when we joke about the newly arrived Cambodians and Vietnamese. The descendants of people who were looked down upon should learn of their past in order not to repeat it.

A CONVERSATION ABOUT RACIAL STEREOTYPES AND SOCIAL DARWINISM

Ana wants to know if Social Darwinism still exists. I ask if the racial stereotypes seem familiar to people, and many students nod. "Why," I ask, "do people adopt these beliefs? Do they just go crazy and fall under their spell?" Here's some of the dialogue that follows:

Kellie: People want scapegoats. If they are busy dumping on someone they see as racially inferior, then they won't try to change things.

Tetteh: People feel safer when they can believe that they are superior. All the "superior" ones can then feel good about belonging to a higher group.

Me: Since wanting to feel safe and wanting to belong are perfectly reasonable human desires, what is wrong with racial stereotyping?

John: I don't know what right and wrong have to do with it. If you don't dominate others, they will dominate you. I don't think the British should have felt guilty for conquering Ireland or India or China. If they hadn't done it, someone else would have.

Joe: But it wasn't okay for the British to sell opium to the Chinese, was it? It wasn't okay to enslave people from Africa and kill forty million people.

Me: John is speaking like a Social Darwinist by describing the world as an arena where only the fittest survive. [Ana nods, and so does John.] What would the Chartists have said about Social Darwinism? How do their ideas fit in?

Anthony: The Chartists talk about justice. They believe that people have a right to be treated fairly. But justice isn't part of Social Darwinism.

It is the end of the hour. Ana is intent, Tetteh is smiling, John looks angry. No one moves for a minute.

"Good," I say. "Let's keep thinking about all this. It's important. We will continue next time."

But John comes up to my desk to ask, "Was I wrong?"

I remember earlier conversations with John, an embattled, Irish, working-class student who fears that he isn't intelligent enough to be in college.

"Well, I don't agree with you," I tell him. "But whether I agree or not, it's worth considering that once you accept the Social Darwinist argument that a small group of people will always dominate the rest, you've taken on a point of view that excludes you."

"I know," John says. "That's what I am struggling with." He shakes his head. "You keep trying to get us to be more self-critical, don't you?"

I nod. He pauses for a moment and smiles broadly: "Well, I sure hope you can bring it off!"

I am silenced.

The odds are against John changing, Tetteh improving his economic situation, Dong returning to class. They have been injured—with no easy cure in sight—by previous schooling that did not nurture their potential and by material needs and time pressures that compel them to choose between a college education and their obligations to children or parents. But Eva is now an honors student, and Anita and Paul have graduated. Joe and Abby are in graduate school, and Eric plays in a band. And Amos, an African American former student whose story is not included here, has come back to teach at UMass/Boston.

Perhaps the failures are not as surprising as the successes. They now seem to me precarious miracles of persistence, intelligence, and luck to which we as teachers can learn to contribute.

NOTES

Acknowledgments: I would like to thank Tim Sieber, Marilyn Hecht, Hubie Jones, Segi Stefanos, Cass Turner, Elizabeth Minnich, Linda Epps, Ed Toomey, and other colleagues and friends for the benefit of deep conversations about teaching over the years, as well as some of the former students whose ideas about teaching and learning have been especially inspiring and helpful: Juan Calo, John Clifford, Sandy Clifford, Cameron Constant, Irene Egan, Tom Gilmore, Frankie Heng, Joanne Kenney, Emily Lopez, Joe Lynch, Barbara Machtinger, Edna Phipher, Cindy Polinsky, Joe Power, Qui Phanh, Michael Quirk, Lauren Craig Redmond, Jeffrey Scott, Lekel St. Fleurose, and Yu-mui Wan.

1. Participants were also without exception "white," but since I shared this background and understood less about it then than I do now, this demographic was not oppressive to me at the time.

2. I had not foreseen their reactions. We quickly improvised an alternative assignment in which they interviewed antiwar activists and read a number of secondary sources dealing with the antiwar movement. But neither their learning experience nor their final papers were comparable to the work of their classmates.

3. Although my scholarly initiation took place over twenty-five years ago, and the experience described above more than a decade ago, a scenario eerily reminiscent of both unfolded at a 1997 session of the national conference of the American Association for the Advancement of Slavic Studies. But by this time, I was the author of three distinguished scholarly monographs and more experienced in the world of academe. I "kept my cool" and spoke clearly and concisely when one of the male panelists finally called on me. Afterward, a female scholar in the audience came over to commiserate, and a male scholar in the row in front of me turned to me and commented, "Good question!" As in teaching, progress toward inclusion seems everywhere to be an uneven and nonlinear process. See Esther Kingston-Mann, preface to *In Search of the True West: Culture, Economics, and Problems of Russian Development* (Princeton, N.J.: Princeton University Press, 1999).

4. Some useful discussions of grading and assessment issues are Georgine Loacker and Marcia Mentkowski, "Creating a Culture Where Assessment Improves Learning," in Trudy W. Banta et al., eds., *Making a Difference: Outcomes of a Decade of Assessment in Higher Education* (San Francisco: Jossey-Bass, 1993), pp. 5–24; and David Smith et al., "Failure's Failure," in Evelyn Jacobs and Cathy Jordan, eds., *Minority Education: Anthropological Perspectives* (Norwood, N.J.: Ablex, 1993), pp. 209–31.

5. See Esther Kingston-Mann, "Multiculturalism Without Political Correctness: The UMass/Boston Model," *Boston Review*, May-June 1992.

ADDITIONAL RESOURCES

Collins, Patricia Hill. "Learning from the Outsider Within: The Sociological Significance of Black Feminist Thought." *Social Problems* 33 (6): 14–32 (1986).

Dews, C. L. Barney, and Carolyn Leste Law, eds. *This Fine Place So Far from Home: Voices of Academics from the Working Class.* Philadelphia: Temple University Press, 1994.

Heath, Shirley Brice. "Work, Class and Categories: Dilemmas of Identity." In Lynn Z. Bloom, Donald A. Daiker, and Edward White, eds. *Composition in the Twenty-First Century: Crisis and Change.* Carbondale: Southern Illinois University Press, 1996.

Kaltner, John, and Andrea Tschemplik. "It's the Format, Stupid! A New Perspective on Teaching Diversity." *Transformations* 4 (1): 51–55 (1993).

Kim, Myung-hee. "Labor Trilogy." In Janet Zandy, ed. *Calling Home: Working-Class Women's Writings.* New Brunswick, N.J.: Rutgers University Press, 1990.

Luttrell, Wendy. "Working-Class Women's Ways of Knowing: Effects of Gender, Race, and Class." *Sociology of Education* 62 (1989): 33–46.

Minnich, Elizabeth. "From the Circle of the Elite to the World of the Whole: Education, Equality, and Excellence." In Carol S. Pearson et al., eds. *Educating the Majority: Women Challenge Tradition in Higher Education.* New York: American Council on Education/Macmillan, 1989, pp. 277–93.

Rose, Mike. *Lives on the Boundary.* New York: Free Press, 1993.

Rothenberg, Paula, ed. *Race, Class, and Gender in the United States: An Integrated Study.* 4th ed. New York: St. Martins, 1998.

Smith, Patricia. "Grandma Went to Smith All Right, But She Went from Nine to Five." Michelle Tokarczyk and Elizabeth Fay, eds. *Working-Class Women in the Academy: Laborers in the Knowledge Factory.* Amherst: University of Massachusetts Press, 1993.

Zandy, Janet, ed. *Calling Home: Working-Class Women's Writings.* New Brunswick, N.J.: Rutgers University Press, 1990.

See also the Library on Inclusive Teaching, Learning, and Curriculum Change of the Center for the Improvement of Teaching, University of Massachusetts Boston. For information, contact *citumb@umb.edu*.

3 Learning to Listen to Students and Oneself

It is in listening to the student that I learn how to speak with him or her.
—Paulo Freire, *Pedagogy of Freedom*

To teach in a manner that respects and cares for the souls of our students is essential if we are to provide the necessary conditions where learning can most deeply and intimately begin.
—bell hooks, *Teaching to Transgress*

AT THE end of one semester, I was reading a student's fairly conventional research paper, "Effects of Adoption on the Family," for my interdisciplinary course Childhood in America and reached that last, unexpected sentence: the student had written, "I'm very familiar with this situation, since my brother is adopted." There it was again—so odd, I thought—that brief mention at the end, almost an afterthought, of a personal connection to the paper topic. I had never imagined that this student had an adopted brother until I read the last sentence.

At first I thought it was a coincidence that students often chose topics of personal interest, even if they alluded to their personal links in such limited ways. Having given them completely free choice on the paper topic so long as it concerned problems of children in the United States, I wondered if this effect was just random. It did seem, however, that students *often* chose topics—adoption, divorce, single-parent families, immigration, and so on—related to their life experiences, even if this only leaked through their work in indirect ways. It crossed my mind, at times, whether this was appropriate, or maybe even an easy way out. If anthropology argued that social and cultural analysis was suitable mainly for applying to the "other," the unfamiliar or the different, did a personal connection with the material hamper, rather than help, effective learning?

Still, papers like this suggested to me in some inchoate way that there was a puzzling disconnect between personal experience and academic analysis in the work that students were doing in my course. Why didn't the students discuss the link earlier and more openly? I spent some years observing this pattern, though remaining a little uncomfortable with it. In my early teaching, two decades or more ago, I had unconsciously assumed that participation in the academic enterprise, and academic achievement itself, required—even depended on—such a disconnection. It was the pattern I had learned earlier as the secret to success and to my own entry as a student into the academic world.

LEARNING TO DISCONNECT AT COLLEGE

I grew up in the country, on the edge of a small town in Appalachia, a white, working-class boy in the 1950s. My mother had quit her job as a receptionist at a country music radio station so that she could stay home with me, and later with my brother, after we were born in quick succession. My father was an electrician who, because of shortages of work in the region, often worked on construction projects in other states and visited home on weekends. My paternal grandparents and teenage aunt and uncle lived next door, all of us forming a closely cooperative extended family. My parents valued education and pushed me strongly to achieve and to enter what was then called the "college-prep" track in high school. From rural, working-class backgrounds themselves, my parents had both been tracked in school away from such a course of study. My mother and father never hesitated to communicate to me their resigned disappointment over their lack of access to all the education they had wanted and felt they were capable of handling.

I did well in high school and was a leader in many extracurricular activities. In that era of great expansion of higher education in the 1960s, I was offered scholarships to attend a small, elite, Quaker, all-men's liberal arts college on the east coast. As a rural, working-class boy and a West Virginian, I was admitted to add diversity to the strongly upper-middle-class, suburban, East-Coast student body at the school. In those days, affirmative action was limited to whites like me and aimed at adding mostly regional and class variety to the fundamentally middle- and upper-class, white student bodies that characterized higher education at the time (there was just one African American in my class of 125).

College changed my life, introducing me for the first time to critical intellectual work, progressive politics, and new class etiquettes, modes of expression, and role models. It was clear to me, though, that little in my background had much to do with the culture of the school or with most of my friends there. Visits back and forth between home and school came to be extremely confusing. I learned how to fit into the college world, but at the expense of keeping that life separate from anything at home. Even short visits home would make me feel that West Virginia was where I belonged, and I wondered why I should even leave to go back to school again. It was disconcerting to live in two such different worlds. It did not help that some old friends at home, who attended the local state teachers' college, told me that the person I was becoming at college was "not the real you." Some of my wider extended family at home disapproved of the intellectual skepticism I was learning, as well as of the radical politics sweeping my campus in those intense times of the 1960s, thinking I was being badly influenced.

At college I often felt ashamed to reveal much about my parents, my family, or my background, even as I continued to love my family and feel longing for them. I felt that my upbringing was a kind of deficit that I had to work hard to overcome, and I was determined to do that. At the time, I felt my family even wanted me to do this, as the necessary price of success. Later I came to understand that, while proud of me, they did not realize that my academic achievements implied that I would probably not return home, either physically or in spirit. At school, I thus learned quickly to try to hide and deny my background, basically to see it as something simply irrelevant to my new life. This was not hard to do. No one at the college was interested in it, nothing in the curriculum had anything to do with it, and in all my four years there, not one of my professors ever asked me about my background or encouraged me to write or talk about it as part of my education. Already being a white male made learning to pass in a new setting and a new class relatively easy for me.

All of this had negative repercussions for my education nonetheless. I often felt confused about my identity, my values, and the kind of life I should live. My studies suffered, my performance was spotty, I wasn't sure why I was in school, and during the middle years I often skipped class and didn't do the reading for my courses. Whenever I applied myself, I could do the work well, and I knew that. Eventually a junior-year escape to neutral territory, a study-abroad program in Berlin, allowed me to pull myself together. I returned for a focused senior year, during which I lived quietly and marginally on the edge of campus. I had decided to dedicate myself to this new life away from home and wanted to enter graduate school with the goal of becoming an academic.

I was well prepared by these early, undergraduate struggles for both graduate school and later struggles to survive the rigors and the terrors of the university's tenure system. While in graduate school, and even as a junior faculty member, I continued to have many of these same identity conflicts, of course, but they had come to seem more "normal," even manageable, by that time. I had learned to disconnect from my past and to fit in, and this arrangement was something I did not question or understand until years later, when I began listening more closely to my students.

LOOKING BACKWARD AND SEEING CHANGE

Twenty-five years later, looking back on my beginnings as a teacher, I know I have changed dramatically the ways I understand and practice teaching, including the way I conduct my course on childhood. I understand better the reasons for the students' disconnection between their lives and what they are studying. For me, the dramatic changes have been more in pedagogy than in content. In the early years of my teaching, I didn't realize how the manner in which I taught the class actually *disinvited* students from tapping their personal experiences and registering their affective—and even their critical and intellectual—responses to the course material in their writing. Over the years, my own process of pedagogical change has involved for me much professional growth as a teacher, especially in understanding the consequences of my actions, in learning how to listen better to my students, and in discovering my own history as a learner and long-time sojourner in academia.

I found that learning to listen to my students and to understand their academic challenges, along with learning to understand my own past, were reciprocal processes: only after I became a witness to my students' struggles could I come to remember and understand what my own had been. This recognition of common struggle has allowed me to be much more supportive to my students. Ironically, as an anthropologist I had long been teaching my students that understanding the self and understanding the other are always a reciprocal process, in fieldwork and in cross-cultural studies. But even while I was "teaching" it, the practical lessons of this disciplinary maxim for my own practice as a teacher took many more years to dawn on me. What follows here, then, is the story of how I have found my way toward these new realizations and struggled to foster a more caring, authentic, and critically challenging environment in my own classes than I ever enjoyed myself as a student.

The Childhood in America Course: Learning from Students

My course Childhood in America is a multidisciplinary treatment of childhood in the United States, cross-listed in American studies and anthropology and drawing broadly on historical, literary, and social scientific (especially anthropological) sources. I developed the course and have taught it for twenty-two years. From the beginning, the course always gave strong attention to race, class, ethnic, and gender differences in childhood and family experiences, and it took a strongly social constructionist, critical, historical perspective toward childhood, contextualizing it within broader U.S. economic and cultural patterns. It's the only course in the university catalog that considers childhood within such a context and that departs from the usual psychological approach, which views childhood as an individual developmental process.

Several of the course's major goals draw on the basic assumptions of anthropology as a discipline, especially its insistence on looking at a widely diverse sample of Euro-American and non-Euro-American childhood and family experiences in U.S. society, historical and contemporary, always in order to create a comparative perspective. (Such an approach is also strongly in keeping with the newer multicultural vision that has emerged in today's field of American studies.) In a society prone to generalization about the universals of good childrearing and family functioning, a comparative perspective reveals the genuine, explainable, and usually sensible diversity of practices that have always existed. A comparative perspective also leads to more insightful, often surprising generalizations about commonalities. The rich ethnographic and autobiographical materials that students study promote understanding and empathy toward the life struggles of people different from themselves, as well as the recognition of unexpected human commonalities among groups. The effort to understand others provides students, of course, with new critical insights into the particular meanings of their own cultural experiences and assumptions.

The course also attempts to shed light on contemporary debates in children's policy in areas such as day care, child abuse, and children's rights, and to show how these are shaped by historically and culturally constructed notions of childhood and family peculiar to the United States. Finally, the course tries to acknowledge children's ambiguous status as an oppressed and a protected group within the nation, and the problems caused for them by the deeply institutionalized age discrimination they encounter in the family and other institutions. Students are asked to consider whether advocacy of children's interests and rights always coincides, in the short run at least, with what is best or most convenient for their caretakers, supervisors, or managers.

The class is always taken by a broad and interesting mix of people. Most have been women, though in recent years a few more men have enrolled. A large number of the mostly working-class and lower-middle-class women who have taken the course have worked or were working while students as child-care workers in preschools or as nannies in wealthy families. Some have been in training to be teachers or nurses, and some have been experienced, working, registered nurses who are back in school to complete their bachelor's degrees. Some have been parents and even, in our age-mixed, older student body, grandparents. Another important segment has been foreign or immigrant students who choose the class, one of a few the university offers that critically examines U.S. cultural patterns, in order to gain more insight into conventional American ways that are still mysterious to them. Another important subgroup is psychology majors, many of whom hope for careers in counseling children and youth. And each class has included some students who are survivors of difficult, often abusive childhoods, for whom a usually unspoken part of their purpose in the educational projects they choose is to gain more insight into their own troubled pasts. More than for any other course I teach, of course, the class material has a special, personal resonance for everyone: by virtue of the fact that all students have been children themselves, they have significant and compelling personal experience with the subject matter. For many, of course, it can be painful to be reminded of their experiences.

As a deeply interdisciplinary effort, my course was innovative for me from the start: I didn't rely simply on anthropological materials, as noted, but used historical and literary materials, as well as social scientific ones, to frame the scope of the subject and to construct interpretations of children and families. Risk-taking in course content, however, did not imply that I was strongly attuned to my students. In fact, two decades ago, questions about who the students were as people, what their motivations were for taking the course, and what the link was between course material and personal experience mattered little to me. I taught the class in the traditional lecture style I had learned and was modeling from my own graduate education: the professor possessed the knowledge and the expert analytic frameworks for approaching the subject, and should patiently, clearly explain and model them for the students. For me, then, teaching involved not so much listening to and responding to students, but preparing formal lectures and making sure I was able to "cover" the subject in the time available. I was clearly a practitioner of what Paulo Freire has called the "banking" system of education[1]—the assumption that the teaching act centers on the professor depositing his expert knowledge in the mind of the passive student and then withdrawing it through examination.

I thought I was being paid and evaluated for sharing my expert knowledge, and there was little in the faculty evaluation system I was subjected to that suggested otherwise. Without being aware of it, I assumed that all credible academic knowledge needed to be taught and learned in a decontextualized manner, removed from personal experience or interest. Accordingly, my assignments asked students to explicate texts, develop and analyze case materials, and draw appropriate conclusions about their relevance for the development of scholarly knowledge. I did not go beyond this to invite students to engage in more critical, sometimes personal, responses to course materials, or to define for themselves the critical intellectual or affective issues they posed.

Finally, after many hints about personal connection in the oblique references to personal family circumstances in student papers I slowly began to invite students to discuss in writing some of the connections between the course material and their own lives. At first I did this in a very circumscribed way, giving them the option on one take-home exam of choosing to write one short essay (out of three) that compared their own families or childhoods to some of those we were studying in the class. When some students actually chose this option, I decided to push the envelope a bit further and "take care" of the issue of personal connection by simply *requiring* that *everyone* in the class write a whole paper on their family histories. This, I thought, would give students ample opportunity to get out of the way whatever issues the course material might be bringing up for them personally, and to appreciate the power of the course's theories and analytic models for illuminating general human experience, including their own. In that way, personal issues would not further "interfere" with the rest of their learning in the course. Of course now I realize that these concerns never really "interfered" with students' learning.

Almost everyone complied with the requirement to write a family history, but it became clear to me in reading the resulting papers that not all students welcomed the assignment or used it to achieve insight into their own family histories. In fact, there was a defensive tone to some of the papers, and the majority were fairly romanticized, nonanalytic paeans to their parents or families that did not achieve the insights I had hoped for. Surprisingly, a few students found the assignment coercive and unfair, an invasion of their privacy. I later heard that the assignment provoked enough of a crisis for at least one student that she needed to resume sessions with her therapist simply to handle it. It had not occurred to me that survivors of abusive families might have a particularly difficult time with this assignment. I see now how threatening this probably was for some; this threat also might explain some of the Pollyannaish reports I got about how good their families were.

It wasn't long after—whether because of my assignment or because of similar ones given by other colleagues—that psychologists in our university Counseling Center offered a friendly advisory to faculty not to require autobiographical work in courses, but instead to make this kind of assignment optional. I realized I had been naive to think that any standard, compulsory assignment would somehow mechanically take care of all the personal issues the course material might raise for the students. I never used this flawed assignment again, though I came to see it as another halting step forward in finding a better way to listen to my students and to recognize the often intense personal issues my courses posed for them.[2]

Learning How to Teach from Supportive Colleagues

Supportive, knowledgeable campus colleagues have always been essential in my growth and learning as a teacher. Several departmental colleagues have always been dedicated teachers, and as friends and collaborators they have always helped me, especially in the years when I was struggling to find new teaching strategies that would work better for me and the students. In the early years of my career, however, the overall faculty understanding of teaching at the university was quite traditional. Teaching was defined as a matter of ensuring that students mastered basic bodies of fixed, expert knowledge, and few departments in the arts and sciences welcomed much critical examination of pedagogy, student learning, or educational philosophy.

Faculty deliberations about teaching were infrequent, usually limited to discussions over what content should be transmitted or even to complaint sessions about students' abilities, unpreparedness, and propensity to evade what the faculty thought they should learn. Colleagues in many departments continually resisted discussing pedagogy or assessment in department meetings, insisting that superior credentials in research are what make faculty good, qualified teachers. Teaching was also seen as decidedly secondary in importance to scholarship: for example, until recently, in yearly merit awards writing one short book review normally brought a higher salary increase than developing and teaching a new course or even creating an entirely new curricular program. Furthermore, faculty did not encourage meaningful critical input or feedback from the students on curriculum matters, or even on individual courses. Student course evaluations were depreciated as unreliable instruments; high marks from students were suspected of measuring popularity, easy grading, or questionable standards. Low marks from students, in contrast, were thought to show that faculty members were "rigorous" teachers with "high standards."

As a specialist at that time in the anthropology of education who had done research on cross-cultural communication and conflict in urban elementary and secondary schools for my doctoral dissertation, I taught several different courses in the university's teacher preparation programs that drew on my field of specialization. The key goals of these courses were to educate prospective teachers about the cultural variability among students in contemporary U.S. schools, the educational problems that resulted from educators' ignorance or neglect of cultural diversity, and the constructive ways that classroom and school organization, curriculum, and pedagogy can be refigured to promote equal opportunity and to allow all students to feel comfortable and affirmed in school and to perform well academically.

Only after a few years of teaching these courses in my usual, traditional lecture format did it begin to dawn on me that these lessons had relevance to my own and my colleagues' teaching practice at the university level. Even though it was obvious that we taught in an urban educational institution with culturally diverse students and an academic culture more or less impermeable to most of the students who arrived to study there, most of us did not think the obvious, standard advice our university was giving to other, lower-level educators was applicable to our own practices. This myopia stemmed from faculty reluctance to define ourselves as educators with interests in common with all other educators. Faculty members were deeply committed to seeing themselves chiefly as scholars, on a superior level of expert understanding, and to upholding a corollary, abstracted conception of education as knowledge transmission.

Anthropologist Josiah Heyman, among many others, has recently remarked on "how little anthropologists (and other academics)" appear to value or write about "teaching and creative institutional service" as important parts of their professional work, despite the fact that these are the main arenas for what he calls "moral practice" by most academics.[3] While Heyman does not specifically offer an explanation for the "invisibility" of these important social engagements for professors, it may be that traditional, disciplinarily defined departments offer relatively barren ground for wrestling with pedagogical matters and the human issues they pose for teaching. Departments' raison d'être and usual preoccupations center all too often on defense of turf—establishing their intellectual authority (and rationalizing their budgets) through sharply bounding and defending their curriculums and academic content areas. Traditional personnel evaluation systems, moreover, privilege such authority through rewarding appropriately narrow ranges of scholarly discourse that typically exclude discussion of everyday academic practice with colleagues, administrators, and students. Most of faculty's community service is under-discussed, if not devalued, for much the same reasons.

Because of this, it has always been chiefly through involvement in multidisciplinary contexts with colleagues and programs *outside* my own department that I have found the most practical help and intellectual support in rethinking and changing my teaching practices. The most important of these involvements was a grassroots faculty, staff, and student movement in the early 1990s. Linked to our Center for the Improvement of Teaching, this group sought to transform the university curriculum to take more account of diversity. I became a part of the effort early on. Our movement and proposals for change did not simply involve curriculum content and academic requirements, but also implied significant attention to pedagogy. I joined a series of ongoing conversations, formal and informal seminars, forums, and conferences with colleagues about making our teaching more responsive, in pedagogy as well as content, to our university's unusual, older, essentially "nontraditional," and culturally diverse student body. A number of these activities were funded by the Ford Foundation. Three times I have been able to discuss my childhood course in detail in faculty seminars, receiving helpful, constructive criticisms from colleagues. My participation in and valuable learning from this supportive collegial network, which includes most of the contributors to this volume, continue today.

Featuring culturally diverse voices and experiences in the curriculum had always been a given for me as anthropologist, as the cross-cultural, comparative approach is the traditional orientation of my field. My greatest changes as a teacher came in the realm of pedagogy. My own department's program, and my own practices within it, made clear to me the limitations of seeing teaching as an issue of content alone, of seeing the core of the teaching act as the professor's transmission of knowledge to the student. Colleagues and my students increasingly helped me to understand how much teaching constitutes a dialogue with students, a dialogue in which who the students are and what they think is central to the learning equation and to shaping the faculty's contributions to the educational encounter. It was becoming more and more clear to me that to be an effective teacher, I had to offer more support for my students to tell me about themselves and their own thinking.

At this same time, I also began teaching a new course on cross-cultural relations within the university's applied linguistics master's program, which trains teachers to work with non-native speakers of English, mostly immigrant minorities. The program is deeply influenced by a Freirean philosophy and is inspiringly directed by Donaldo Macedo, a close collaborator of Paolo Freire.[4] Participation in this program allowed me to rediscover Freire, who visited campus a number of times, and, with the encouragement of colleagues such as Donaldo, to examine the relevance of his critical pedagogy for my own teaching.

Freire's critique of the "banking" model of education had pointed directly to the teaching practices modeled in my own education. Freire's emphasis on seeing teaching as a dialogue in which both teacher and student learn made increasing sense to me, as did his other key ideas, especially his advocacy of grounding learning in themes culturally relevant to the lives and daily practice of students and his emphasis on the need that all learners have to critically construct new information in the light of their existing knowledge and experience. Freire's teachings confirmed that I should include materials, wherever possible, that are relevant to areas of problem-solving, application, and experience in students' lives: this was not hard to do in courses on educational application or on childhood. He also made clear that I should welcome students' interrogation of new information, through writing and discussion, in the light of their previous learning and experience, as well as their need for active critical understanding and practice in remaking their worlds outside of school.

Most of all, the students in applied linguistics were a key impetus for making me rethink my approaches to teaching. These were the first classes on culture that I had ever taught where students of color, often immigrant students who spoke two, three, or more languages, usually made up the majority. Material I taught on multicultural relations that seemed more abstract and conceptually cut-and-dried in my predominantly white, undergraduate classes had much more resonance in this class, for most of the students had lived those multicultural realities concretely for their entire lives, and most were already practicing teachers themselves, with students who were also linguistic and usually ethnic/"racial" minorities.

My students had a lot to say, and their insights often confirmed, augmented, expanded, illustrated, explained, and sometimes revised the course materials. Minority students were not so quiet as they were in my predominantly white classes; they made their voices and perspectives heard, for example, by explaining their experiences of racial barriers and their own or their students' struggles over identity. In this class, it became more obvious to me than ever before that my students had much to teach me and one another, and that the most educationally productive class would be one in which all our voices—students' as well as my own—were strongly represented in recurrent written and spoken dialogue on the issues at hand. In all of this, the irony of my being a white man teaching this mixed class did not escape me.

In my early years of teaching that course, especially the first time, I had to struggle mightily with a feeling that I was somehow neglecting my duty by not monopolizing the class communication: Was it irresponsible not to work harder toward asserting my authority as an expert, even in the face of the recognition that my expertise in handling these issues was still limited? I had all these doubts despite my students' positive evaluations of the course and my own high satisfaction, even excitement, with the level of engagement and quality of work the students had offered. Old models of teaching die hard.

Meanwhile, learning from workshops with English department colleagues conversant in composition theory and process-writing, I began experimenting with asking students to do more informal types of writing that would encourage them to register more freely their thinking about the course material, first in my class on childhood, and eventually in all my classes. The channel of written communication that proved the most useful to me was the weekly, ungraded reading journal. The broad guidelines I gave students asked them to critically engage with the course material and to reflect on their learning process in the course and on how their new learning connected with what they already knew, both from their wider studies and from their professional or life experiences. The students could choose each week which issues to address and how to write about them.

Discovering Students' Realities Through Their Journals

I was surprised and delighted to find in their journals some of the most eloquent, honest, and clear writing students had ever given me. It has been wonderful and enlightening to read of the reflections, hopes, frustrations, angers, and epiphanies that my students arrive at while in my class. I have had the opportunity to learn from their reflections and to use these learnings as the basis for engaging in more focused dialogue with the students, not only in my weekly, written responses to their journals, but also with them as a group, during class meetings. I came to understand and to appreciate much better the diversity of preoccupations they had and the directions they were following in their lives as people and as students. As Freire's work has long suggested, such knowledge allows the educator to know how to speak more clearly to students.

Sometimes the students' preoccupations centered on difficulties feeling at home in the academy, with being "heard" by professors, due to language and cultural differences. I recognized myself in some of these expressions of estrangement.

> ESMERALDA, a Salvadoran student in her late twenties, wrote eloquently of her own feelings of being discriminated against in school—including the university—on account of her less-than-perfect English, as well as of the subtleties of the rejection that her teachers had displayed toward her and her sister. When I remarked on how beautifully she wrote, she broke into tears in my office, saying that in her entire school career, no teacher had ever told her she was a good writer.

In Esmeralda's case I was struck by how much journal writing opened a way for her to write from the heart about issues that truly concerned her, as well as opening a way for me to welcome her into the university in a way she had never been welcomed before.

In the case of Brian, an outstanding student and a brilliant writer, the materials from the childhood class posed other kinds of personal issues that I would never have known about except through what he wrote in his journal entries.

> A WHITE, Irish-American male in and out of school for many years as he struggled with an alcohol problem and a history of childhood abuse, Brian wrote frequently of his attempts to be a supportive uncle to the nieces and nephews he often had to care for. He did not trust himself to be loving with those children. Fortunately, the course materials on the wide variability in styles of good caretaking and my responses to his journal helped him to demythologize the caretaking role he was playing, to see that he did not need to be perfect to contribute to those children's care.

His journal entries, like those of so many others, suggested topics important for handling in class—in his case, putting on the agenda for class discussion the facts that, as our course materials indicated, there is no one "perfect" formula to use in caring for children and that all children need different kinds of adults who support them in varying ways.

On class days when I had read his journal, I found myself shifting emphasis toward questions he raised.

In their journals, I also saw that students' ideas are always deeply inflected by who they are as people—by their gender, class, race, and other cultural characteristics whose salience varies from student to student. The different intense responses to the same materials, often in the same classroom, can be stunning, and they make it clear that students learn differently from the "same" content. As examples, I can cite the responses of classmates Lateesha, Patrick, and Kadiatou to materials on race in a recent class.

CLASS MATERIAL on the impacts of societal racism and the development of racial identity among children was not just a theoretical matter for Lateesha, who wrote of her and her family's experiences with discrimination, and of the alarm and pain she felt in class over the complacency she perceived among the white students about the material we were reading. She could only imagine that white students must be writing overtly racially hostile comments about African Americans in their journals. I did what I could to tell her I understood and to reassure her that the white students were not as actively or consciously racist as she suspected they were. I read to her some passages from white students' journals showing their shame, alarm, and sometimes self-blame over continuing racism in society.

PATRICK HAD grown up poor in a Boston housing project and had a difficult childhood and youth, when he was in and out of trouble with the law. He had struggled hard and now, at thirty, he was working as an office manager with a small trucking company, hoping to finish his business degree and to advance his career. Our conversations, always in writing and through the journals, centered on his fury over the neglect of white poverty and struggle that he perceived in social science literature and academic culture in general, as well as on his difficulty acceding to the idea that he had gained much from "white skin privilege" in his life.

KADIATOU, FROM Guinea, wrote a great deal about the intersection of class and race. An exchange student from an affluent family in West Africa, she wrote about all she was newly learning about racism from living in the United States, about how long it had taken her to understand its subtleties, and about her new appreciation, and shock, at all that her executive father must have faced in his international travels to France and the United States as a businessman.

Although class discussions on issues such as racism allow valuable exchanges of viewpoint and much learning, I have found that journal writing allows more thoughtful, extended development of students' reflections on controversial issues. Without reading their journals on these topics, it's impossible to know what students really think about the issues at hand, or to realize how differently these materials touch different students. Knowing more about the range of student reaction to some material has allowed me to anticipate and moderate potentially volatile class discussions more effectively, to acknowledge more respectfully the enormous diversity within the class, and finally to offer supplementary individual tutorial sessions for some students when needed.

The depth and complexity of students' responses to course issues and their understanding of the subject matter was revealed to me in many journals, which in turn allowed me to support the students as individuals and to encourage them to feel comfortable serving as resources—through class discussion—for other students in the course. An example was Julia.

WHEN A GIRL, Julia had been sexually abused by her father while living in a well-respected, conventional family in a middle-class suburb. One of the most courageous students I have ever known, she worked as a therapist in a prison hospital for criminal sexual offenders and struggled in her journals to find the humanity in the men she was working with, trying to imagine how they could face living, knowing the crimes they had committed. She also wrote about the challenge and the promise of her new marriage, and her attempts to help her husband admit to his own emotional vulnerabilities and overcome the limitations of his traditional male gender socialization. Our communication was only in writing, and Julia never once visited my office or even spoke with me after class, but she told me in her last journal entry that she had felt safe to write about these things, that it was both educational and healing for her to do so, and that she had told me more about these issues than she had ever revealed to her therapist. Without ever revealing personal secrets to the class, Julia was especially vocal and persuasive in classroom discussion whenever we discussed whether the nuclear or any other particular family form could guarantee loving care of children, as well as when we talked about issues of childhood abuse. It was clear to me, and perhaps to the other students as well, that her compelling ideas on these questions were more than casual opinions.

Student journals such as Julia's remind me of our great responsibility as teachers, especially in the social and human sciences, where the issues we teach about are not removed from students' lives, but can be volatile and can force them to confront painful issues in their own experience.

MARIA AND BRIDGET, Portuguese-Mexican and Irish-American respectively, were in their thirties and both mothers of several children. Like the other students, they were reading anthropologist Myra Bluebond-Langner's *The Private Worlds of Dying Children*, a work about the struggles of terminally ill children that I have always assigned in my childhood class. I was shocked to discover after reading their journals that Maria and Bridget had each lost a small child to death, one by disease and the other by an electrocution accident. They used their journals to tell me about their children—what they had been like as people, how they had died, and what that loss had meant to them. For Maria, this proved a cleansing experience, and she finished the course with flying colors. For Bridget, however, it seemed too much to bear, and she disappeared from class in the midst of this unit, never to return.

TRAN WAS forty, a refugee from Vietnam who hoped to become a Catholic priest. He regularly used his journal to compare his childhood experiences in Vietnam during the American war there with the quite different childhoods we read about in the United States. When we were studying how conceptions of motherhood have changed significantly throughout American history, for example, he was prompted to write a journal entry about the great comfort his mother had given him as an eight-year-old during terrifying bombings of his village, the loss of family members and his home, and a five-day, secret flight to the border under cover of night. When we read about African American slave children, Tran remembered his own life in a refugee camp, where he worked in street commerce as a nine-year-old to help his parents and made daily visits to the garbage dump of an American military base to look for food and other items that might be useful to his family.

Students from the class often have personal stories that augment in effective ways the published case materials I put on the reading list, and they can wind up sharing these with fellow students in interesting ways.

WHEN WE were reading about children with disabilities, Kate, from a wealthy, upper-class Yankee background, wrote a journal about the lack of trust and support she felt from her family during her life-threatening illness and the eventual amputation of one of her legs. Her account of the onset of her disability and of her long struggle to accept it was stunning in its honesty and eloquence, and with my encouragement she published it shortly afterward in a feminist magazine. It is now a regular reading in the course, and current students tell me in their journals how much they learn from reading her account.

The challenges students face as a result of being at the university often include the rethinking of life goals and commitments, especially those related to career planning. These concerns also come through frequently in journals. The intellectual discoveries made in a class can prompt the reorientation of a life's course. Learning is often more complex and bears more significances than the idea of simply "mastering" the material might suggest.

ANNE MARIE had a good job working as a hostess in one of Boston's most elegant downtown restaurants, but she found her job empty and was in school—as many of our students are—to find a way to more meaningful work. She was an outstanding writer who empathized deeply with the struggles and achievements of the children we read about in the course. She registered her own surprise at how much the course materials moved her, and through her journal entries explored the possibility of—and made the decision to—change careers and seek work as a "child life specialist" in a hospital setting. Not long after the course, she applied to graduate programs that would allow her to achieve this goal.

My experience of reading and responding to student journals has increasingly taught me the limitations of my earlier writing standard for students. The disembodied, unreflexive academic discourse I had been trained in myself as a student was not the only writing that I wanted them to do. It made less and less sense to try to turn them all into "junior anthropologists" or especially to hold up myself and my scholarly identity as a role model that all needed to emulate in order to feel successful or to feel they belonged in the class.

I began to see that there are many different forms of critical, engaged thinking and expression that can be recognized and valued as evidence of committed student learning. I realized that students as a group—and as individuals—were beginning in very different places in their encounters with the course material and were asking very different kinds of questions of it, and that their learning outcomes would also be quite different for these reasons. The need for and the possibility of working closely with them as individuals became much more evident to me through reading their journals.

Feedback the students themselves have given me has convinced me that acknowledgment of their own particularity is an important moment. It fosters their engagement with the university, their recognition of where their own understandings do and do not overlap with others', and their assumption of new ways of growing and learning. Awareness of their own particularities, their own differences, if you like, can offer students important critical leverage in engaging with their learning, if they are actually welcomed to use it in this way.

In my classes, journals are now a crucial part of the writing that students do. I understand how journal writing enhances many types of student learning that I have been trying to encourage in the course—writing more clearly; making analytical connections; applying theoretical material to their own lives, communities, and society; and engaging in self-reflective, cross-cultural comparisons. I also continue to assign writing exercises that involve more traditional academic genres, such as analytic essays evaluating theories or drawing generalizations across comparative cases, thus offering a range of writing opportunities in the course as a whole. Students who stay engaged on an ongoing basis with the course materials via the journals stand in better stead when handling more traditional writing genres, and perform better at them. Most, in fact, use their journals as springboards in extending their thinking in longer, more formal analytic essays.

Many students use their journals exclusively, in fact, to rehearse their thinking along fairly traditional academic lines. Like Jonathan, probably half of my students never delve into personal issues at all.

I KNEW from a few brief conversations with him after class that Jonathan was Jewish, came originally from upstate New York, was HIV-positive, and worked as a hospital ward clerk in Boston, but he never discussed his life in his journal writings. He planned on attending graduate school in sociology after graduating, and he used his journal to meticulously evaluate the theoretical assumptions behind the readings, based on all that he had been studying in his sociology courses, and to further refine his application of sociological theory to the new field of investigation represented by the course.

The realm of journal writing, then, and the critical dialogue that it allows between me and my students—some have told me they feel they are "pen pals" with me—offer a substrate of informal, open, fresh communication that can serve varied purposes within the class. I try to let the students take the lead in setting the terms of the communication, and I'm very rarely disappointed in what they offer.

Because uncovering and entering into this substrate of informal communication with my students has been the most surprising and valuable pedagogical discovery I have had as a professor, the foregoing discussion has emphasized this process more than the teaching and learning of formal course content. In that more "visible" domain, my students look conventional, and the casual observer (who is sometimes the professor) cannot imagine how much is going on beneath the surface—unless he or she looks and listens carefully. Indeed, the students too seem to realize there is a separate, somewhat private domain in the class. They seldom overtly mention journal issues in their formal writing for the course; nor do they do so in classroom discussions, except in more intimate, small groups. They seem to appreciate the space offered in the course for making affective and experiential connections with the material; for recognizing discomforting questions provoked by class readings or discussions; for testing more authentic, critical styles of writing; and finally for rehearsing new ideas and analyses that will usually take final form in more formal essays. I'm pleased and gratified to be knowledgeable, supportive, and indeed *part* of my class on this level. Now I have a better sense of what the students' learning processes really are in my course and am better able to encourage students to carry their efforts further.

Conclusions: What Can a Professor Be for Students?

As I began to be more open to hearing and responding to students' own stories, whatever they might be, I came to ask myself more and more why it was that they were able to move me so, why I—a white, middle-class, Anglo-Saxon Protestant male and professor—was able to understand and empathize with their struggles. I had, after all, succeeded, or at least become established, in this academic world. Listening to my students, pondering what I could understand in their experiences, and participating in a number of diversity-oriented and antiracism workshops on and off campus provoked me increasingly to remember and to re-examine my own uneasy history as a student and long-term sojourner within academia. This self-discovery has given me a basis for supporting my students in their own broad intellectual and social struggles to make sense, and good use, of the particular academic world we share together.

What I can do to help my students is not reducible to something so simple as being a "role model." As an older, white, Anglo-Saxon male from a background unlike those of almost all my students, I really don't think I can be a role model for many of them. There are obvious, great differences of culture, of outlook, and now of generation (in most cases) between them and me. It would be presumptuous, if not preposterous, for me to claim an identity of experience with them, or to think that I or any one person could have shared their enormous variety of struggles and achievements, or especially to think that they either could or should try to recapitulate mine. It's essential for me to be accessible and supportive to *all* the students, in any case, and not just the ones who are most like me, the white, working-class males who are a tiny portion of the students I teach, or the additional, almost miniscule number who want to be what I have become myself—an academic anthropologist.

The state of having felt and been different, of having been an "outsider within,"[5] as Patricia Hill Collins has phrased it, is something that I know I *do* share with most of my students, and that helps me know how to be supportive of them, regardless of the particular differences among them or between us. In fact, knowing them well in their particularities as people, and knowing precisely their own great *differences* from me and so many other of my colleagues on the faculty, helps me to empathize with their struggles and to understand their aspirations so much better. To be able to mentor, support, and teach does not depend on cultural likeness with one's students. I've come to think it involves more the recognition that we, faculty and students alike, even across all the differences that separate us, are all involved in the same fundamental human struggles—to learn what is worth learning, to understand the meaning our lives have within larger schemes, to use our knowledge to make our world better, and—as best as we can—to find ways of helping one another in these endeavors.

NOTES

Acknowledgments: I thank Craig Jackson for sharing with me his insightful reflections on Paulo Freire's ideas, which have helped much to clarify my own understandings. (See his 1997 master's thesis for the University of Massachusetts Boston, "Cross-Cultural Teaching and Learning: Teaching Environmental Education in Costa Rica.") Esther Kingston-Mann and Estelle Disch also offered much valuable critical editorial advice on earlier versions of this chapter. I also greatly appreciate the reading and encouragement given by Mariah Sieber and Angela Cacciarru-Sieber. Lastly, for the insights they have helped me arrive at, I thank all the students I have had the privilege of teaching, including the many students whose stories I have cited here and the many others who have helped me understand teaching better, including José Fernandez, Alex Costley, Vicky Nuñez, Yvonne Hultman, Lynda Lattke, Mike Blasi, Tasha Baizerman, Lidan Pan, Carmen Pineda, Mary Concannon, Diane D'Arrigo, Craig Jackson, Teresa Miranda, Teresa Quinton, Kelye Stowell, Marlyse Baptista, Paula Burns, Darlinda Moreira, Jim Longergan, Paul Harrington, Jean Mackinnon, and Ann Colageo. All names of students given in the text are pseudonyms.

1. Paulo Freire, *Pedagogy of the Oppressed*, Myra Bergman Ramos, trans. (New York: Continuum, 1970), pp. 57–74.

2. Through Association of American Colleges and Universities (AACU) networks, my childhood course materials were added to its extensive bank of diversity-related curriculum resources. This assignment was noticed by Robert Diamond, who cited and reprinted it as a model "pluralism assignment" in *Designing and Assessing Courses and Curricula: A Practical Guide* (San Francisco: Jossey Bass, 1997), pp. 210–12. The assignment did make very good intellectual sense as an assignment; but unfortunately it retained serious pedagogical and ethical limitations when considered within the social-psychological ecology of the course.

3. Josiah McC. Heyman, *Finding a Moral Heart for U.S. Immigration Policy*, American Ethnological Society Monograph Series, No. 7 (Washington, D.C.: American Anthropological Association), p. 12.

4. Donaldo Macedo, *Literacies of Power: What Americans Are Not Allowed to Know* (Boulder, Colo.: Westview, 1994).

5. Patricia Hill Collins, "Learning from the Outside Within: The Sociological Significance of Black Feminist Thought," *Social Problems* 33 (6): 14–32 (1986).

REYES COLL-TELLECHEA

TRANSLATED BY MARK ZOLA

4   Language and Cultural Capital

Reflections of a "Junior" Professor

Here in the United States we have perhaps the most brutal form of social discrimination: some, as a matter of course, are awarded the full enjoyment of life; many are not.

—John K. Galbraith, *The Good Society*

Middle class societies will remain highly inegalitarian in certain respects, but the sources of inequality will increasingly be attributable to the natural inequality of talents, the economically necessary division of labor, and to culture.

—Francis Fukuyama, *The End of History and the Last Man*

WHAT IS EDUCATION FOR?

These are the days of a global economy, neoconservatism, global warming, neoliberalism, feminism, anti-immigration laws, genocidal wars, affirmative action protests, identity politics, gay rights, the welfare crisis, AIDS, famine, and so on. A horrible century has just ended. We all hope the new one will ease human suffering. Politicians speak of education as the means for a better future; at the same time, there is a public clamor about the crisis in education. It hits close to home.

I am a foreign-born professor, working at a public university in the United States of America. I believe that producing and distributing knowledge are at the core of intellectual labor and that intellectuals have the social responsibility to explore the world, analyze its complexities, evaluate possible solutions to real problems, and communicate all of that to their communities. I also believe that powerful social forces prevent the production and distribution of knowledge to whole sectors of the population.

As public education is transformed to meet the goals of new, private interest groups and economic elites, it stands to reason that intellectuals who work in the field of public education—or public transmission of knowledge—have to speak up. This essay is the story of how I arrived at these convictions and how, in turn, these convictions gave me the strength to work—against the odds—alongside my students and colleagues.

Born, raised, and educated outside of the United States, I arrived in this country in 1988. I entered graduate school at a public institution and received a Ph.D. five years later. That is to say, I spent a number of years accumulating knowledge and learning how to produce it. I then accepted a job offer in Boston and entered academia. As I went from being a student to being a professor in a matter of months, I was confused about every aspect of my new career: teaching, research, service. I know now that this happens to most "junior" faculty who re-enter the university right after they finish graduate school. But in those days, I was frustrated and lost.

From my mentors I had learnt that distributing and producing *knowledge*[1] were not only my goals as a teacher and a scholar but also my responsibility and obligation. I was to teach, produce scholarly articles and books, develop new courses, attend professional conferences, serve on university committees, and contribute to the well-being of the community at large. By accepting the UMass/Boston job offer, I was agreeing to do it all to the best of my abilities. But how in the world was I to perform so many tasks at once? Did other junior faculty manage to do them better? Perhaps I was not "that good" after all. At times, I must confess, I felt like a fraud.

I found it hard to "descend" to the undergraduate level and even harder to "rise" to the level of the scholarly world. Was scholarship more important than teaching, or vice versa? Since the teaching and the scholarly worlds seemed so far apart, I felt that I had to adjust my priorities in order to survive in my brand new, tenure-track job.

Trying to get closer to the real level of my students, I abandoned my "ideal syllabi" and increased my efforts to develop a sophisticated theoretical framework for my research. At this point, I caught myself thinking that perhaps the production and distribution of knowledge were indeed separate activities that were impossible to reconcile. It seemed to me that my students would not understand or benefit from my research and vice versa. I went through phases where I saw myself as a good teacher and frustrated scholar, then as a good scholar and frustrated teacher. I produced new knowledge in the form of articles and books, but found myself teaching mainly skills (a little grammar here, techniques of interpretation there). It was all very puzzling and dissatisfying. Why was I an educator? What was education for?

Something happened when I began to raise these basic questions. Up to then I had felt controlled by external forces. But when I challenged the framework and assumptions supplied to me in graduate school, I began reading in the field of education, observed my senior colleagues carefully, and enrolled in a semester-long seminar for junior faculty organized by the Center for the Improvement of Teaching.

After much work, research, reflection, and observation, I came to realize that my professional career did not require me to abandon my beliefs. I could draw on the works and example of my most admired intellectuals—Hannah Arendt, Theodor Adorno, Edward Said, John K. Galbraith, Frank Lentricchia, Pierre Bourdieu, and John Guillory, who had written extensively on the function of education.[2] Their writings reminded me that intellectual labor demands that we produce and distribute knowledge ethically—according to the professional and moral standards agreed upon within our communities. The knowledge we produce should be shared inside as well as outside our institutions and should contribute to the solution of some of the most painful features of past and present social systems: hunger, drought, slavery, unemployment, poverty, inequality, violence, greed, physical and emotional pain, injustice, fanaticism, alienation, illness, discrimination, totalitarianism, and so on. In the words of Hannah Arendt,

> Basically we are always educating for a world that is or is becoming out of joint, for this is the basic human situation. . . . Because the world is made by mortals it wears out. . . . To preserve the world against the mortality of its creators . . . it must be constantly set right anew. . . . Our hope always hangs on the new which every generation brings.[3]

This, I believe, is what education is for, and this is precisely why I am an educator.

"Cultural Capital": The Production, Distribution, and Consumption of Knowledge and the Role of the Teacher-Scholar

French sociologist Pierre Bourdieu has developed a concept of cultural capital that distinguishes economic from symbolic capital. Symbolic capital is not reducible to economic capital; it includes cultural capital, which, like its economic counterpart, modern capitalist society distributes unequally among its classes.[4]

During my graduate school years, I had studied and applied the ideas of Bourdieu to the field of literary production. At UMass/Boston, it seemed to me time to consider what those ideas could do for me and for my students in the much different field of everyday life. If I wanted to be true to my beliefs, I had to admit that lowering my expectations of students' abilities through adjusted syllabi was wrong. Given the limitations that our society imposes on the distribution of and access to cultural capital, such a strategy would undermine my mission as an educator.

I had chosen to work at a nonelite university, a public institution significantly underfunded and located next to some of the top private universities in the world. One can describe its students as nontraditional: They are "ethnic minorities," working class, mature, and first-, second-, and third-generation immigrants who often hold full-time jobs and are responsible for families. They bring a variety of educational backgrounds, needs, and abilities. They are full-fledged human beings who, while at times located at the margins of society, strive to succeed by accessing the necessary knowledge. It is because these students place their trust and hopes in my hands that I, as a teacher-scholar, could no longer accept as inevitable the contemporary academic divisions between producing and distributing cultural capital.

An era dominated by computers and the drive for scientific progress has somehow characterized the study of the humanities as a useless practice that does not contribute to the students' social success outside the university, in the so-called real world. In my opinion, this argument serves to protect and perpetuate a social system that survives by regulating access to the means of cultural production as well as its distribution and consumption. When schools and teachers implement teaching systems that concentrate on the most superficial practices (skills), they do enormous damage to students coming from the least privileged social sectors. For instance, it is one thing to learn enough of a foreign language to rent a room or buy a meal, and another to be able to interpret and precisely evaluate the intentions, values, and needs of other peoples by *knowing* their languages, ideas, myths, arts, and histories.

Providing access to language, history, ideas, arts, and myths to the least privileged citizens requires a combination of research (production of knowledge) *and* teaching (distribution of knowledge). It also requires struggling against the idea that our students are only consumers of knowledge. As I see it, the university is neither a flashy supermarket of knowledge nor a museum of impractical ideas, and the students are not our clients. Instead, a teacher-scholar is someone who provides access to knowledge as the "means of production"—not only the product of research (knowledge), but also the means to improve it to the satisfaction of present and future generations. The work of the teacher-scholar thus serves a purpose for the community. The key would be his or her awareness regarding the specific needs of each community.

In practical terms, a recognition of this possibility would require me to transform my habits of thinking and working in order to concentrate on the intellectual needs of my students and our communities. This could mean that my research plan (carefully drafted in graduate school) would have to be revised (this possibility increased my fears about getting tenure). In theory, this seemed like the right thing to do, but I hesitated. Then, again, something happened.

LANGUAGE AS CULTURAL CAPITAL

Like all professors, I teach language. That is to say, my area of specialization is neither language nor linguistics; I channel what I teach through language, and I require students to master a series of concepts, terms, and skills that constitute a particular language. Although I teach Spanish as a native and foreign language, my area of specialization is literature. It is not unusual these days to find professors whose research fields are literature, art, or philosophy teaching language courses. This is, in part, due to the scarcity of full-time jobs in those fields and to the university's requirement that we teach courses for which there is a high demand, such as foreign languages. But humanists have been teaching language for centuries, whatever the conditions of the market. Mastering a language and using it to interpret, evaluate, and express ideas is essential to our task. Teaching how to do it can indeed be a pleasure.

Time, however, changes everything. Nowadays, one has to teach Spanish 101, for instance, and at the same time produce "cutting edge" research in, let us say, Latin American women writers of the nineteenth century in order to get tenure. It is extremely hard to deliver one's specialized knowledge to beginning language students. This is not due only to the students' lack of linguistic skills in Spanish, but also to the apparent disdain that many individuals show toward what is perceived as "extra" or "useless" knowledge. I refer here to the view of professors as producers, universities as distributors, and students as consumers of education.

Many times in my classes I felt students were interested only in rules that help them say what they already think (and get a grade or fulfill a language requirement) rather than increasing their critical thinking skills. Anything beyond concrete, "scientific" grammar rules was considered a distraction and a deviation from the syllabus. Language became for them a mere commodity, and that, to me, was a sign that knowledge altogether had been reduced—in their minds—to an object that could be acquired for a fee and then used to obtain a private benefit. So much for the centuries-old humanist tradition of teaching language as a means to knowledge. So much for Adorno, Said, and Bourdieu. Should I simply concentrate on publishing my research and teaching grammar rules?

Fortunately, we go through experiences that show that it is in fact worthwhile trying to be a teacher-scholar. These experiences convince us that we can develop a mechanism for conveying to students the practical knowledge that they desire and that we possess, combined with other cultural capital that will enhance their ability to think, interpret, evaluate, and act as informed, educated individuals. That is to say, we can figure out how to convey the cultural capital that will provide students with the privileges and rights that society distributes so unequally.

If one thinks of language as a form of cultural capital, it is clear that the consequences of unequal distribution of and access to language are tremendous. Effective control over language as a means of communication guarantees, for whoever possesses it, the possibility of access to the production and distribution of knowledge. This control not only determines whether or not one can represent oneself; it also assures the individual's entry to specific social (cultural, economic, etc.) circles. Knowledge of and control over language also determine the individual's opportunity to participate in the public exchange of ideas that gives shape and order to this society. Language is, in fact, one of the few essential tools needed to succeed and survive in our society.

BECOMING A TEACHER-SCHOLAR: SPANISH Z289

It happened, of course, in a language class. Spanish Z289: Composition for Native Speakers is designed to teach the practice of writing in Spanish to individuals who already write in Spanish but who want to achieve greater control. When the department assigned me to teach this course, my main objective was to help students partially or completely schooled in English to achieve a level of written expression equivalent to that of a person educated entirely in Spanish. My syllabus, tests, and direct instruction were consistent with this objective. Dictionaries, spelling and punctuation rules, style exercises, and so on were aids to reach the desired goal.

Although nowadays it is not unusual to find Spanish courses for Spanish speakers in the catalogs of many universities, my department developed such a course twenty years ago as part of a pioneering sequence of courses dedicated to the education of increasing numbers of second-generation Spanish-speaking students. Twenty years ago, my colleagues had already responded to an important need of the Spanish-speaking community in the area; over the years, and thanks to their work and dedication, these courses attracted hundreds of native speakers from a wide range of majors. I was told that this course was very important, and I understood what was meant: I had to do it better than well. This was my second year at the university. I knew how to teach Spanish as a foreign language, I knew how to teach literature, but Spanish for native speakers was not in my repertoire. I was in for a big surprise.

The first shock hit me when I entered the classroom on the first day of classes. The room was full of Spanish-speaking students of various national origins, classes, "races," ages, interests, and education levels, all grouped under the label *native speakers* and all of Latin American origins. There were at least thirty, and I had to go out and get more chairs. To complicate things a little more, everybody (myself included) was suddenly painfully aware of an important detail: the professor happened to be a *Spaniard*. Five hundred years of history face to face. We all thought it was going to be a very long semester.

Our first, common reaction—as we later confessed—was shame. They were ashamed of not writing "properly," ashamed of having forgotten or never achieved precision in and command of a language in which, according to the university, they were native speakers. I was ashamed of having enjoyed many educational privileges and, in a certain sense, of witnessing their shame. I was, for the first time in my life, acutely aware of being a Spaniard trying to "teach" Spanish in the Americas. The historical parallels were unavoidable, making us all feel very uncomfortable toward each other. I did not want to be perceived as a new conquistador, and the students would have never tolerated such a violent approach. We had a problem.

Without a doubt, a course like this presents numerous obstacles. In the first place, there are those who think that such a course is counterproductive, since to be successful in this country one must master English, not Spanish. But my students were in the class because they wanted to be; it is not a departmental or university requirement. In the second place, this kind of course usually brings together individuals with many diverse needs and different areas of specialization. From the first minutes it was clear that my students' proficiency in Spanish ranged from exclusively oral to a total command of the language. Finally, as there continue to be people in this country who equate the Spanish language with a stigma (poverty, immigration, etc.). I detected a number of students whose attitude toward the course was, at least, ambivalent.

In a somewhat intuitive way, I had prepared a syllabus to bring my students toward an advanced level of literacy in a language that was already their own. To do this, I had taken into consideration the possible difficulties that they might have had gaining access to the highest levels of mastery of written Spanish: emigration, limited schooling, access to monolingual (that is, English) school systems, limited opportunities to practice the written form of the language, economic and social pressures, and so on. But I had not foreseen that the first and most important of the obstacles was the very real and inescapable weight of history.

Under normal circumstances, a professor does not have to justify to students why s/he is teaching a particular course. The reason is that s/he is trained and authorized to do so, and that, moreover, s/he wants to teach that course. Although my status as a native speaker of Spanish almost automatically projects a certain image of competence to language students, in this particular instance, I found that it was precisely my origins that might pollute the atmosphere. I immediately realized that the short introduction that I had prepared for the first day of classes would not have the desired effect. After several minutes of questions and answers (who were they, why were they taking this course, and so on), I noticed on the class roster that many of their names were English, that others were Spanish, and that some had mixed names (English-Spanish or vice versa). I thought that this was normal and interesting and did not make any comments about it. Then, I wrote some basic information on the blackboard—my office hours, my office location and telephone number, and my full, original name: María de los Reyes Coll Tellechea. There was a murmur in the class. Somebody asked me, "What kind of Spanish name is that?" When I began explaining why I had three different languages (Spanish, Catalan, and Basque) within my name, the murmur died. My students' eyes were fixed on me. They were paying great attention to my words. That, I thought, was curious, because my name had nothing to do with the subject matter of the course.

Anyway, I told them that my parents were bilingual, but that I did not learn Catalan or Basque. I speak Castilian (also known, outside of Spain, as Spanish), and I teach it. By the time I was born, the Franco regime had banned the public and private use of all the vernacular languages of Spain except for Castilian-Spanish. In addition, after the Spanish Civil War (1936–1939), my parents and their families had left their original lands and emigrated to the capital of Spain, Madrid. There they met, and after their marriage they moved again. This time they went to a different region known as Old Castille. There, in a small town named Béjar, they settled for the rest of their lives. In Béjar I learned what is now my native language. When Franco died and it was legal again to learn Basque and Catalan, I enrolled in some language courses at my university. In spite of all of my good intentions, it proved to be too hard to learn those languages in addition to everything else. So I abandoned them and concentrated all of my efforts on learning the intricacies of Castilian Spanish. I regret not knowing more about my parents' languages, but I make my living teaching Spanish.

My answer had taken five minutes. Some students raised their hands to ask more questions, but according to my syllabus, I was running out of time. I had to assign the first composition. "Literacy," I thought, and proceeded to give them that first task in order to assess their levels and abilities in Spanish composition. "Write a brief autobiography. Typed, please."

A few days later, I began to correct those pages, expecting to find spelling errors, syntax errors, and so forth. I was in for another big surprise. I found mistakes, it is true, but I also discovered an unmistakable message from every composition: their enormous personal investment in learning more about the language that happened to be their parents' native tongue, the language spoken in those lands from which their families had come.

After reading pages and pages full of Spanish and Native American words unknown to me (those of plants, cities, animals, smells, and textures that I had never experienced), I had to pause to call a friend. I needed to talk, not about the unknown vocabulary, but about a shocking experience: as my students were writing their own short autobiographies (loves, struggles, secrets, and all), they all left space for mine. They all wanted to tell me that they knew what I meant when I was talking about my bittersweet feelings regarding Spanish, and some wanted to advise me on how to deal with them.

Soon I realized I had stopped correcting mistakes; I had forgotten to add the missing accents, letters, and punctuation. I was simply reading, carefully, as if listening to someone who speaks in a very soft voice.

When I was finished, I took a look at my syllabus and smiled. It was not a bad syllabus; I had covered every aspect of the language, at least technically. My students, however, were pointing out that there was something missing. I knew they were leading me then, waiting for me to arrive where they already were: at a place of understanding language as a source of power. One student had written that she knew that Spanish was her native language only because it had been violently imposed in America five hundred years ago by the Spanish conquistadors. Nevertheless, she continued, it was her only native language, and that of her parents. Finally, she recommended that I, too, make peace with my past.

I was a very shocked language professor. As a teacher, I pride myself in self-control; and as much as I can, I like to keep emotions out of the way. So I was immediately concerned about taking things too personally, getting too involved, letting personal feelings (my own and those of my students) take charge of the class.

I kept the syllabus as it was and kept teaching grammatical rules, style variations, and so on. But the class was as much about thinking and talking as about writing a particular assignment over and over again in order to achieve perfect orthography and a polished syntax. I accepted their challenge. The course was about our language, and we had much to say and to think about the different ways each of us owns that language and about the consequences of that ownership. Having spent years exploring the relationship between language and power, language and cultural capital, language and history, I could offer much more than practical knowledge. I knew more. I had written about it, and I had experienced first hand some of the private and public effects of not having access to certain domains because of a limited linguistic control.

Over the next weeks and months, we discussed many issues related to language as cultural capital. We talked and wrote in Spanish about symbolic capital, the function of education, the problems of emigration, and the English labels Latino and Hispanic, Spanish and Spaniard, and their Spanish counterparts; we discussed language and social class, language and the construction of social reality, language and "race." To be sure, we never lost sight of grammar. We discussed what a linguistic norm is and means, and we paid close attention to rules by doing dictation (they often laughed at my "Spanish accent," and I often got a little uncomfortable about it, too), writing and rewriting essays, and so on.

I worked, talked, and read with a passion, and so did they. At times, it was frustrating for all of us, especially when we got stuck trying to define who "we" were. It turned out that some defined themselves as Latinos, other as Hispanics, some as Argentinean, and some as Colombian, Chicanos, or simply American citizens. I told them that I was a foreigner. Not knowing what to do about my self-definition, each of them had different advice about what I should call myself. This unfinished conversation, like many others, kept coming up so often that I decided to explore the possibility of sharing with the students what I knew about concepts such as identity and subjectivity, identification and subjection, subject and citizen. We talked about them in Spanish. They sincerely appreciated the opportunity to think and express themselves *in Spanish* on what they considered to be highly sophisticated matters. Needless to say, at times things got very complicated and extremely interesting. There was a general sense of satisfaction. Their language could indeed explore and express the intricacies of their lives as daughters, husbands, workers, and thinkers. All that was needed was access to the language capital.

One day, when the issue of "our voices" came up, I became worried. Was this kind of discourse sincere, mere imitation of some public discourses, totally superficial? "Language and voice are not the same thing!" I had hoped that they would be more critical, less inclined to clichés, and more daring in their propositions. By this time I was not very enthusiastic about any discussion of "we," or "us," or "our" (I remind the reader that I was determined to remain a foreigner). So I challenged them. "Why do you want your voices heard?" They accepted the challenge. Soon after, the student newspaper appeared with a new feature, a page written in Spanish by my students, *Página*

Latina. It lasted until the end of our semester and indeed proved that they had a lot to say. The first issue featured an essay on pre-Columbian history and cultures, including the power of language and language struggles during the Spanish Conquest.

On the last day of classes, we reviewed our discussions. Usually I do not say much on the last day when it is time for me to close a course. I thank the students, offer my help for the future, wish them good luck, and go back to my office. On this day, I tried to do exactly the same, but it did not turn out quite that way. I told them that I had never had better or more patient teachers; and I dared to say that I was more than thankful for their generous knowledge and gentle manner. I also confessed that I was as worried about their self-definitions as they were about mine. Then I tried to leave the room, but they stopped me. Somebody had brought a camera. The students came toward my desk and placed themselves behind it and on top of it, with me sitting down. Then one of them took a picture. Only after I had left the classroom and was on my way back to my office did I understand. This had not been one of those emotional reactions that sometimes bothered me. Simply put, the desk was not mine, not anymore; they were laying claim to their own space and their own language, even if I did not understand or approve of some of their choices. I had reacted emotionally, not my students.

This experience and my reflection on what happened in this course had an immediate effect on my being able to reconcile myself to my work as a teacher-scholar. Finally, the distance between producing and distributing knowledge has begun to disappear for me. Furthermore, I am not worried any more about it. What my students want from me is access to knowledge in the form of language and a clear understanding of how to use language as a means of production. They want to discuss what language is, how it works, and how one enters (or is excluded from) the domain of power through one's ability to convey needs, goals, opinions, and rights; they want to lay claim to their own territories, in their own ways, using an array of shared tools, techniques, and values.

The effect of my experience on my courses in language, literature, and culture, as well as on my research has been tremendous. From the explanation of how Spanish pronouns work to complex issues regarding the political function of literary texts, there is now a common theme. I teach *and* study, explicitly, the old and new social practices of production, distribution, and consumption of cultural capital in the form of language, as well as how those practices affect all individuals and their societies. The Spanish Conquest, the Franco Regime, the Semitic roots of the Iberian languages and cultures, the effect of rapid modernization ("Europeanization") on the Spanish language and literature, and so forth, all rely on particular practices of production, distribution, and consumption of cultural (and economic) capital.

Eight years have passed since my arrival at UMass/Boston. I am no longer, officially at least, a "junior" professor. I am tenured now. And my students are living proof that access to knowledge is not—contrary to Fukuyama's formulation—a matter of the "natural inequality of talents," but a matter of social justice. Justice understood as equal opportunity to produce, distribute, and consume, ethically, the enormous riches accumulated by humankind. For this lesson I will be always grateful to the students at the University of Massachusetts Boston.

NOTES

Acknowledgments: This chapter is dedicated to Jesse, Maruja, and Shannon. It was originally written in a mixture of Spanish and English (Spanglish). I wish to thank Mark Zola and the editors of this volume for their kind and patient work. I also have a debt of gratitude for their support and wisdom over the years to the following colleagues and friends: Professors Clara Estow, Adorna Walia, Esther Torrego, Estelle Disch, Janis Kapler, Catherine Lynde, Cindy Schuster, and Susan Wolf from UMass/Boston; Professor Constance Sullivan from the University of Minnesota; Professor Donna Lazarus (NY), Professor Patricia Powell from UMass/Boston and Harvard University, and Professor Shaary Neretin from Lesley College. Thank you also to Elizabeth Wirth, Crystal Murray, Tomy, and Espe.

1. With the term "knowledge" I refer to "the body of facts, principles, etc. accumulated by mankind," *Webster's New World College Dictionary*, 1996.

2. My readings included Hannah Arendt, "The Crisis in Education," in *Between Past and Present* (New York: Penguin Books: 1977), pp. 173–96; Theodore W. Adorno, "Taboos on the Teaching Vocation," in *Critical Models* (New York: Columbia University Press, 1998), pp. 177–90; Edward. W. Said, *Representations of the Intellectuals* (New York: Vintage Books, 1994); Pierre Bourdieu, *The Field of Cultural Production* (New York: Columbia University Press, 1993); Pierre Bourdieu and Jean Claude Passeron, *Reproduction in Education, Society, and Culture* (London: Sage Publications, 1990); John Guillory, *Cultural Capital: The Problem of Literary Canon Formation* (Chicago: University of Chicago Press, 1993); Frank Lentricchia, "Provocations," in *Criticism and Social Change* (Chicago: University of Chicago Press, 1985), pp. 1–20; John K. Galbraith, *The Good Society: The Humane Agenda* (Boston: Houghton Mifflin, 1996); Michael

Bérubé and Cary Nelson, eds., *Higher Education under Fire: Politics, Economics, and the Crisis of the Humanities* (New York and London: Routledge, 1995). In order to balance my readings, I selected other approaches to society and education, such as Francis Fukuyama, *The End of History and the Last Man* (New York: Avon Books, 1992); Christopher Lasch, *The Revolt of the Elites and the Betrayal of Democracy* (New York: W. W. Norton, 1995), and even Newt Gingrich, *To Renew America* (New York: Harper Paperbacks, 1996).

3. Hannah Arendt, "The Crisis in Education," p. 192.

4. For different applications of the concept of cultural capital to education, see Guillory, *Cultural Capital*, and Michael Apple, "Cultural Capital and Official Knowledge," in M. Bérubé and Cary Nelson, eds., *Higher Education under Fire*, pp. 91–107.

CASTELLANO B. TURNER

5   Racial Problems in Society and in the Classroom

THE MAJOR aim of this chapter is to discuss how the dynamics of race relations as they exist in U.S. society at large also appear in the college classroom. A second aim is to explore ways in which the dynamics of race and race relations can be made explicit and worked on in the college classroom. (I focus on race in this chapter, but other intergroup problems and social problems might be considered in similar ways.) Some of what I relate is based on personal experiences, but I begin with the premise that my experiences have not been unique and that the lives of most Americans (not only African Americans and other peoples of color) exemplify at least some aspects of the racial problem we share. This is because race and racial conflicts have been defining elements of our country from its beginning. Although material abounds to support such an assertion from both history and contemporary social analysis, I find quite sufficient evidence in the span of my own life. We are all carriers of our cultures and the internal social structural maps drawn by experience.

A second premise is that when we enter classrooms (here I focus on college classrooms), we all bring our selves along—our experiences, cultures, and maps. Moreover, it is both what we share in common and how our perspectives differ that make race relations in the classroom problematic—and also full of opportunities. The *problem* is that we may simply find in the classroom yet another venue for racial conflict. The *opportunity* is that, in the context of the classroom, sharing perspectives and learning the perspectives of others may be valued and used to reduce racial conflict.

Among the differences between blacks and whites in the United States are their perspectives on the extent and pace of change in race relations—in all its aspects, including racial bias, discrimination, opportunities, and so on. Over the last thirty years of teaching undergraduate and graduate students and interacting with colleagues, I have found remarkable consistency in this difference. African Americans (and other people of color) who I have met believe that examples and evidence of racial bias are readily apparent and have changed only modestly over time. It appears that some consider the subtlety and indirection of "modern racism" even more offensive than "old-fashioned" racism. The range of perspectives among whites is perhaps greater. Some react with shocked indignation or disbelief at the notion that blacks might still consider themselves at all disadvantaged. Others may be aware of continuing inequities but regard them as vestiges of historical racism that are rapidly receding. My own perceptions of the state of race relations necessarily reflect the perspective of an African American. In my own case, the extent and pace of change may be exemplified by the following two experiences.

At the age of thirty, soon after finishing graduate school, I left Chicago, where I was born, grew up, and received almost all of my education. I have been away almost thirty years now, but like many adults with such long formative periods in one place, I have never quite abandoned my identity as a Chicagoan. My memories of Chicago are both bitter and sweet, but on balance I think of the city with the kind of deep fondness that many adults eventually feel toward their aging parents.

Whenever I run across articles that focus on Chicago in local newspapers or national magazines, I attend to them automatically, without self-conscious reflection. (My loyalty to the Bears, the White Sox, and the Bulls has never been threatened.) Sometimes what I read causes me to feel sad or embarrassed. Recently a front page story about Chicago appeared in the major local newspaper. The story: three African American teenagers rode their bikes out of their black community on the near west side (where I grew up) into a bordering white community. They were attacked by three white teenagers. One black thirteen-year-old was beaten so severely that he remained in a coma throughout the following week. The article described the sense of horror expressed at every level of the city— from the local citizens (black and white) and community organizations to the city's mayor, who had grown up and spent most of his life in that particular white community. I had two reactions. First, I resented the expressions of outrage from adults in the city, because I saw them as attempts to deny complicity rather than to recognize that they constituted an important part of the problem. The local politics of Chicago, the racial organization of its neighborhoods, and the hostilities across racial boundaries are not new. Nor should it be shocking to find young people acting out what is said by their parents at home, by their neighbors in the clubs, and by the political leaders at their community rallies.

My second reaction was much more personal. Reading the story transported me back fifty years, to a similar episode in that same community. One warm spring Saturday, a friend and I decided to take a long bike ride to a park frequented by African Americans on the south side of the city. Without thinking about it, we took the most direct route, which from our neighborhood began at a long, dark viaduct under railroad tracks running east and west through the city. The viaduct was one of the unmarked but unchallenged boundaries between blacks and whites in that part of the city. Was this simply a youthful adventure on a warm spring day? Were we unconsciously challenging the boundary, believing that surely no one would bother us as we simply passed through? Well beyond the viaduct, we passed a park where white children were playing softball. My friend and I had no inclination to stop, but soon I heard stones bouncing off our bikes and the pavement near us. When I looked around, I saw a group of the children from the park running in our direction and throwing. No stones hit me, but I was powerfully struck by the meaning of what was happening. We were black. They were white. We were in their part of town and in mortal danger. We peddled faster and probably did not slow down until we saw a dark face on the street.

When I made the connection between the newspaper article and my flashback, I said out loud: "Fifty years later!" I was distressed and saddened at the thought that the racially divided city I grew up in was so unchanged.

Chicago is not unique, and on any given day I am as likely to read about some racial incident taking place in Boston, where I now teach and live. And, although the larger urban centers of the country are the likeliest places for manifestations of racial conflict, they may simply be the most visible. Some rural areas have always been inhospitable to African Americans and other people of color. In some parts of the country, suburban communities have grown dramatically, in part because of "white flight" from the inner city. So what can we in the safety of academia conclude? Racism, racial conflict, and inequality are abiding problems in the United States. The nature and extent of the problems depend, in part, on one's perspective, which in turn depends, in part, on one's own racial group. But how can these problems affect the college classroom? The simplest answer is that such problems are there because we are there.

The second experience, more closely tied to the issue of race in the classroom, serves to bridge off-campus social realities and the teaching and learning enterprise. Early in my academic career, I made the self-conscious decision to try to contribute to the well-being of minority communities, both in my research and in my teaching. Research questions were readily available, and I found colleagues and students with whom I shared idealism and ideas. Projects on racial and cultural differences in early childhood experiences, socialization, aspirations, and personality were followed by research studies on the formation of social stereotypes and cultural barriers. Whenever possible, I have encouraged both undergraduate and graduate students to lead me to the particularly exciting research questions that arise from their own racial and/or cultural experiences. It has been through this process that they and I have contributed most to minority communities and to the discipline of psychology. The vehicle for this contribution has been their diversity.

As recently as thirty years ago, there was no black psychology, Latino psychology, or Asian psychology. There was no psychology of women. There was no psychology of gay and lesbian issues. No psychology of disability. There was hardly a subfield of cross-cultural psychology. Like many academic disciplines, the faculties of psychology departments around the country were overwhelmingly populated by white males, who (not surprisingly) considered the variability across white men (and white mice) quite sufficient for defining our science and understanding human behavior. The field of psychology in this country was sometimes criticized for its lack of research in cultures outside the white middle class. Ours was said to be "the science of white male college sophomore behavior," because that social group dominated the population of our human research subjects. Still, psychology purported to study and describe human behavior. But even that study was carried out largely without regard to social or cultural context. In order to be a science of human beings, the sampling of behavior clearly needed to be extended—to the universe of humans if possible, but certainly well beyond the white middle class of the contiguous United States.

The national movements toward diversity of all kinds in schools and in the workplace have benefited higher education enormously. But for psychology as an academic discipline, however, diversity has triggered something closer to a paradigm shift. Since the 1960s, as students of color entered graduate psychology programs in larger numbers all over the United States, many sought mentors who would help them carry out research projects relevant to their cultures and communities. African American students working with me have completed master's theses and doctoral dissertations on such topics as coping strategies of African Americans, the psychohistory of black elderly, the role of spirituality among African Americans, the relationship of racial identity and family formation decisions, and the relative significance of gender and racial identity among African American women. Latino students have completed graduate research projects investigating acculturation and adjustment among Puerto Ricans, maternal functioning and depression among Dominican women, resilience and school achievement among Latino youth, psychopathology and spiritism among Cubans, and the role of collectivism and individualism in the well-being of Latinos. Students of Asian background have done projects on questions of assertiveness, empathy, individualism and collectivism, sex roles, coping, acculturation, family relationships, and responses to immigration in Asian communities. I have mentored students from India, Pakistan, Algeria, South Africa, and Zimbabwe; they have all done research projects comparing their cultures to others. If students from these cultural backgrounds had not carried out these research projects, it is very unlikely that anyone else would have done so. These students and their projects have extended the data base of psychology, incorporated new perspectives, and helped us to understand more profoundly what difference culture makes in behavior. As a consequence of their efforts, the discipline of psychology has become a more valid and empirically grounded science of human behavior.

Making a difference as a teacher has been even more challenging than encouraging multicultural research in psychology. My teaching experiences have been almost entirely in predominantly white institutions. In my thirty years of teaching, I have had numerous opportunities to speak with African American, Asian American, and Latino students and faculty who have related many stories of abuse (insults, rejection, bigotry, and bias) on campuses and in classrooms. Some of the stories reflected real but subtle racism, and sometimes an incident might even be considered open to interpretation. The majority, however, were neither subtle nor open to generous interpretations. My personal experiences with such abuse are too numerous to recount here, and on the whole are less horrific than those of others.

Recently I conversed with an African American sociology instructor who had taught in prestigious public and private institutions. One of several shocking experiences he related had taken place in his first job at a private university: in teaching a large lecture course on the urban family, he found that whenever he alluded to racial inequities and oppression in the United States, he was met with general hostility from the students. At a class soon after the Challenger disaster of 1986, in which eight astronauts died, he contrasted the grief-stricken national response to that loss with the lack of response to the daily loss of life among the homeless in urban centers. As he turned toward the class, an eraser came at his face. The heckling and threats that followed were so intense that he had to end the class. I had heard before of rare instances of African American instructors being physically assaulted by students, but this was the first time I had spoken personally with someone who had been attacked.

A flood of memories washed over me after that conversation. Some reached back as far as my own undergraduate years, but most were from my years at a large state university in the Northeast. I remembered the young instructor in my own department who told me that he intended to resign from teaching, partly because he was worn down by the unrelenting hostility of white students, who baited him in class and wrote racial insults on his posted grades and anonymous course evaluations. I remembered the many times when African American instructors were ignored by their colleagues because they had no interest in "black psychology." I remembered the many undergraduate and graduate students who told me of insults in and outside of class from white instructors and students. When reporting to authorities, the students were most often met with responses like "You're being too sensitive" or "Such people are unusual and cannot be controlled at any rate." I remembered the frequent reports of racial harassment and physical assaults on students in the dormitories.

Therefore, I argue that racial conflicts are as apparent on our campuses and in our classrooms as they are in the larger society. Perhaps they are even more regularly apparent, because the college classroom is a meeting place for individuals from diverse backgrounds and conflicting perspectives. Have things changed? Those of us who have been victims of this conflict have difficulty seeing substantial improvement over time. Those who have not tend to see the situation differently.

What can be done? In my teaching I have infused the content of all courses with questions of relevance to social problems, particularly problems of intergroup relations. General Psychology provides rich opportunities to demonstrate both the oneness of our species and its behaviors and the important impact of physical, biological, and social ecology. Abnormal Psychology leads many students to challenge their conceptions of deviance and, by inference, to see our general tendency to distance "the other." In my courses on counseling and psychotherapy, the students frequently find themselves in a classroom that is a laboratory for seeing how they can be touched emotionally and communicate concern. Race and other invidious distinctions create barriers to understanding even in the helping professions. Seeing what it takes to get through those barriers can open many to an even deeper understanding of intergroup alienation.

In these and other courses, my attempts to raise the problems of race and racial conflict produce fairly predictable (but not universal) responses from white students. Sometimes they ask, "What does this have to do with . . . ?" or "I thought this was a class on. . . ." Discussion usually leads to a better understanding of what the point is. More frequently I face nonverbal signs of discontent. One of the most painful signals of rejection for me is the rolling of eyes when I speak about race, especially inequity. For several years I would ask myself after this occurred, "Is a black person suspected of being self-serving for mentioning such things?" For a time I felt constrained and began to limit and moderate such comments.

My initial resentment at feeling so limited gave way to a recognition that the students' perspectives were as legitimate as mine. That is, their own needs, history, and cultural maps were informing their views of the world, much as my own were informing my views. I realized that I was disappointed that I could not convince them to think my way or that they were not receptive to my ideas. Over time I have found that, in listening to students, I eventually hear much of what I want to say. Students are also struggling with the dilemmas of race. When confronted, for example, with the question of how to rectify racial inequities in opportunity without considering race, students are guided by vested interests, which, when threatened, lead them to defensiveness and hostility. They ask me, "Is it fair for a white man to be discriminated against just because blacks have been discriminated against in the past?" I accept this as a reasonable question. The burden of answering it, however, should not rest solely on me (or on any African American). When students are invited to struggle with the dilemma and formulate solutions, they often begin to express themselves rather than react to my assertions, and they begin to learn. They are willing to express themselves on these issues when they are listened to. Taking a receptive stance rather than professing too much has, I believe, made me a better teacher. It has certainly helped me to enjoy teaching more. If I do not expect myself to have all the answers to our dilemmas, then I can share the burden and the struggles.

I have also taught two courses specifically focused on issues of race and culture. The first, which I began teaching fifteen years ago at both the undergraduate and graduate levels, is called The Psychology of Cross-Cultural Relations. In recent years I have also supervised advanced graduate students in teaching the course to undergraduates. As originally designed, this was a multidisciplinary course in which materials from history, sociology, political science, economics, and anthropology were joined with a psychological perspective on cross-cultural and cross-racial relations. Among the themes that invariably arose from the readings and discussions were cultural invasion, domination, oppression, and ethnic stratification. Both white and black students typically had little difficulty understanding these processes in historical terms. On the other hand, for white students to perceive these processes as they related to current social structural arrangements was more difficult. Students in general found this type of analysis both difficult and irrelevant to their lives and interests. The first few times I taught the course to undergraduates, I discovered that some had signed up thinking that a course on cross-cultural relations was about inter-ethnic dating and mating! Perhaps the title was ambiguous, but how could they imagine that I would teach something about their real-life and age-appropriate concerns?

I had made a fundamental pedagogical error: I expected the students to meet me where I was, presenting abstractions such as stratification and domination, rather than meeting students where they were—struggling with the developmental transition from family into the larger world of intimacy and of getting along with others. As I had expected, they were animated and involved when they shared their observations about "mixed marriages" and disagreement between different racial groups in the dormitories. Gradually, and especially after the graduate students began teaching the undergraduate version, the course took on a more participatory format and began to emphasize personal experiences. When students see themselves as agents within an interpersonal encounter, they become more open to accepting the general dynamics of intergroup relations, especially in terms of power. In owning their ethnic/cultural backgrounds and discovering those of others, they seem more willing to lower the barrier to authentic encounter. This makes it more possible to discuss issues of stratification, as well as to understand how a view of the world from a position of privilege may differ from the perspective of a person who is marginalized.

The second course, Cuture and Mental Health, was designed specifically as a graduate course and is a required course in a program that emphasizes social-cultural context in understanding normal and abnormal human development. The students are from diverse racial and cultural backgrounds, and they are chosen because, in part, they share the faculty's belief that social and cultural context are important in understanding psychological disorder and its amelioration. I have taught the course for seven years, and each time the experience has been somewhat different.

In such a small group (usually eight, but ranging from six to twelve students), variations in group composition are important. The difference, for instance, between having one and two African American students in a class is remarkable. The single African American is invariably viewed as the exemplar, the spokesperson, the exception, and even the target of unacknowledged resentments from white students and faculty. The "singleton" carries the full burden of stated or implied assumptions that s/he was accepted without adequate credentials and in order to fill a racial quota. On the other hand, when students of color make up half of a class, a subtle tension is present. Everyone seems to experience pressure to choose sides. A white student may complain of feeling like the "outsider" when all of the other students (including other white students) are sharing personal feelings about racial and ethnic identity. Among the most common problems in this course is that some students have real difficulty seeing themselves in racial/ethnic/cultural terms. While other people are "ethnics" or "racial minorities," they themselves are simply American, middle class, without culture, "white bread." Fortunately, it is rare for a student to refuse to explore previously hidden aspects of their personal identity. I have learned much about race, ethnicity, and culture by witnessing students' stories and self discoveries.

For example, my first real understanding of problems of acculturation came from students who related stories about being caught between parents demanding the maintenance of the traditional culture and friends pressuring conformity to American peer culture.

My own place in the dynamics of this class is complex. I have based this course on several premises. First, I believe that it is important for helping professionals to become competent to work with individuals from diverse social and cultural backgrounds. Second, in spite of much theory and some research to the contrary, I believe that it is possible for people from different racial/ethnic groups to work together in productive therapeutic alliances. Third, as in any sphere of competence, I believe that becoming an adequate therapeutic agent requires effort, training, and practice.

Using a modification of the public health model of change, I consider three elements important in therapy training: knowledge, attitude, and practice (of skills or behavior). Many students wish to jump over the first two. They want to be told or shown "how to." They reason that knowledge never will be adequate, since we cannot know about all the groups we might encounter, and then they erroneously conclude, "Why bother?" Attitude change is particularly resisted, although in my view it is the most important element. It is a paradox that attitude change, although an essential element of learning, cannot be made the goal or content of academic instruction. But a pedagogy that allows students to observe and appreciate the changes in themselves and others is clearly desirable.

Students typically believe that their attitudes are "just fine, thank you." They are, after all, good people who want to help those in distress—without regard to race, creed, religion, color, sex, sexual orientation, disability, or national origin. Revealing, exploring, or discovering their own attitudes puts a threatening burden on them. Fortunately, these are burdens that students can and do handle. They are good people, and given our help and expectations for growth beyond mere skills, they do become better able to provide appropriate services.

Some years ago, early in the semester of this course, two black women complained to me that they were upset by several things happening in class. They felt most aggrieved by white students repeatedly addressing each of them by the other one's name. I suggested that bringing their feelings up in the class might occasion a learning experience for everyone— "Just what we are there for." They did, and they explained to their classmates that such mistakes disturbed them because they harked back to the notion that whites think "all black people look alike" and that blacks do not deserve the respect implicit in being called their own names. I did not expect the defensiveness from white students that followed: "You are being too sensitive," "That's a natural mistake," and "I've never been good at names." More disturbing to me were the comments directed to one of the black students: "I consider you distant, arrogant, and condescending," and "You addressed me by the wrong name once, too." Finally, most disturbing were the comments, "I have many friends [relatives, etc.] who are black [people of color]," "I resent being thought of as a racist," and "Some things you have said in class suggest to me that you are homophobic." The black students responded with defensiveness themselves and then brought forth their whole litany of complaints against the white students, who responded in kind.

The discussion deteriorated into an exchange of accusations. I suggested that the class might want to plan one whole day just to work this through. They agreed, we met, and it turned into an extended period of the same destructive process. My exhortations to share honest feelings and to listen to each other undefensively went nowhere. By the end of the meeting everyone had expressed feelings, but there was little evidence of listening. I tried to put as positive a face on this failure as I could, suggesting that each person take responsibility to work it through with others. They never did. Instead, several of the students came to me to complain in private or to report some other malfeasance of an antagonist.

Over the years that followed, I was aware that the conflicts that began in that class continued to fester and emerge repeatedly in this particular cohort of students. I had always felt that what had happened was my fault. I did not, however, understand my failure fully until years later, when members of the group took another course with me. The two black students made it clear that they had been disappointed in my lack of support for them. The white students said they felt that I had both favored the black students in the conflict and given preferential treatment to them over the years. More significantly, I was made to understand for the first time that the defensiveness in everyone arose out of my presence. They did not want to be labeled white/black racists (or any other kind of bigot) in front of the instructor, who was also the director of their program. The resulting threat had led to their defensiveness. I had not acknowledged this obvious possibility. I had not, for that matter, noticed or noted that I was in the classroom. I had simply been mystified and frustrated by their defensiveness and lack of empathy for each other. If I had invited them to express their fears about what I thought, they might have felt safe enough to acknowledge those fears, and we might have been able to work them through.

So what complicates my role in the classroom? I am the instructor. I am an African American. The students see me both as an authority and as the personification of a set of stereotypes. Students of color tend to expect a champion of their perspectives. White students may believe that I will use my authority to push unwanted change on them. I have my own agenda, my perspective, my ideals, and my own defensiveness. These several perspectives are not so much complications as reflections of reality. We have all met in the classroom, and we have indeed brought ourselves. The country's drama of race is played out there.

Over the last few years, with the help of colleagues facing similar questions and problems, I have been able to face that reality more completely. I believe that I have a much better sense now of how an African American instructor's presence might make a difference. Fortunately, my realization has not led me to either ignore or run away from the racial dynamics of the classroom. In recent courses (one team-taught with a white colleague), I have tried to be even more present, more personally available in the classroom, and more receptive to the individual perspectives of my students. This has not always been easy, and the results have sometimes left me distressed, but I believe that it is the correct way for me as a teacher and as a person. I believe that it will be correct for the students as well.

Vivian Zamel

6   Teaching (as) Composing

As I think back to my English classes, I recall being taught about parts of speech, parts of sentences, and diagramming sentences. I remember being told what writing should be, what it should look like, what to do, and what not to do with writing. Always do this, never do that, do not think, just follow the rules. The problem here was that all of this is what I was *taught*, but I do not think I ever *learned*.

—an undergraduate writing tutor

When I started college, I had to write papers for my courses using a second language. . . . I remember my first paper topic for English. It was an essay I remember with dread. I recall obsessing about making the essay perfectly organized and—above all—grammatically correct. I edited, edited and edited, never leaving any room for myself to explore my thought or develop them further, because I was too distracted with getting the right form. In the process, I also lost my own voice.

—an undergraduate ESL student

Why do so many of our schools, and most of our textbooks, urge us to hold only one opinion? Like so many other people I know, my education always urged me to find the "right answer," always pressured me to believe that every question had one right answer (and that all others led to disaster). . . . We were pushed to find the "correct" interpretation to our reading. Reading was indoctrination. . . . I wasn't urged to think for myself.

—a graduate student

THESE ACCOUNTS are representative of those written by under-graduate students, many of whom are in English as a Second Language (ESL) classes, as well as by graduate students in courses on the teaching of ESL.[1] In all of the courses I teach, I ask students to reflect on their past educational experiences, particularly as these are related to reading and writing. These reflections reveal the backgrounds, perspectives, and attitudes students are bringing with them and suggest what I need to do to build on these. Importantly, these recollected experiences inform and contribute to my own ongoing research and reflection on writing, language acquisition, and pedagogy.

What I continue to learn from students underlines the extent to which their educations have focused on the correct response, form, and interpretation and reveals the ways that this pedagogical orientation has affected them. Despite theory and research on the factors that promote learning, language, and literacy, and despite the rhetoric surrounding educational reform, much schooling seems to be characterized by a transmission model of education intended to reproduce the "right answer."[2] For students who are struggling with the acquisition of English and written discourse, such a reductionist stance ultimately silences these students and actually subverts the process of learning. Focusing on and prioritizing correct language use keeps students from understanding that we use language to make sense of the world, to learn, to engage in academic work, and that it is when we use language in these ways that we acquire it. In the case of prospective and practicing teachers of ESL, their past histories as learners, not surprisingly, serve as models for their own teaching and thus perpetuate the very problematic approaches that limited their learning.

My Own Education and Early Career

It is interesting, given the professional choices I have come to make, that I can see myself in both the ESL students and teachers I work with. As a non-native speaker of English myself (I was born in Germany, and my first languages were Yiddish and German), and as a young child who emigrated to the United States and attended a school that expected me to learn in two new languages (English and Hebrew), I remember the hours of memorization of language and content, the obsession with figuring out what the tests would cover, the need to display, to the teacher's satisfaction, what she wanted. In one vivid and symbolic memory, I see myself concentrating on reproducing those perfectly rounded cursive letters, careful not to go outside the lines printed on the manuscript paper, convinced, as was my teacher, that these shapes constituted writing. I came to believe, I see now in retrospect, that this is how one learns, oblivious of the influence of the books my parents and I read at home or the impact of the complex language negotiations I was involved in as I shifted between home and school languages. I am startled by how much of this belief about learning persisted and was reinforced throughout my own education. Years of Spanish instruction in high school and college consisted of the drilling and memorization of segmented and decontextualized language, of the conventional separation of speaking, reading, and writing, with no attempts at genuine reading and writing (or speaking, for that matter) until I reached very advanced levels of language study.

Of particular importance, given the research and teaching I eventually came to do, was my first-semester college composition course. I can still feel and see the onion skin paper on which I typed my essays, completely unsure of how to fulfill the professor's expectations. These papers, returned with the most devastating grades I had ever received and filled with responses that consisted of thick red circles around errors and cryptic comments about my logic and thinking, frustrated and embarrassed me, disabused me of the idea that I could major in English, and reinforced the notion that writing had to be "right." I had just never really learned that lesson, I thought. As a result of this unsettling experience, I put off taking a second required composition course as long as I could. And though I was reassured through my experiences in other courses that I indeed *could* write, that first experience with college writing left an indelible impression on me.

In graduate school, as I studied linguistics, theories of language acquisition, and pedagogy, and as I came to understand the ways in which these needed to be brought to bear on working with students who spoke an array of different first languages, I remember the comfort I felt when I read about specific methods of teaching English, proven techniques for promoting better pronunciation and reading and writing skills. Even when my mentor encouraged us to recognize the complexity of teaching and learning language, even when the research I undertook as a graduate assistant, observing and analyzing ESL classrooms, revealed the messiness and unpredictability of classroom dynamics and processes, I resisted incorporating my observations into a new perspective on teaching writing. And so, not surprisingly, my early experiences with teaching college-level ESL classes reflected a deeply ingrained belief about the systematic nature of language and language learning and a pervasive concern with grammar, form, and structure. Students were expected to remember and display particular language items. After all, I believed, in order for these learners to do anything with English, they first needed to master its components. All I needed to do, I was convinced, was find the right textbook, the right set of worksheets. I was very much like one of the tutors in a class I recently taught whose experiences led her to write, "Am I the only one who feels overwhelmed when working with ESL students? What are the steps? The procedures? The secrets?"

It is this kind of "magical thinking," this belief that there are steps, procedures, and secrets that will ensure that students will learn what we teach, that I embraced and brought with me to my first years of teaching composition at UMass/Boston. The textbooks that I examined for adoption confirmed that this rule-driven and mechanistic approach to teaching writing and language was indeed what students needed in order to succeed in the academic world. I insisted on correct language and expected papers that followed a set of predetermined formats. Students mimicked these formats, and their papers were evaluated on the basis of how closely they approximated the models presented in their textbooks. My responses, in red, pointed out their errors, and my comments were limited to amorphous remarks about organizational issues. I had become the kind of teacher so many of the students in my courses tend to recollect. I had become the professor I had had when I took freshman composition.

Given students' previous instructional experiences, and given the roles they assume in our classrooms, it is not surprising that students did not question my curricular decisions. During one semester, however, a student who had written well-organized papers that imitated the models I provided made a remark that led me to raise questions about my teaching. As Sabena handed in her course evaluation, she indicated how much she had liked me as a teacher but felt that I had not been interested in what she and the other students had been thinking. This struck me as odd, given that I had believed that I had invited students to share their concerns and thoughts in their writing. But clearly, students like Sabena understood that the real agenda for the course (a focus on conventions, formats, and correct language) transcended my suggestion that they write about issues that mattered to them, about their own observations, opinions, and interpretations. The ways I responded to their writing reinforced what they came to understand as my real agenda. Sabena's comment, I now believe, represented a critical moment in my teaching. Her concern led me to begin to question the extent to which engagement, inquiry, and using language to learn and make sense of that learning played a role in the work I asked student to do. Furthermore, I began to see my own work had not involved me in exploring, inquiring into, and making sense of students' learning processes and experiences. Like the students in my classroom, I too had adopted someone else's predetermined framework and curriculum and, in doing so, saw learning/teaching as static, fixed, and closed processes.

TAKING RISKS AS A TEACHER

At around the same time as Sabena's remark raised these concerns, the discipline of composition studies, much like the field of language acquisition, was experiencing what has since come to be viewed as a paradigm shift.[3] In both of these disciplines, researchers were interrogating the extent to which the product orientation of language and writing classrooms reflected and took into account the actual processes involved in the acquisition of language and literacy. Language and discourse had been fragmented into their basic components and structures, but this, it came to be recognized, had little to do with either what we actually do when we use language or what we actually need in order to acquire it. Curricular approaches had been designed on the basis of how language could be broken down rather than on the basis of how each of us, in genuine attempts to use language and in contexts that support these attempts, builds our own language/literacy repertoire.

It was in this context that I began to take risks with making my classroom a site of inquiry and to investigate the writing processes and experiences of the ESL students in my composition courses.[4] This research became the basis for my later scholarship and utterly transformed my teaching since it draws so heavily on what students have taught me. What I discovered during these investigations allowed me to understand the struggles that students were experiencing as they tried to put pen to paper in a language that they were still in the process of acquiring. One graduate student, an English teacher from Vietnam, captures the struggle she experiences, this despite how accomplished a writer she so obviously is:

> Writing has always been excruciating to me. I often start my writing process with a given topic in mind and think about what I know and am able to say about it, usually not much apart from my emotional reactions. Then I'll do some reading, take notes, and feel miserable for not being able

to sit down and write something, even a few words. I keep procrastinating—the hardest part for me is to put words on paper and organize ideas and arguments. I often wonder why both professional and amateur writers are obsessed with getting the words right. Even Hemingway admitted such obsession. I would stop in the middle of a sentence to look up in the dictionary for the spelling of a word, or the uses of another to choose the one I think most appropriate, most meaningful. What also seems to be problematic to me is when I have so much to say about a topic or theme that I can't put my thoughts in order. They all get messed up and tumble in my head like the snowballs in a powerful nor'eastern storm! Then I tend to shun the drudgery of sorting out my ideas, put them into words and organize them in paper.

Many students in my classes have shared similar accounts, which, in turn, have contributed to my thinking and learning about teaching. As I continued to attend to what these accounts revealed, I began to experiment. Gradually I came to see that, once I gave students multiple opportunities to use writing to think through their ideas, to offer their interpretations, to take risks with language, and to engage with the issues we were studying, they could begin to see writing and the use of English in more positive and productive ways. For example, they began to appreciate what all of us who write understand about writing, that writing is messy and unruly, and that not only is it useful for recording what we already know and think, but that it generates ideas and language. Although they are still in the process of acquiring English, these students began to use written language as a means for exploring their ideas, discovering, in the very process of doing so, what they want to say. As some of them put it,

> Unless you write about something, you can't find out exactly what you know about it.

> I don't even know what I'm thinking sometimes, but I'm finding out by writing.

> At the beginning I have some order in mind, but I don't really know what's going to happen.

Along with understanding how writing provides students with a powerful way to construct meaning for themselves, I have come to see that their ongoing struggles with the English language do not necessarily preclude this process from getting underway. Students speak of the importance of focusing on their ideas and of finding strategies for dealing with the challenges of writing in English:

If I have an idea, but I don't have the words, I write in Chinese so I don't lose it. Language is not the big problem. Most of the difficulty is how to put the ideas together.

I may write a word in Portuguese, but I know I'll find it later. It doesn't affect my writing in stopping me. Sometimes it helps to have two languages because you can write it down in another language and get on with your ideas without stopping. You have another way to say it.

Students may even come to see writing in English as beneficial, as liberating, giving them, in those situations where they are encouraged to use writing to engage and grapple with course material, a sense of freedom and accomplishment:

Personally, I love writing in English. . . . I much prefer writing in English than in my native language. I feel very rhythmical when writing in English.

Writing in English is great. I feel comfortable and free. I grew up in Vietnam. I still remember I had no choice and no way to write a paper. I couldn't write what I thought and saw in society.

These discoveries about students' experiences with writing in English, made when these students felt safe to use language to make meaning, have led me to other investigations of students' experiences in courses across the curriculum.[5] Again, what is revealed is the essential relationship between student engagement and learning. When the goal of instruction is to transmit and cover course content, when students are left out of the process of constructing knowledge, when pedagogical approaches do not take into account what students already know and the ways in which they are making sense of the course material, there is little opportunity for students to see this course in relationship to themselves. The process of learning is thus undermined. Martha, a former student in one of my composition courses who had found in writing a particularly powerful way for both reflecting on her learning and acquiring English, attests to her experience in a course that seemingly did little to draw her in, to make her "visible." Her frustration and disappointment are palpable:

I only heard dates and facts. Facts, dates. I reacted by sitting quiet and feeling very frustrated. I did not feel like sharing any of my opinions. . . . The lectures were missing the combination of creativity of my classmates' reflections. I started to lose the grounded self I carried with me from my ESL class experiences. I tried several times to become visible during the lectures by letting out my voice. But I found myself lost because the lectures were without writing. . . . I remember that silent students in the classroom started to feel like a normal part of the lecture. Many times two or three words were my contributions in class. They were replacing the long and sometimes unclear sentences that previously in my ESL class were disentangled to reveal a powerful thought. . . . My writing started to experience a metamorphosis because I was only copying dates and facts from the blackboard. There was not a drop of motivation to enjoy my journey of learning. I felt illiterate at the end of that semester. I did not learn a single new word.

In stark contrast to this discouraging situation is the following account, written by Motoko, another former student, who is commenting here about the first day in an introductory philosophy course:

The first day of the course, the professor gave us an ungraded paper assignment. The subject was about our image toward philosophy. On the second day, he posed the same question to the class and started to call on the students from the front row. Since I was sitting in the left corner of the front row, he called on me by verifying my first name. I was nervous to speak up in front of everybody whom I had yet known, but because I already organized my idea and image toward philosophy last night in my assignment, though it was far from the fluent English, I somehow managed to bring my self to the end. After I finished, the professor briefly summarized what I just said by using more sophisticated and philosophical sounding words. Then he raised two important issues from my statement and wrote them down on the blackboard. I felt so delighted. I felt I was included. I felt my existence was affirmed.

   The reason why I was and still am hesitated to raise my voice in the classroom is because I am always intimidated by two big worries which are "Will everybody be able to understand what I say" and "Does my idea is important enough to be raised?" Most of the time these two ideas envelop my mind so that I cannot release my words, especially when I sense that the class circumstance is neither comfortable nor worthy enough to take a risk. But this time, the professor displayed very warm and sensitive conduct before me. Perhaps that was really trivial matter for other people, but because I was always worried about my English deficiency, even such a small matter became a big deal in my mind. A kind of hope was gradually growing in my mind and I sensed that something urged me to take future chances in the class. I felt fortunate to take this course.

Much is revealed here about the kind of pedagogy that makes it possible for students to be included and heard, even when their own struggles and fears often lead to self-censorship, as is the case with this student. Using writing as a source for exploring, in a safe way, the subject matter of the course, the teacher was able to build on Motoko's "image toward philosophy." Drawing on and validating her attempt at understanding, the teacher offered language and concepts, seemingly new to this student, that probably complicated and enriched her initial understanding. Importantly, this process allowed Motoko to take the kinds of risk that are critical for learning and gave her reason to believe that she could take "future chances" of this sort.

TEACHING COMPOSING

This research into students' learning experiences and perspectives both confirms and contributes to what I have come to understand about composing. The act of writing does not involve only recording what we know, think, or mean at the moment (or what someone else knows, thinks, or means). It is not limited to retrieving information and transmitting it onto paper. It is not the typographical transcription of what we are already capable of articulating aloud. (I point here to what writing is *not* precisely because I continue to see so many writing assignments, both in writing classrooms and in courses across the curriculum, that are informed by just such misconceptions.) Rather, writing is a means for composing at the most fundamental level, for it allows us to explore, uncover, and actually make meaning. It allows us to discover what might otherwise have remained inchoate, elusive, unarticulated thought. It is for this reason that writing is such a powerful means for learning, for making sense of and connecting with course content, for understanding our understandings. This accounts, no doubt, for Martha's conviction that the absence of writing excluded her from the "journey of learning." It helps us see why Motoko benefited from the invitation to use writing as a way of exploring her ideas about philosophy, especially since, in her case, it is very likely that, had it not been for the exploratory writing assignment, she might not have taken the opportunity to respond to the question posed and to share her response in class.

The act of authorship confers authority. (Indeed, "author" is in the word "authority.") By inviting students to bring themselves to the texts they write, they begin to see themselves as making legitimate and constructive contributions to their studies. They become invested in their learning, and the more legitimacy their contributions are given, the more committed they become. However, learning to use writing in this meaningful and purposeful way is neither an easy nor a straightforward process. Writing is a convoluted and often chaotic undertaking precisely because being engaged in meaning-making is such a challenging and associative process.

The same is true of reading.[6] Reading is a dynamic, exploratory process whereby the reader composes (rather than merely retrieves and reiterates information), drawing on what she brings and contributes to the text. It, too, is generative, requiring the reader to find and make connections and to figure out, on the basis of what one knows and thinks, what speaks to the reader and why. Reading often necessitates a degree of tentativeness and guessing, as we revise our readings in light of our newly acquired understanding. One student characterized the process in the following way:

> While reading, I'm saying to myself, I understand exactly what he's saying, but if you ask me exactly what I agree with, I don't know yet. I think I have to write it out myself before I can internalize the points I agree with. It's still very fuzzy in my mind what I agree with. By writing, I have to consciously think out what I've read, and by writing it down, I internalize the meaning in my own words to make the ideas real to me—so that I own the words.

I'm convinced that, because reading involves this interactive, dialogic process, writing is critical for understanding, learning from, and reflecting on texts, especially in the case of less experienced readers and writers who assume that reading is a matter of decoding and marking a text, yellow marker in hand. Writing, because it gives rise to our own ways of probing and working with texts, is not only an ideal way for composing and constructing the reading: it also helps us to understand that this process is what reading entails. The following account, written by a graduate student, reflects this very understanding:

> For those courses where we have to write [in response to reading], I am infinitely more involved with the readings than those courses where no writing is required and I do my obligatory underlining and marginal writing. One course I am thinking about has an enormous amount of extremely technical reading. No writing. As a result, it's almost as if the readings are one activity; class discussion is a separate activity and somehow, although the course is based on the readings, they are never effectively integrated into the course. In the article on reading, Freire says, "Reading always involves critical perception, interpretation, and rewriting what is read." I have come to see that "re-writing" what one has read is essential in interpreting and understanding that text.

Another student in my undergraduate seminar for writing tutors echoes this realization as she comments on the process of keeping a reading journal throughout the semester:

> Writing is like a journey of self-discovery and exploration of ideas. Being free and encouraged to ask questions, analyze, reflect, disagree with and make sense of what one is reading helps one to connect with the text in some way. So the reader is doing more than just reading a piece—he/she is examining it and essentially talking with the text. That dialogue that one has when reading/writing is so important in understanding what one is reading in relation to one's own life. And that is the whole point of reading and doing anything. It has to have meaning for the individual as a reader, writer, person. . . . I wish more professors would recognize what a powerful and positive tool journal entries can be for the student as well as the teacher. Not only can the student make sense of it all—the professor can, too! The professor can see what his/her students are struggling with and respond directly to their questions. Professors also have the opportunity to build a foundation of confidence by positively responding and asking further questions that show that they care about what the students took the time to write. . . . [Those classes] that I have had where we were asked to do journal entries about the readings I did much better in and enjoyed more. I think journal entries really help you get the most out of the class because one is given the opportunity and freedom to "play" with and challenge what he/she is reading without being confined to or burdened with writing grammatically correct, perfect prose. Each journal entry is truly a reflection of one's progress and a reminder of one's initial feelings and attitudes when responding to a piece. When I look back on this course, I can see my growth simply by reading my journal entries. I've learned so much because I was asked to respond and reflect on what I was reading. There were no "right" or "wrong" answers. There were only *my* answers and ideas that emerged as I was challenging what I read. I was able to connect the "word" of the text with my "world."[7]

This is a rich and compelling account of how reading and writing as interactive and integrated processes benefited her understanding and learning. It urges us to rethink teaching that stresses the "right answer," teaching that fails to take into account the inextricable relationship between a student's "word" (her ongoing acquisition of literacy) and her "world" (her knowledge, understanding, experiences). It further suggests that this pedagogical approach not only helps the student "make sense of it all," but that "the professor can, too." I believe that this is a critical moment in this account, for it suggests that the ways in which I have been characterizing writing and reading can be applied to the process of teaching.

TEACHING AS COMPOSING

Teaching, too, I have come to understand, is a process of composing, one that involves what we bring to the "text" of our classes and what we do in order to create meaning for ourselves and in response to students (who, along with us, are reading and writing the "text" of the classroom). Like reading and writing, teaching requires that we engage with and commit ourselves to this work (much as we do when we undertake our scholarly projects), seeing teaching as a site of inquiry, exploration, and discovery, and as a means for making sense of what we and our students do in the classroom. Responsive teaching takes into account the dynamic interplay of participants (teachers and students alike) as they send each other messages about their emerging understandings; it assumes that learning is dependent upon and enabled by the particular and local conditions of each classroom. Teaching circles back and reconsiders previous experiences in order to move forward. Rather than being predictable, linear, and orderly, it depends on posing questions and testing out tentative and alternative hypotheses in an ongoing way, revising them in light of what is produced and how students respond. It anticipates that these responses, like our own, may be variable and idiosyncratic, tied as they are to individual background, experience, and understanding. Like reading and writing, teaching is generative, recursive, contingent, dialogic.

Once I came to see teaching in this way, as an act of composing, I could let go of the "search-for-the-right-answer" mentality, in both my students' work and my own, and turn my attention to making teaching and learning a project for research (literally, the process of searching and searching again). I turned to investigating students' literacy, language, and schooling experiences, collecting accounts of the sort included in this chapter, and considering the implications of these discoveries for my own teaching. I invited students to share with one another in class their (mis)understandings of the texts they read, including the texts (assignments and paper comments) that I write. My pedagogical approach has been transformed as a result of my attempts to "author" my teaching (by constructing courses that draw and build on students' experiences and understanding) and to help students become "authors" of their own learning (by encouraging them to construct knowledge on the basis of their experiences and knowledge). In teaching ESL students, this has meant a shift from a fixed set of curricular goals driven by absolute standards and mechanistic assumptions about language and literacy to the creation of courses that engage students in challenging and rich work that they would find meaningful.[8] It is this kind of work that, by its very nature, makes it possible for these students to acquire and construct knowledge and enables them to do so in a language that has so often served to exclude them. By involving students in course work in which reading, writing, and classroom discussion are inextricably linked, contributing and fostering one another, students are able to acquire the language of the content in which they are engaged.

As I (re)search the ways in which students' reading, writing, and use of language play into one another, I note, too, that individual students respond very differently and with great variability to the tasks I assign. I observe, for example, that some students participate more fully in class, while some who are less vocal demonstrate their strength in their writing, and still others, while they may have written an impressive response to one assignment, are derailed by a subsequent assignment. I therefore provide students with multiple and extensive opportunities to inquire into, raise questions about, and critically examine course material, and I use these opportunities as a means for exploring and responding to student learning. I invite them to see connections between their own perspectives and experiences and course content, help them develop new frameworks of understanding, and encourage them to actively construct knowledge by locating meaning in their observations and interpretations, bringing these into the classroom as a resource to be considered along with other course material. For example, in one course that was focused on the theme of work, students wrote about their work-related experiences, were introduced to several of the interviews that Studs Terkel published in *Working;* conducted their own interviews, which they shared with one another as texts; explored ways to characterize and represent both Terkel's interviews and their own; and then applied this frame of understanding to the work experiences they wrote about initially, revising their texts in light of the knowledge they had constructed together. Throughout all of this, I urge students to take risks with new language and discourses, because this kind of risk-taking is essential for learning.

As a result of my explorations of students' experiences across an array of college courses, I have come to realize that students need this sort of work not only in their English/composition courses, but across the curriculum, as a means for introducing students to unfamiliar subject matter, new concepts and terms, and differing approaches to course content. This notion is central to my collaborations with faculty both at UMass/Boston and at other institutions where classrooms have become increasingly linguistically diverse. What I try to give faculty to understand is that each course brings with it content, language, and sets of assumptions that are tied to and embedded within the specific concerns and issues of that course, just as all language and conventions are situated within specific cultural contexts. The very conditions that make it possible to acquire language and literacy, conditions I have tried to enact in my own teaching, are those that promote learning across all classes. Note how an undergraduate writing tutor, recognizing the context-specific nature of academic work, captures this notion:

> Academic discourse is a foreign language for a lot of people. . . . It is like traveling to different parts of the world. Every student, like a tourist or foreigner in another land, needs time to adjust to the academic world, to learn the language, the culture. I think a lot of professors are aware that learning academic discourse can be powerful but from my own experiences, I think that some professors' methods don't allow students enough time to "play" in and question this new language and other world.

Although the recent frustrations and tensions voiced in our institutions suggest that the growing diversity of students who are "strangers in academia" makes *us* feel like strangers in academia and challenges us to rethink our teaching, the project of transforming pedagogy ought not to be viewed as a necessary concession to this diversity. Rather, teaching that is responsive and dialogic, that builds on and connects with students' knowledge and understanding, that allows classroom participants to "play" with new language and construct knowledge in collaborative ways, that recognizes the context-dependent nature of learning, is good pedagogy for everyone.

In my composition courses for ESL students, I have experimented with a number of themes related to language, education, or work that have particular significance for them. One two-semester sequence of courses (the same group of students moved from one composition course to the next) involved students in exploring the myth and reality of the "American Dream" and in analyzing those situations and conditions that enable or constrain the dreams that so many of them had embraced.

In addition to the fact that I anticipated that this theme would have charged meaning for these students, this course grew out of and was inspired by ongoing conversations with my colleague Lois Rudnick, who had created a course on the American Dream for the American Studies Program.[9] Interestingly, since that time, Lois has worked with ESL faculty on a collaborative project whereby students in American studies courses and ESL courses write to and respond to one another about their understanding of and experiences with such issues as immigration, ethnicity, and multiculturalism. As a result of this collaboration, students in American studies examine and consider course issues as these are brought to bear on what the ESL students share with them through their written exchanges. And the ESL students not only learn about the issues and questions addressed in American studies, but they also, because they are "insiders," become authoritative sources for the American studies students.

Students in this course examined key documents such as the Declaration of Independence and the Gettysburg Address and important court decisions such as *Brown v. Board of Education*. They read newspaper accounts and analyzed media reports related to immigration experiences and issues. They read revealing interviews in Studs Terkel's *American Dreams: Lost and Found* and carried out interviews of their own. They read poetry by Langston Hughes and Martín Espada, speeches by Martin Luther King, Jr., and autobiographical pieces by Ann Moody and Rosa Parks, and considered the civil rights movement in light of the promises of the American Dream. They read selections by Amy Tan, Maxine Hong Kingston, Richard Rodriguez, and Sandra Cisneros, pieces that illustrate the complicated relationship between language, cultural identity, and power. They read about research that corroborated the firsthand experiences of these authors and that linked them with a far more complex set of societal factors than students had previously realized. Through all of this work, I expected students to compose their writing, reading, and learning. I invited students' reactions, their analyses and interpretations, and their attempts to make connections between this work and their own assumptions and experiences. I encouraged them to bring their own knowledge and cultural background into play so that they could approach the authors they read as other voices (rather than as definitive authorities) to which they could add their own. Intrinsic to this work was a sequence of reading and writing that I composed, examining, taking into account, and building on what students produced, referring, along with them, to their previous work, and sharing with the class students' growing expertise.

What this kind of work produced was not the kind of neat and predictable essays that I requested of students like Sabena much earlier in my teaching career, essays that could be evaluated and plotted along some standardized continuum. Rather, this more engaged work generated rich, compelling, and memorable pieces that reflected the questions and issues students were grappling with, their active involvement with and investment in the material, their use of the material to think about and make sense of the world around them, to think about the ways in which this material and its words and their worlds intersected. Students became authors alongside the authors they read, thus reclaiming authority for themselves. In short, their work represented the dialectical interplay between themselves and the course content, indicating not only the way the material affected them, but also the ways in which they were contributing to the material.

As I read and responded to students' work, looking for interesting, provocative, and even puzzling reactions, insights and questions, I was often struck by the powerful nature of the connections they were making, not only to their own experiences and backgrounds, but also to previous course content. In one journal entry, a student wrote the following response to a passage by Rosa Parks, a response enriched by her previous reading of Hughes and her experiences with racism in China:

> When Rosa Parks talks about African Americans, I had a horrible feeling. No other immigrants can feel about that. Think if you were kidnapped to be a slavery from your country, how difficult the situation would be? "This is not the home of the blacks" is the poem written by Langston Hughes had expressed. Rosa had showed her progressive action 12 years before she arrested. But she was taken off the bus. I was shocked by the humiliating segregation law. You have to stand up and give the seat to somebody else because you are black. What racism! When I was in China, even though there was discrimination to the north people who came down to the south, the south people at most could call them bad names and cheat them, but could never show out.

In another journal entry, a student's moving reaction to a text by Maxine Hong Kingston revealed her own complicated thoughts about language, voice, and inclusion and allowed her to speak about and make sense of the silent world she inhabits.

I identify with her experience and feelings about voices. More than once in my life, I had to deal with that. Like her, before I picked up the phone to talk to someone in English, I spent more than 15 minutes to prepare what I was going to say but when my fearful voice came out, word by word as a stutter and I forgot all. . . . Also I have shared with Kingston her experience of going to school. Right now, around me is silent too. I want to make friends but my English doesn't allow me to do that. I'm afraid of asking people and of being asked as well, so I keep quiet and do things by myself. I'm always thinking of my old friends and my own happy, lovely world I left behind. (I had studied chemistry for 4 years in college in Vietnam.) For 4 years, my class was home and my friends were sisters, brothers and now the more I think of them, the more I feel lonely. Got into the lab, looked around, but only strangers and only English. More silence covered me up.

Yet another text, written in response to one of Cisneros's stories in *The House on Mango Street*, "Mango Says Goodbye Sometimes," demonstrated the startling way students came to (re)compose not only their reading/writing (drawing, for example, on Cisneros' revelation in another story that she was born in the Chinese year of the horse), but also their understanding of themselves, bringing all of this to bear on their reflections about identity and belonging:

The house on Mango Street is not a house that Cisneros dreamed about. She likes to tell stories because when she writes, "the ghost"—her spirit "does not ache so much." Mango sets her free at this moment. She flies to wherever she belong to. But her dream is not just to get out of Mango. Her dream is to come back, bring "the ones [she] left behind," bring "the ones who cannot out." Cisneros is such a strong woman who was born in the Chinese year of a horse. She has such a strong dream that one day she can write and fight for her people. I was born in the Chinese year of a goat. Perhaps because of this, my dream is ambiguous. America is where now I do not belong. I write letters to my friend in China. My pen gives me wings to fly. My words give me strength to survive. America says goodbye. But when I go back, friends and neighbors will ask, Did you find gold there? Are you happy there? Can you bring me there? I say, I don't know. . . . One day I will go back to China, for balancing my identity. But American dream hold me so tight with her arms. America, when can I belong?

Providing students with multiple opportunities to compose their thinking made it possible for them to extend themselves and their use of language to make meaning. To borrow the poetic language of this response to Cisneros, it gave them "wings to fly." In one rich and powerful text, a paper written subsequent to a sequence of integrated and recursive reading and writing experiences that involved students in reconsidering texts they had already read and written earlier in the semester as they themselves read and wrote other texts, one student used a refrain from one of Langston Hughes's poems to punctuate her paper, thereby raising questions about the American Dream, and also quoted an original verse that another student had composed. Her remarkable paper also incorporated references to the Declaration of Independence and the U.S. civil rights movement and concluded with a retelling of a Vietnamese folktale, a folktale she had written about prior to our consideration of civil rights issues but now reframed in light of the critical perspective she had developed:

> I remember a story which my grandmother told me in my childhood. "A long time ago, people are the same color and live lovely together. Some of them are lazy and some others are gluttonous. One day they gather and bake a cake. The gluttonous ones eat their part of the cake when it is still not well-done yet. So the color of their skin changes to white. Meanwhile, the lazy ones eat their part of the cake when it is burned. And their skin color changes to black." Of course, it is just a popular story of my childhood. But after studying the issue of Blacks and Whites in class, everything changed in my mind. I felt bad for this unfair world. If you ask me my dream, I would say that I dream one day the color of skin changes back to that of a long time before, so all people may gather and make a cake again, but eat the cake together at the same time.

By shifting among and responding to the different texts she had read and reconsidered and by bringing her own text into dialogue with them, she created new relationships among them. As we read her paper together, her own re-vision of these texts influenced other readers (teacher and students), thus contributing and enriching (and composing) the course.

TEACHING, LEARNING, AND RESEARCH

The course I have described and the writing students produced speak to the benefits of approaching teaching as a learner and researcher, posing questions, allowing for exploration, attempting to make sense of the classroom and the work of its participants. Naturally, this stance brings with it a level of uncertainty and confusion and requires us to struggle with complex issues of power and authority. Negotiating the tensions that come with a shifting perspective can be challenging, disorienting even, both for teacher and students. Students in my classes, for example, graduates and undergraduates alike, are initially puzzled by and wary of my exhortation that they use writing as a way to make sense of, offer interpretations of, and raise questions about the course readings. But this change in perspective is also freeing and productive. No longer consumed by the exigencies of covering a prescribed or predetermined curriculum, we begin to uncover what is genuinely at stake in our classes, looking closely at students and their work and at what this work reveals about their understandings. Rather than being distracted by and frustrated by the ways in which students' work has fallen short, we can look for evidence of students' intelligence, read their attempts as coherent efforts, and consider the extent to which our assignments and expectations have contributed to or compromised students' attempts at understanding.

This very principle, that we see our work as well as that of our students as intersecting works-in-progress, is central to my graduate courses for teachers—teachers who enter my classes looking for proven solutions and viewing their own questions, tensions, and doubts as problems to be done away with, as signs of failure (the same misconception held by the students they teach). As they explore their own experiences as learners who consider and interrogate the theories and research presented in the course, and write "literacy narratives" that give them the opportunity to literally compose their lives as readers and writers, these teachers are asked to undertake their own classroom research. They raise questions about what they do and why; investigate students' assumptions, expectations, and understandings; test out alternative approaches; and study their consequences. They examine the dynamics of classroom interchanges, follow particular students' performance and progress over time, look for the underlying logic of the work students produce, and ask students for help in understanding this work. And they come to realize that the discoveries they make about learning—that it is an ongoing process of (re)constructing knowledge—apply to them as well. Note how one teacher who remembers that in her own educational experiences as a learner "we were pushed to find the 'correct' interpretation to our reading," an interpretation that was "doled out to us," now finds writing an appropriate metaphor for the teaching of writing:

> Like writing, a good education is not simple, not linear, not clear-cut. Whose rules we follow and what rules we choose to retain, and how we choose to teach them as well as honor them in our own work, is a complicated subject.

Part of writing, and certainly part of teaching, is not to shy away from these complicated questions.

In considering the implications of these realizations for her own teaching, she writes,

I want my students' writing to sound like them. I urge them to write their own opinions. I applaud their opinions, and I enjoy their opinions. But I haven't always taught like this. I used to use a very Socratic method—ask a question whose answer I know and wait until one student gives the "right" answer. I remember the first time a student ever expressed an opinion I wasn't prepared for. My whole lesson was upset! Her ideas were brilliant and totally alien to my way of thinking. The colonialist inside my brain was toppled off her throne. The class became a very interesting place. My students had points of view widely divergent from mine, and instead of trying to sway them to see things my way, I learned to honor their points of view, to let go of some of my power and privilege, and to let some real learning happen.

As this account makes clear, this teacher has given up the wait for the "right answer," sees the classroom as an "interesting place" for exploring "divergent" points of view, and recognizes that "real learning" often springs from the unexpected and anomalous contributions of students. This is what I, too, have discovered in my teaching, and the more I see teaching as a site of inquiry, the more students learn. Teaching and learning have thus become reconceptualized as overlapping, reciprocal, and mutually transformative. Teaching, like the very learning I am trying to enable, has become a process of composing.

NOTES

1. It should be noted that, while ESL is the commonly adopted term for students whose first language is not English, for many students designated in this way, English is a third or fourth language. All students' accounts are reproduced as they were written so as to retain these writers' voices and syntactic choices.

2. Numerous works address the problematic nature of such instruction and argue for a more transformative approach. Several authors who speak to this issue as it relates to higher education are Elizabeth Chiseri-Strater, *Academic Literacies: The Public and Private Discourse of University Students* (Portsmouth, N.H.: Boyton/Cook, 1991); Eleanor Kutz, Suzie Q. Groden, and Vivian Zamel, *The Discovery of Competence: Teaching and Learning with Diverse Student Writers* (Portsmouth, N.H.: Boyton/Cook, 1993); Mike Rose, *Lives on the Boundary: The Struggles and Achievements of America's Underprepared* (New York: Free Press, 1989); and Marilyn S. Sternglass, *Time to Know Them: A Lon-*

gitudinal Study of Writing and Learning at the College Level (Mahwah, N.J.: Lawrence Erlbaum, 1997).

3. For a discussion of this paradigm shift in composition, see Maxine Hairston, "The Winds of Change: Thomas Kuhn and the Revolution in the Teaching of Writing," *College Composition and Communication* 33: 76–88 (1982). For an overview of parallel changes in the field of ESL, see Ann Raimes, "Tradition and Revolution in ESL Teaching," *TESOL Quarterly* 17: 535–52 (1983). Perl's recent volume reflects the kind of composing process research that contributed to the transformation of composition teaching; see Sondra Perl, ed., *Landmark Essays on Writing Process* (Mahwah, N.J.: Lawrence Erlbaum, 1994).

4. These initial explorations were reported in Vivian Zamel, "Writing: The Process of Discovering Meaning," *TESOL Quarterly* 16: 195–209 (1982), and Vivian Zamel, "The Composing Processes of Advanced ESL Students: Six Case Studies," *TESOL Quarterly* 17: 165–87 (1983).

5. Some of this research is reported in Vivian Zamel, "Strangers in Academia: The Experiences of Faculty and ESL Students Across the Curriculum," *College Composition and Communication* 46: 506–21 (1995).

6. My own understanding of reading as an act of composing is reflected in Vivian Zamel, "Writing One's Way into Reading," *TESOL Quarterly* 26: 463–85 (1992).

7. The connection this student refers to draws on the work of Paulo Freire and Donaldo Macedo, *Literacy: Reading the Word and Reading the World* (South Hadley, Mass.: Bergin and Garvey, 1987), who underlined the inextricable relationship between "reading the word" and "reading the world."

8. For further elaboration about courses that my colleagues Eleanor Kutz and Suzie Groden and I have developed, see Kutz, Groden, and Zamel, *The Discovery of Competence.*

9. This course is described in detail by Lois Rudnick in Chapter 8 of the present volume.

ADDITIONAL RESOURCES

Cisneros, Sandra. *The House on Mango Street* (New York: Vintage Books, 1989).
Elbow, Peter. "Reflections on Academic Discourse: How It Relates to Freshmen and Colleagues." *College English* 53: 131–55 (1991).
Fulwiler, Toby. *Teaching with Writing* (Portsmouth, N.H.: Boynton/Cook, 1987).
———, ed. *The Journal Book* (Portsmouth, N.H.: Boynton/Cook, 1987).
Hull, Glynda, and Mike Rose. " 'This Wooden Shack Place': The Logic of an Unconventional Reading." *College Composition and Communication* 41: 287–98 (1990).
Lu, Min-zhan. "From Silence to Words: Writing as Struggle." *College English* 49: 437–48 (1987).
Rose, Mike. "The Language of Exclusion: Writing Instruction at the University." *College English* 47: 341–59 (1985).

Shaughnessy, Mina. "Diving In: An Introduction to Basic Writing." *College Composition and Communication* 27: 234–39 (1976).

Terkel, Studs. *American Dreams: Lost and Found* (New York: Ballantine Books, 1980).

———. *Working* (New York: Avon Books, 1975).

Walvoord, Barbara E., Linda Lawrence Hunt, H. Fil Dowling Jr., and Joan D. McMahon. *In the Long Run: A Study of Faculty in Three Writing-Across-the-Curriculum Programs* (Urbana, Ill.: NCTE, 1987).

Walvoord, Barbara E., and Lucille B. McCarthy. *Thinking and Writing in College: A Naturalistic Study of Students in Four Disciplines* (Urbana, Ill.: NCTE, 1990).

Zamel, Vivian, and Ruth Spack. *Negotiating Academic Literacies: Teaching and Learning Across Languages and Cultures* (Mahwah, N.J.: Lawrence Erlbaum, 1998).

PETER NIEN-CHU KIANG

7   Teaching, Tenure, and Institutional Transformation

Reflections on Race, Culture, and Resilience at an Urban Public University

I WANT TO GO ON

I want to go on.

Her words broke a long silence from the front of the room. A few moments earlier, she had faltered in her project presentation about the experiences of Vietnamese Amerasians and had begun to cry quietly.

Usually, Trang sat in the back with one or two other Vietnamese friends, trying to remain safe and unobtrusive. Had the pressure of speaking her second language in front of everyone in class overwhelmed her? Perhaps she was reliving the memories of her own life in Vietnam. Maybe she recalled how hard it was to arrive here five years ago in the land of her father, still not knowing who or where he was.

Are you sure?

Yes, I want to go on.

She completed her presentation, filled with emotion in accented English, teaching the class about struggle and survival.

On the last day of the semester, I reminded the class of the context and meaning of those words, "*I want to go on.*" There are strengths to be shared and lessons to be learned from Southeast Asian refugees, especially in facing and overcoming obstacles.

From the back of the room, Trang looked up for a moment and smiled. Everyone nodded in recognition.

This example of Trang's determination to go on, in spite of her struggle to speak at the front of the room, captures some of the shared learning that has defined my work since 1987 at an urban, public, doctoral-granting university. I, too, have tried to go on—as a teacher, an advocate, and an organizer across the fields of education and Asian American studies.

Inspired by students like Trang and her classmates, I have resisted the compartmentalized categories of scholarship, teaching, and service that traditionally define faculty roles and responsibilities, and have used the following integrative themes of *sharing voices, crossing boundaries,* and *building communities* as more accurate, authentic ways to describe my commitments and contributions in the university.

SHARING VOICES

Much of my work as a researcher and teacher centers on *sharing voices*—creating contexts in which immigrant voices, student voices, women's voices, Asian American voices, and so forth, can be expressed and appreciated. The voices of those who are traditionally silenced or structurally marginalized, like the Vietnamese refugee high-school student who states in one of my articles, "We don't feel like our voice the authority would ever think of,"[1] literally fill my curricula, publications, and projects, as well as my classroom and office.

The purpose, process, and presentation of my research and writing—whether with Vietnamese children in a bilingual fourth-grade classroom or Vietnamese American high-school students or Cambodian college students or Chinese adult immigrant learners in a community-based ESL program—document and authorize student and community voices. In turn, those voices serve to challenge the validity of dominant paradigms (race relations paradigms or models of student persistence, for example) and enable alternative theories to be grounded.

In addition, by sharing voices in the classroom through both the content and pedagogy of my teaching, students consistently report that they can "speak up" and "feel heard," unlike in other school settings, where they are frequently silent or silenced. This is particularly significant in my undergraduate classes, where immigrant students of color are the majority. In my graduate education courses as well, sharing voices models a student-centered pedagogy and reinforces the importance of drawing from primary sources for content—crucial principles in our teacher education program.

CROSSING BOUNDARIES

The structure of my faculty appointment and my teaching responsibilities purposefully cross both disciplinary and bureaucratic, institutional lines. My day-to-day practice is multidisciplinary on many levels—reflecting the nature of my dual professional fields in Asian American studies and education as well as my commitment to seek connections across boundaries that isolate subject matter or separate people. In my relationships with colleagues and communities, I find that my own organizing experience, biracial background, and connections to the various worlds of K through 12, undergraduate, and graduate education enable me to move comfortably and productively across boundaries of race, culture, gender, and class to facilitate collaboration and forge coalitions.

BUILDING COMMUNITIES

Nearly every aspect of my research, teaching, and service relate to community-building. My studies in Boston's Chinatown or with Cambodians and Latinos in Lowell, Massachusetts, for example, explicitly examine the dynamics of immigrant community development, while my research and service within educational institutions invariably point to the importance of communities as a survival strategy for addressing student needs or as an anchor for curriculum transformation. Furthermore, as a teacher, I consciously strive to create community in the classroom, based in part on the mutual understanding and respect that result from *sharing voices* and *crossing boundaries* together. This process has special meaning at an urban commuter school because the day-to-day realities of life facing our students, combined with the institution's resource constraints, limit opportunities to develop a cohesive sense of identity and connections on campus.

TRANSFORMING CRABS IN A POT

In using these three themes to frame my tenure statement in 1994, I challenged the problematic "scholarship-teaching-service" design of the tenure review process itself and modeled an alternative approach to make the review more valid and conceptually meaningful, both for my own case and for colleagues who would follow me. I was, of course, careful to provide adequate documentation of excellence in the separate categories of teaching, service, and scholarship that are traditionally evaluated, but I also explicitly argued that the compartmentalized structure of the traditional evaluation was inappropriate to accurately assess or interpret the intent and impact of my work. By interrogating my own review process individually, I tried to offer a vision to transform it institutionally.

My critical disposition toward the tenure process had hardened many years before facing my own review because of a situation I witnessed at an Ivy League school where students were actively demanding Asian American studies in the curriculum. The school at that time offered no courses, but did have one Asian American in a tenure-track position in international politics who, coincidentally, had been an outspoken activist for Asian American studies as a graduate student at another elite university. Students had repeatedly asked him to consider offering a special topics course or, at the very least, to publicly support their demands to the administration, but he had become increasingly distant, even defensive. Once, when I visited the campus to meet with the students about their strategies, I found him alone in his office. He sighed:

Can you tell the students to stop coming to me? I just can't deal with them till I get tenure. After that, maybe I can do something, but not now . . .

Like sociologist Felix Padilla,[2] who has critiqued this same dynamic among some Latino faculty, I could not have disagreed more with my colleague's assessment of priorities. Not only was there nobody else for the students to approach, but, even from pure self-interest, I told him, this was a fundamental error in political judgment because he was "protecting" himself from the population that would potentially care most about his being there. He insisted on his distance, however, and was denied tenure two years later anyway. Sadly, but not surprisingly, no one rallied in his defense.

At the time, I felt quite self-conscious for criticizing his stance, as if I were his elder, when he was actually half a generation older than me. But I could not accept leaving the students without support, even though I had no affiliation to the campus myself. That moment in his office crystallized a personal vow I made never to sacrifice my own core commitments for the sake of professional status. It also reminded me of hearing community members' talk-story about how crabs struggle in a pot—each one crawling over the next, trying to save itself, without regard for those it passes over or pushes out of the way. The crabs-in-the-pot metaphor is a warning for us to examine the impact of our individual ambitions and actions in relation to our collective groups, to recognize how we help *or* hurt each other, and to question more fundamentally—What is the nature of this pot, and how did we all get here in the first place?

I often raise these questions now as I recruit and mentor new faculty of color. Out of seven new junior faculty hired in the College of Education during 1996 and 1997, for example, all were people of color (one African American, three Latina/o, and three Asian American). I purposely served on six of those seven search committees and am convinced that my presence, perspective, and power (as I have tenure now) positively influenced the process and outcomes for each case. Gaining critical mass in a mainstream institution is essential, as we all know. But it matters less if we still act like crabs in a pot. We need to transform ourselves. . . .

TRANSFORMING THE POT

Another crystallizing moment occurred at a 1993 national conference in Los Angeles on diversifying the university curriculum. I listened to a panel of nontenured faculty of color from local institutions who vented deep frustration in the wake of the previous year's riot/rebellion. Having responded to relentless demands from communities, government agencies, and the media to provide analysis and assistance in relation to the complex racial, cultural, economic, and political dynamics during that crisis period, they discovered that their heroic interventions counted for little in their annual reviews. Penalized by the traditional reward systems of their institutions, each had privately concluded that universities were not serious about responding to Rodney King's question of the decade— Can we all get along? As a result, communities were left without access to crucial resources and follow-up, while a cadre of energetic junior faculty found themselves increasingly cynical about their own roles.

If those faculty of color, regardless of their own disciplines, had established relationships with their schools' ethnic studies programs, they might have found greater individual support as well as more productive models of community-university collaboration. Although ethnic studies programs are themselves often marginalized by institutional racism in universities, they nevertheless represent institutionalized spaces that value faculty and student engagement in communities. Ironically, however, at the national level, references to lessons and models from ethnic studies programs are completely absent from the formal literature on faculty professional outreach, service-learning.[3]

Furthermore, if the late Ernest Boyer's definition of applied scholarship or the late Ernest Lynton's criteria for evaluating faculty professional service[4] had influenced the reviews of those faculty of color in post-uprising Los Angeles, the outcomes would certainly have been more positive. Boyer's compelling call to redefine how to evaluate and reward faculty scholarship and other national trends in higher education reform have direct relevance to the professional lives of faculty of color. By connecting visions and priorities from our own campuses with these larger policy discussions, such as the recent, millennial call by the Kellogg Commission on the Future of State and Land-Grant Universities[5] for public higher education institutions to become "engaged" by responding to the diverse demographic profiles of students, by connecting students' learning with real world research and practice, and by allocating resources to address the critical issues of communities—all of which mirrors the commitments that individual faculty of color and ethnic studies programs have sustained and institutionalized within universities over the past thirty years—we not only strengthen our process of change inside the pot, but also find strategies and allies with which to transform the pot itself.

Trusting Students

Still another crystallizing moment emerged in a conversation about curriculum and pedagogy several years ago with Vivian Zamel, the director of the ESL program at UMass/Boston. Over the years, Vivian and I have had many students in common, and we have collaborated frequently on student and faculty development projects. At that time, Vivian was rethinking her plans for an English composition course with ESL students and wrestling with the question of how much to focus on issues of oppression and inequality as subjects for reading, writing, and class discussion. She wondered, "I'm just not sure if it will be too depressing or discouraging for them."

Reflecting for a moment on my own choices with similar students in Asian American studies courses, I urged her to have the class critically engage with those issues, even if dynamics became emotionally intense and pedagogically risky. She could trust her students—predominantly nonwhite, working-class immigrants—to draw on the realities of their daily lives as rich resources for meaningful teaching and learning.

Much to her credit, Vivian took the risk. By the end of an unforgettable semester of shared learning and inspired writing, the students in Vivian's class crafted a collective poem titled "*Mis Palabras* (My Words)" that articulated the multiple ways in which they resisted oppression in their lives. Many found connections with each other's name stories—those experiences in which their names and, by extension, their identities, had been ignored, disrespected, or changed because of the dominant culture's hegemony. In the process, they touched a hidden dimension of Vivian's own identity and survival that none of us had ever known. Vivian's beautiful given name, she revealed, is *Aviva*, which, in Hebrew, means *spring*. But, like so many of her students, she had adopted *Vivian* at an early age to be more acceptable to others. Through her words in "*Mis Palabras*," I recalled my own story as well.[6]

The Return of Spring
(*for Vivian Zamel*)

Aviva shares secrets,
returning me to second grade.
Writing our names,
practicing penmanship.

> At least no one has to say it,
> always sounding so funny.
> I fill a page quickly.

> *Use your middle name, too,* Mrs. Shapiro commands.
> My pencil slows, my hand reluctant.

> *Ni e n—c h u*

> In the next row,
> Gordon Clay steals a glance at my desk
> and explodes in laughter.
> I hate Gordon Clay. I hate Mrs. Shapiro.
> I hate everyone looking at me.

> Humiliation lasts forever in a child's heart.

I use my full name
in publications now,

> Knowing *Nien-chu* means
> *Honor your ancestors.*
>
> I think of Aviva.
>
> *Mis palabras* come to life
>
> as the cold of winter turns to spring.

Trusting Oneself

Two years earlier, I had begun a full-time, "target-of-opportunity"[7] appointment in the Graduate College of Education at UMass/Boston and started teaching graduate courses in multicultural education and social studies curriculum design, in addition to teaching undergraduate Asian American studies courses. I was the only tenure-track faculty of color in the entire College of Education at that time. My appointment signaled the beginning of a dramatic intellectual and cultural shift to realign the mission and activities of the college with the realities of urban schools. *I wanted to go on.*

For many years prior, the college had been exclusionary and out of touch, particularly in relation to the students, families, and communities of color who comprised the majority in Boston's public schools. One student described a revealing example of instruction in the elementary education program from that time in the following way:

> The art [curriculum design] teacher left a lasting impression on me. She discussed various art supplies and told the class that she takes all the little black and brown watercolor paints out of the sets because they were not very nice colors. . . . When I think of this woman, my stomach turns and I feel guilty because I did and said nothing to make her realize how damaging and ignorant her words were.

Another student from that time lamented,

> Why would anyone of any background other than white middle class want to attend the current program when they are excluded from nearly every discussion in nearly every class?

Driving the institutional change process was the college's acting dean, a courageous and resilient African American man of faith, steeped in principles of respectful collaboration and urban educational practice. Through a deliberative strategic planning process, reinforced by the dean's calm but steadfast insistence, all aspects of policy and culture in the college were on the table—from the outdated design, sequence, and assessment of courses to the lack of diversity within the faculty and student demographic profiles to the haphazard arrangements with practitioners and school sites. We wanted to transform the entire pot. In addition, through attrition and targeted new hires following a cluster of impending retirements, we knew time was on our side. We intended to transform the crabs as well.

Perhaps with good reason, some senior faculty viewed our visions and our presence as threatening. Feeling the chill from several senior colleagues and trying to read the power dynamics in my first few department meetings, I remained relatively silent until we reviewed a formal proposal for a new course on teaching children's literature. The syllabus presented "multicultural children's literature" as a one-session topic at the end of the semester, following different literary genres such as poetry, historical novels, and readers' theater. Pushing aggressively for course approval was a full professor who also happened to be director of the Teacher Education Program in which I was based.

Calculating that her retirement would precede my tenure review and remembering my vow about not sacrificing core commitments, I asserted in the meeting, and later in a long memo to the department, that we should not approve the course as proposed because the multicultural reality of children's literature needed to be infused throughout the entire course across every genre, rather than being mistakenly treated as one of several token topics to cover. As teachers of future teachers, I asked, what are the educational practices and principles that we are choosing to model within our own teaching and curriculum design? Not surprisingly, the chill in the room grew much more severe. But that moment created space for another junior faculty member to speak up as well—a white male colleague committed to antiracist pedagogy, who became my closest ally in strategizing how to implement educational practices that we believed in while also surviving the tenure process in our increasingly contentious department. *We both wanted to go on.*

All Students Can Learn

Students from that time also acted out the tensions and contradictions in our shifting institutional culture. During my first semester, for example, graduate students in my weekly social studies curriculum design course openly rebelled after the first class meeting, in which I described my broad commitment to antiracist, multicultural education and my specific intent to use the Japanese American internment experience as the focus for a major course assignment to design curriculum units for fifth graders. A core of students actually circulated a petition to have me removed as the instructor, although I later discovered that they had come to the first class with that intention, encouraged by the Teacher Education Program director. One student outside of that core explained:

> On the first day, I sat in the rear corner of the class and was surrounded by three women who had come in together. According to them, our teacher for the course was not the person we were supposed to have. Maybe, if the class was quickly identified as a disaster, we could get rid of him and have him replaced in time to salvage our education and our futures. That was how my first five minutes of school went.

Being a teacher committed to student empowerment, and considering my own background as a student activist, the irony of being the object of student protest challenged me on many levels. As a young teacher, I tried not to take the criticisms personally or obsessively. As a responsible teacher with grading power, I tried not to respond by unfairly punishing those who disagreed with my ideas. As a teacher of teachers, I tried to remain committed to the principle of having high expectations for all students to learn—mindful of realities in urban schools where low teacher expectations, especially for students of color, are daily self-fulfilling prophecies. And as a teacher of color, I tried not to view the problematic classroom dynamics simply as racist resistance by white students who could not accept my position or perspective.

I did not share any of these dilemmas with my colleagues and instead turned deeply inward to search for strategies and inspiration. Reflecting on many past transformative teaching experiences with white students, including two remarkable working-class, white men who were the first students at UMass/Boston to design and complete individual majors in Asian American studies, I knew I had to reach the class emotionally by directly connecting with their own lives. This helped me reaffirm my decision to use the Japanese American internment experience as a case study to model powerful teaching and learning across subject areas and grade levels—having experienced its impact with undergraduates of all backgrounds in Asian American studies courses year after year.

Nevertheless, because of the active campaign being waged against me both inside and outside my course, I was unsure if emotional content and a caring pedagogy would be enough to shift the hostile dynamic in the classroom, which also reflected larger issues of race, power, and contention over culture in the college. Instinctively, I responded to the situation in political terms and recalled Mao Tse Tung's basic organizing principle in the Chinese revolution: *Unite with the advanced to win over the middle and isolate the backward.* From that guiding slogan, I regrounded myself in the strengths of my own political training and my skills as a community organizer. Rather than utilizing arbitrary faculty power to crush the core of students challenging my presence, I chose to develop tactics and a strategy to out-organize them.

The students I wanted to reach emotionally were those in the middle. Indeed, most students were there—heavily influenced by the prevailing climate in the college and the strong views of the backwards core, but hardly consolidated or actively resistant themselves. Winning them over meant showing, during the second week, that I had listened to their sincere, initial concerns that the Japanese American internment seemed to be a narrow focus taking a lot of time in the course, perhaps at the expense of other important social studies topics that they might need for their preparation as teachers. In the third week, using the internment as a case study, I raised core questions about race, war, loyalty, ethnicity, family, immigration, the Constitution, and the media with curricular connections to economics, politics, geography, history, and psychology as well as to art, literature, music, health science, and mathematics. I wanted students to see that exploring this one case in depth offered far more powerful learning than skimming the surface of several topics.

Furthermore, by using oral histories, poems, video excerpts, role plays, and reflective writing activities within our own class, I used teaching methods designed to have emotional impact and moved many students to realize how little they themselves had been taught about the causes and consequences of the internment experience.[8] As a result, they began to reflect more critically and concretely about their own responsibilities to become effective teachers. The internment example challenged and inspired those in the middle to engage with me and the course. *They wanted to go on.*

Meanwhile, to isolate the backward core of students, I structured many small group activities and discussions that, on the surface, modeled effective collaborative learning/teaching practices, but that also served to split up the core group, whose members were otherwise always sitting together, talking among themselves during class and asserting themselves as a collective force. I also used some of their statements and questions as reference points for class reflection as the semester progressed. For example, during the second week, one of the resistant students directly challenged my plans with this question:

> Maybe you can teach some of this stuff in high school, but not in elementary school. Children don't know anything about war or racism. Why do you have to ruin their innocence?

At the time, I had swallowed my own immediate response of "Excuse me, whose children are you talking about?" and simply replied, "Well, that's a really important question that we're going to examine much more in this course." I returned to that question during the fourth week, after some of the lessons from the internment case had been internalized, and found several students from the middle who could respond thoughtfully. This fulcrum shift in the balance of classroom dynamics also served to isolate the resistant core. I referenced the same question again at the end of the course to serve as a reminder of where we had started and how far we had come.

Unite with the Advanced

Although my political organizing methods had opened the learning environment sufficiently so that the pedagogy and emotional content built into the course design could reach most in the class, I did not realize until reading students' final reflection papers that I had failed to implement the essential first step in Chairman Mao's framework—*to unite with the advanced.* With tremendous guilt, I learned that I had taken for granted my responsibility to meet the academic and social needs of those two or three students who were initially thrilled to have an instructor finally offer multicultural perspectives and commitments to urban schools. The lone African American student from the class wrote,

> I am not surprised that you as an instructor were greeted with such hostility. . . . I found the atmosphere in this class to be quite uncomfortable, but then again, this is how most of my classes have been.

While appreciating my efforts, she and a white student with long-standing commitments to cultural democracy wrote about feeling uncomfortable and silenced by their peers throughout the semester. I had mistakenly assumed that they saw themselves included in both the content and process of my organizing and teaching, but I had not talked directly to either of them about what I was doing or why. I was so concerned with reaching the middle and neutralizing the resistant core that I failed to affirm and invest in those students who could most benefit from working together with me. The course had not empowered them, and their feelings of frustration and disappointment still move me today, nearly a decade later, to think clearly about my priorities as a teacher and mentor.

Thankfully, the College of Education is a completely different environment now, due to retirements, new hiring, and the impact of our transformative visions taking root. The graduate program directors of teacher education, special education, and family counseling are all faculty of color, as are the department chairs for educational leadership and for counseling and school psychology. More importantly, the commitment to urban education is explicit and generally shared by most faculty, staff, and students. At the same time, the students in our M.Ed. teacher education program are still predominantly white—in sharp contrast to the large majority of black, Latino, and Asian students in Boston's schools. While we are now able to recruit and support significantly more students of color, the urgent reality remains that students who wish to become effective and relevant teachers need deep and sustained immersion in antiracist, multicultural learning environments themselves. This agenda, and our capacity to make it happen, were barely imaginable just a few years earlier.

Teaching graduate education courses side by side with my undergraduate Asian American studies courses, however, I constantly confront choices about where to prioritize, what to affirm, and who to support. Who are the advanced that I must not take for granted? Where can I have the most meaningful impact for both the short term and the long term? Although I have no easy ways to resolve these daily questions, my gut feelings and political sensibilities often converge in choosing to invest in students like Trang, whose simple but profound assertion, *I want to go on,* echoes in these pages. Those are the students who move me most and whose lives and futures I affect most directly and deeply.

I have passionately advocated elsewhere that the content and pedagogy of Asian American studies courses represent powerful curricular interventions that facilitate the integration of students who are often otherwise marginalized within both the academic and social domains of the university.[9] Because the extent of students' social and academic integration within the university is so closely associated with their persistence and retention,[10] the role played by Asian American studies courses—and other courses, programs, or structures with comparable commitments—has profound implications for urban, commuter campuses where enabling students' institutional integration is an urgent and fundamental challenge.

In this essay, however, I am arguing that those curricular interventions also represent resilient survival strategies for faculty of color, in particular, to deal productively with issues of race, culture, and power in the processes of teaching, gaining tenure, and driving institutional change. Due to the highly stratified structure of higher education, however, urban, working-class institutions and their constituents are rarely recognized for their strengths in these areas. But, if my own reflections in this brief essay connect at all with the experiences of others, then perhaps it is a sign that we have many more lessons and models to offer. *We all need to go on.*

NOTES

Acknowledgments: This chapter draws substantially on material published in the article "Crossing Boundaries, Building Community," *Thought & Action* 15(1): 49–60 (1999), and from a longer essay, "Wanting to Go On: Healing and Transformation at an Urban Public University," in Enrique T. Trueba and Lilia I. Bartolomé, eds., *Immigrant Voices: In Search of Educational Equity* (Lanham, Md.: Rowman and Littlefield, 2000), pp. 137–66. I thank my students in Asian American studies, who daily inspire me as a teacher-learner, and my colleagues involved with UMass/Boston's Center for Improvement of Teaching for their support over the years. All names of students in this essay are pseudonyms.

1. See Peter N. Kiang and J. Kaplan, "Where Do We Stand: Views of Racial Conflict by Vietnamese American High School Students in a Black-and-White Context," *Urban Review* 26 (2): 95–119 (1994).

2. Felix M. Padilla, *The Struggle of Latino/a University Students* (New York: Routledge, 1997).

3. Joan Arches, M. Darlington-Hope, J. Gerson, J. Gibson, S. Habana-Hafner, and P. Kiang, "New Voices in University-Community Transformation," *Change* 29 (1): 36–41 (1997).

4. See C. E. Glassick, M. Taylor Huber, and G. I. Maeroff, *Scholarship Assessed*, Carnegie Foundation for the Advancement of Teaching (San Francisco: Jossey-Bass, 1997); Ernest L. Boyer, *Scholarship Reconsidered*, Carnegie Foundation for the Advancement of Teaching (San Francisco: Jossey-Bass, 1990); and

Ernest A. Lynton, *Making the Case for Professional Service* (Washington, D.C.: American Association for Higher Education, 1995).

5. Kellogg Commission on the Future of State and Land-Grant Universities, *Returning to Our Roots: The Engaged Institution*, Third Report, February 1999.

6. Capturing the meaning and significance embedded in Asian names became the focus of a semester project in one of my introductory Asian American studies course two years later. With funding from the provost, students produced a booklet, "Recognizing Names: Student Perspectives and Suggestions for Pronouncing Asian Names—A Guide for the Community," with guidelines on how to pronounce Asian names, along with essays on pedagogy and student learning related to their name stories. See Peter Nien-chu Kiang, "Pedagogies of Life and Death: Transforming Immigrant/Refugee Students and Asian American Studies," *Positions* 5 (2): 529–55 (1997) for further discussion about the pedagogical issues involved. To order the booklet, contact UMass/Boston's Asian American Studies Program at <http://omega.cc.umb.edu/~aast/>.

7. A specific affirmative action strategy that I strongly support and acknowledge with appreciation.

8. Many new books, exhibits, performances, videos, CD-ROMs, World Wide Web resources, and curriculum guides about the Japanese American internment experience are now available through the support of the Civil Liberties Public Education Fund—a body established by Congress in 1997 to fulfill the final component of the U.S. government's redress commitment (in addition to a formal apology and individual monetary payments to survivors). See <http://www.acon.org/clpef/>. Other suggestions for available materials include Commission on Wartime Relocation and Internment of Civilians, *Personal Justice Denied* (Washington, D.C.: Government Printing Office, 1982); Peter Irons, *Justice at War: The Story of the Japanese American Internment Cases* (New York: Oxford University Press, 1983); Deborah Gesenway and Mindy Roseman, *Beyond Words: Images from America's Concentration Camps* (Ithaca: Cornell University Press, 1989); Maisie and Richard Conrat, *Executive Order 9066* (Los Angeles: University of California, 1992); Tule Lake Committee, *Kinenhi: Reflections on Tule Lake* (San Francisco, 1980); Sheila Hamanaka, *The Journey: Japanese Americans, Racism, and Renewal* (New York: Orchard Books, 1990); Yoshiko Uchida, *Journey to Topaz* (New York: Scribners, 1971, 1985), and *Journey Home* (New York: Atheneum, 1978). Media suggestions include *The Color of Honor* (90 minutes) by Loni Ding; *Unfinished Business* (60 minutes) by Steven Okazaki; *Family Gathering* (28 minutes) by Lise Yasui; and *Honor Bound* (60 minutes) by Wendy Hanamura. Contact the National Asian American Telecommunications Association (NAATA) for these and other relevant media sources: <http://www.naatanet.org/distrib/>.

9. See Peter Nien-chu Kiang, "Stratification of Public Higher Education," in Linda A. Revilla, Gail M. Nomura, Shawn Wong, and Shirley Hune, eds., *Bearing Dreams, Shaping Visions* (Pullman: Washington State University Press, 1993), pp. 233–45; "Bicultural Strengths and Struggles of Southeast Asian American Students," in Antonia Darder, ed., *Culture and Difference: Critical Perspectives on the Bicultural Experience in the United States* (New York: Bergin and Garvey, 1995),

pp. 201–25; "Persistence Stories and Survival Strategies of Cambodian Americans in College," *Journal of Narrative and Life History* 6 (1): 39–64 (1996); "Pedagogies of Life and Death"; and "Writing from the Past, Writing for the Future: Healing Effects of Asian American Studies in the Curriculum," *Transformations: A Resource for Curriculum Transformation and Scholarship* 9 (2): 132–49 (1998).

10. V. Tinto, *Leaving College: Rethinking the Causes and Cures of Student Attrition* (Chicago: University of Chicago Press, 1987).

LOIS RUDNICK

8 Teaching American Dreams/ American Realities

Students' Lives and Faculty Agendas

My American dream is to fit in the American society, be Americanized without losing my cultural heritage, inhale the freedom and human rights, and have my own "home page" in the American history as an active individual.
—fall 1996 student response to the question, "What is the American Dream?"

IF I were not an academic, I might argue that I was fated to title my survey course in American Studies, American Dreams/American Realities. My life is, from one perspective, a paradigm of the middle-class norm of the American Dream. I am a third-generation Jewish American who started life with my parents and grandparents in a double-decker in Dorchester, Massachusetts (a few miles from UMass/Boston). My family moved to the suburban wilderness of West Roxbury in the early 1950s and became a part of the great white American escape from the cities. Here I lived an almost entirely sheltered life, innocent of issues of race, class, and gender, except for my forays to Girls' Latin School, where I experienced some ethnic and class diversity. At Girls' Latin, I was given an almost messianic vision of what a young woman could accomplish, which reinforced my faith that I could do and be anything I wanted (except a mathematician or a scientist).

It wasn't until I was in my twenties that the veil drawn over American history—and the history of my own family—first lifted, as my father regaled me with tales of his days as a member of the Communist and Progressive Parties, including stories of me as a four-year-old standing on a Dorchester street corner, handing out Henry Wallace for President leaflets. My dad's radicalism was a taboo subject in my household during the McCarthy era: he had been contacted by the FBI just at the point when he had achieved his American Dream by receiving an academic appointment in an engineering department at a local university. My father was one of the lucky ones who survived, and my family thrived during the expansive 1950s and 1960s.

My college years at Tufts University in the early 1960s were almost as sheltered as my childhood. As a liberal Democrat, I noticed with approval that there were students organizing for voter registration drives in the South, but that didn't concern me personally—not to mention the fact that my mother would have had heart failure if I had so much as mentioned putting myself in any kind of danger. My academic awakening to the tensions that existed between the American Dream and its realities came in a course called Introduction to American Literature, taught by Jesper Rosenmeier, a Danish immigrant and student of the historian Perry Miller (one of the founding fathers of American studies). Rosenmeier's course committed me to a lifelong fascination with the idea of the United States as a "city upon a hill," whose "errand in the wilderness" was supposed to achieve "the last, best hope of man," a utopian promise that left both wonder and havoc in its wake.

However, it wasn't until after my semi-bucolic college years that I learned to face the race and class vectors of that wake. Between 1966 and 1972, although I couldn't have known this at the time, I was preparing myself for teaching at UMass/Boston: formally by studying for a Ph.D. in American Civilization at Brown University, and experientially through involvement in learning environments far removed from my own elite education. I was a reading teacher in an Upward Bound Program in which some of the urban students I worked with distrusted me because of my class, race, and religion; a composition teacher at a junior college whose working-class students challenged my "lecture" format; an antiwar activist living under suspicion (though unharrassed) in a Republican suburb of Boston; an instructor in an Introduction to Black Studies course at Brown University who was boycotted by my black and white students in protest against my race.

My most important epiphany came the summer after the black studies course, when I was employed as the only white instructor of inner-city high-school students. After one of my students called me "a jive-ass nigger-loving honky" in front of the class, I decided to quit my job. I could no longer stand being put into a "category" that had nothing to do with me as a person. Then, as they say, the light dawned. I had intellectually comprehended this posture for years—that stereotyping results in judging a person by her group classification—but I never *felt* what that meant until this moment. Nor had I realized before that as an educated, middle-class white woman I could walk away from this situation, but that my students did not have that choice. And so I stayed.

When I came to UMass/Boston in 1974, I was my father's daughter but also a child of the times, with a visceral knowledge of how the historical moment shapes individual lives. I was fortunate to bring with me a rudimentary understanding of some of my students' lives and an appreciation for the lived experience against which textbook learning must be measured and refined. What I couldn't possibly have anticipated was how challenging I would find the struggle between my agenda as a teacher and my students' widely diverse needs, interests, life histories, and political and social values. I have students in the same classroom who range in age from eighteen to sixty: welfare mothers and grandmothers, suburban women whose children are grown, recent high-school graduates, savvy union organizers and Mayflower descendants, immigrants from Columbia and Iran, South Boston Irish and Roxbury African Americans, high achievers and those just struggling to get by.

If my primary professional identity today is that of a "teacher," it is largely because of my UMass/Boston students, who have pushed me to channel a substantial amount of my creative energy into finding ways to make learning meaningful, a task that required me to overcome my own forms of resistance, as well as those of my students.

AMERICAN DREAMS, AMERICAN REALITIES: MEN AND WOMEN IN AMERICAN SOCIETY AND CULTURE, 1620 TO 1860

I have chosen to write about my American Dreams course because it has become for me a kind of litmus test of the state of the academic profession, as well as the site in which I find myself facing the most frustrating and interesting negotiations among the contesting dreams and realities of my students' needs and lives and my own interests and desires. It is the course in which I have been most resistant to giving up standard academic practices and the one in which I have been most open to experimenting with alternative forms of classroom performance and assessment. What has taken me the longest time to accept is that my students' agendas are not and do not have to be the same as mine. It is this course, which begins and ends with student definitions of the American Dream, that has taught me this hard-earned lesson.

Let me begin with my "dream" agenda and then describe its rationale and relationship to the ways I have structured the course content and pedagogy, in which the diverse dreams and realities of my students have played an increasingly larger role. My original agenda began with my desire to offer students the best introduction to American social and cultural history that money could buy (as good as what they'd get at one of the more prestigious schools in the greater Boston area). That agenda has been revised and expanded over the past two decades to include the following goals for my students:

1. to find cohesion and depth in a three-hundred-year survey that examines the dialectical relationship between cultural and social history—the ways that the ideals and norms of a culture both shape and are shaped by material realities;
2. to engage with history in ways that are analytic and imaginative so that they can understand the past, in so far as it is possible, on its own terms, before judging it by their own contemporary standards;
3. to recognize the similarities and differences in the origins and evolution of the American dreams and realities of Native, African, and Anglo Americans, as well as the continuities and changes in these dreams over time;
4. to confront the pain, violence, and various oppressions of the American past without dichotomizing various cultural groups into demons and victims;
5. to understand the different varieties of evidence that can be used in constructing interpretations of the past—literary as well as historical, visual as well as textual;
6. to recognize that any interpretation of the past is always a construction, never a final "truth," but not to have students alienated by this knowledge into taking a stance that "it's all a matter of opinion"; and
7. to acknowledge their own embeddedness in history and the significance of their roles as citizens with a responsibility to shape the history of their time.

WHOSE DREAMS AND REALITIES?

I first taught this course in 1977 as American Literature I, when it included the standard canonical fare of mostly white male writers, from the Puritans through Walt Whitman. When I reinvented it as the introductory survey course for American studies and changed the title, I took my first risk—handing over the definition of the American Dream to my students. It was a risk well worth taking. The thematics of the course have proved to be a compelling way for students to explore potent cultural myths and symbols with which they are already familiar. Through them they can test the similarities and differences of dreams and realities among and between men, women, and different classes and racial groups in the formative years of U.S. history.

The one disadvantage of the title is that it does not attract more than a handful of students of color. A few students always drop the course after they come to the first class and read the "fine print"—that they will be studying literary and historical texts from and about the seventeenth through the nineteenth centuries. But the title itself may keep students away who believe that the American Dream "belongs" to the white middle class. There is no doubt from the data I've gathered that minority students are among the more skeptical evaluators of the American Dream.

Students begin the first day of class by writing their own definitions of the American Dream, which I then place in the following categories: *life* (personal and material security and gain), *liberty* (personal and political freedom, equality of opportunity), *the pursuit of happiness* (personal and communal), and *doubters of the dream.* I use their definitions (some students write their own personal definitions and others write what they think the dream means to most Americans) to frame the course and their final take-home exam question. During the years that I have been collecting these definitions, in classes that average thirty-five students, the responses have been at once consistent and diverse; in fact, each class pretty much represents the range of ideas about the American Dream one can find throughout U.S. history. Thus they are able, from the beginning, to see the link between their own ideas of what the dream is and where that idea originated in the past. They are also confronted from the start with the plural nature of the concept—that there is not and never has been one dream shared by all Americans—and that there are serious conflicts embedded both within and between their different definitions.

What has been most surprising and interesting to me is the tenacity of what has remained the overwhelmingly largest category of student responses, which is closely related to the American success myth. The *life* category of responses has, in fact, increased over the years, while definitions of social equality and humanitarian ideals have decreased in number, perhaps in keeping with both the expanding economic insecurity and the materialism of the 1980s and 1990s:

> The land of opportunity, ability to go from rags to riches through hard work and determination

> The "white middle class" seem to view it as a married couple with two children, a home in suburbia, a two-car garage, and a dog

> To have a better life than my parents did . . . finishing school, having an education to lead me to a rewarding career

> A universal desire for all Americans to acquire wealth, success, fame, and power over others, and not have a need for anything else

The next largest category is *liberty*, which my students have increasingly defined in terms of personal liberties:

> Discovering new paths and frontiers, always pushing forward into the unknown . . . there is no end boundary to anyone's imaginations and abilities

> I am free to go any place that my spirit guides me, I can change my society and my country, or only myself if I choose

> The freedom that we Americans have of saying, thinking, doing, believing, and writing anything that we wish

Happiness is an all-encompassing category that includes the noblest humanitarian goals and the most individualist aspirations to total fulfillment:

> A harmonious community of all people of all religions, races, sexual preferences living together in peace, that is a real dream

> That there is a place, at last, where all peoples can come together and have the freedom to be and act how they are as well as to help develop a new culture embroidered with or tapestried by the differences brought by the individual

> To be happy, healthy, wise, to love and be loved, to be successful, have my own home and family, finish college, get a job, and make lots of money

My final category includes the *doubters of the dream*, who are the smallest number (but from my point of view some of the most interesting) of respondents (typically no more than four or five out of thirty-five):

> America to me as a child who emigrated here at the age of ten was to be the land of golden opportunity. Everyone was going to be friendly,

happy, and rich. It was to be a melting pot where all peoples and classes got along well and respected one another. The reality, of course, was very different. I feel that I was lied to by my parents and by the myth of America. Of course they were lied to also. It has been hard for me to integrate the myth with the reality.

Is there an American Dream, or is this a "catch phrase," a product of political gibberish, sentimental patriotism, and greeting card prose . . . I find the phrase trite and now meaningless—far too general and catering to the clichés of the U.S. history books.

There is no such thing as the "American Dream" anymore—it has become a nightmare! In today's modern post-industrial society, people just try to survive; the old dream of marrying, having children and owning a home is a fading memory in the midst of escalating housing costs, health care costs, and increasing divorce rates.

As you can see, the students' definitions provide them with a modicum of authority when they begin their engagement with readings that are difficult and alien to many of them. Just as they voice disparate and discordant definitions of the dream, so do the historic figures they encounter. The Spanish conquistadors' credo, *"Fé y Oro"* (Faith and Gold), is easier to recognize for its contradictory intentions once they've wrestled with their own contradictory and sometimes self-contradictory credos. Just as some of them "want it all" while others hope for a less materialistic nation that is more equitable in its distribution of resources, so do many of the historic figures they encounter differ in how they define the pursuit of happiness and at whose expense they believe their own success should be achieved.

It may seem ironic that my students' definitions of the American Dream have become increasingly more individualistic and less political over the past few years, despite the increased difficulties they encounter. I have always been both awed and dismayed by the complexity of my students' lives. The majority work twenty to forty hours a week and carry a load of three to five courses per semester; many care for families, as well. Over the past few years, I have noticed a greater incidence of physical and psychological stress, as students have had to pay higher fees and carry more courses per semester than many can adequately handle. In one recent class, I had a twenty-one-year-old student who miscarried and learned she had cancer; a student who suffered severe depression after getting married; a student whose wife walked out on him the second week of class; a senior who had serious panic attacks and was frequently unable to come to class; and another with an unnamed disease that so enervated her that she was absent for one-third of the semester—and these are only the students whose problems I knew about.

Course Design

It is nice to have the utopian ideal of giving my students the best course that money can buy. But what I have had to learn over the years is how to reach a reasonable compromise between what I can realistically ask of my students and what I want them to learn. This has meant giving up (some of) what my colleague Vivian Zamel calls the "obsession with content coverage"; using class time for students to do their work; finding alternative assignments and performances to assess their learning; and, most challenging of all, figuring out how to engage the majority of students who take this course to fulfill a "general education" requirement in historical inquiry to believe in their own historical agency.

The opening up of the canon to include the voices and visions of the broad spectrum of Americans who have actually shaped our history has certainly allowed me to structure a more honest and interesting course, although it has also created problems. The "great white male" voices that were part of the traditional canon are heard throughout my course, but over the past two decades they have spoken increasingly in dialogue with newer, lesser known voices: Anglican playboy Thomas Morton of Merrymount confronts Puritan diehard William Bradford of Plymouth; Jane Franklin Mecom's spirited but humble life is juxtaposed to that of her illustrious brother, Benjamin; African American mathematician Benjamin Banneker contests Thomas Jefferson's application of "natural rights" philosophy to whites only in the new republic; Native American orator William Apess calls into question Emerson's paeans to American individualism and self-reliance; Fanny Fern's satirical sketches of middle-class married life challenge Catherine Beecher's notions of the middle-class Christian home as heaven on earth.

From the early 1980s through the present, I have struggled with the issue of representation, which can never be entirely satisfactorily resolved, but which I have come to feel very strongly must accomplish three goals.

1. The voices of the mainstream and the margin can't be segregated from one another.

They have to be present throughout the course, which means that not every group that was a part of the making of early American history is heard in my course. I sacrifice one kind of diversity for another—looking at a variety of forms of expression and ideas by and about women and men from Native, African, and Anglo American cultures. What I hope to accomplish by this is to complicate students' understanding of all three cultures and to avoid the tendency of nonminority students to see any one minority figure as representative of the whole group.

Because I want students to experience a modicum of cohesion in the course, I make other sacrifices of coverage beyond the limitation of the themes and cultural groups we study. I have given up geographical diversity to focus primarily on the Northeast, New England in particular, both because I want to encourage my students to know the area in which they live (which very few of them have explored in terms of its history) and because I want them to experience a greater sense of "ownership" of that space, particularly in terms of the evolution of the themes of the course.

I also make sacrifices of chronology in order to provide students with greater depth and diversity. Rather than trying to cover the entire three hundred years, I focus attention and readings on sociocultural watersheds defined by important shifts in ideology and social practice: the first contacts between Europeans and Natives, the Enlightenment and the American Revolution, and the era of Romantic literature and Reform. To introduce each of these historic periods, I use visuals that offer allegorical and mythical representations of "America," a concept we deconstruct during the first slide show, which consists of European visions of the western hemisphere as utopia/dystopia, symbolized by Indian women as fecund goddesses and seductive demons. These visual exercises reinforce one of my primary goals throughout the course: to encourage students to grapple with the role of preconceptions and perspective in historical and cultural interpretation.

2. Multiculturalism needs to be balanced with interculturalism.

In the beginning of our recovery of lost and marginalized literatures and histories, it was inevitable that our emphasis would be placed on difference. But some of the most exciting work in my field in the last few years has been the recognition of the syncretic and hybrid nature of U.S. history and culture; the *fact* that from first contact our dreams and realities, and our concepts of race, class, gender and sexuality, have been constructed in the "contact zone" of intercultural exchange.[1]

The thematics of American Dreams provide an opportunity for students to "connect the differences" because the conflicting dreams they encounter—of wealth, community, freedom, success, and happiness—often cross gender, class, and racial boundaries.[2] The "realities" against which these dreams are tested in the course are often determined by the constraints placed upon women and minorities by a dominant white, patriarchal culture whose self-definition is very much dependent on its definition of the "others" who do not share their economic, social, and political power. Yet both the promise of American life and the bonds that constrain women and men with little or no power from achieving their dreams have also been used by them for individual advantage and group advancement. Students are as fascinated by the parallels as they are by the differences between the autobiographies of Ben Franklin and Frederick Douglass, the two figures with whom the majority of them (men and women) seem most consistently to identify in the course. Given their own life circumstances and the sacrifices they are making to obtain an education, their wish to believe in the power of individuals to overcome difficult obstacles and achieve their dreams is hardly surprising.

3. Representation must include his/stories that emphasize the complex interrelationship between agency and victimization.

We must emphasize the precarious and sometimes elusive balance between individual ability and motivation, and the socioeconomic, political, and historical circumstances that both enable and disable individuals and groups who seek to achieve their dreams. In this regard, it is not difficult to encourage students to identify with minorities who had to struggle harder and longer to achieve freedom and success, but it *is* hard to dissuade them from demonizing those who tried to keep them from succeeding. It is the Anglos who are the "bad guys" for my students, not Native or African Americans.

Two unanticipated consequences of opening up the canon that have bedeviled me for some years are (1) how easily students reverse the dichotomies that I try to help them undermine, and (2) how readily their exposure to various forms of past oppressions leads students to confirm their cynicism about the efficacy of government. That the European conquest and settlement of North America was accompanied by the ruthless destruction of Native American cultures and the enslavement of Africans is a fact of history that we can and should not explain away. The problem is that many students use that fact to make categorical judgments that obscure deeper understanding of the differences and complexities within (and between) the groups involved, so that condemnation substitutes for analysis. I insist throughout the course that students take into consideration the social and cultural frameworks available to different groups at any particular historical moment, while providing them with diverse voices from each group. For example, students have ample opportunities to see (and hear through lectures) that the majority of Anglo-American women living in the colonial and post-colonial era did not appear to see wifehood and motherhood as constraints on their identity. But that doesn't prevent a substantial minority of my students from insisting that *all* white women were oppressed.

One of the most important challenges for me in reshaping the course over the years has been to figure out ways to mitigate these sins of presentism: to help students distinguish their worldviews from those of the past, so that they do not project back their own contemporary proclivities, including their increasingly noticeable political apathy. At the same time, I do want students to be able to make moral judgments and to discover the links that exist between past practices and beliefs and present behaviors and values, theirs as well as those of other Americans.

PEDAGOGICAL STRATEGIES

I have the good fortune to be at a university where the improvement of teaching is taken seriously and where Title III and Ford Foundation grants have given me released time and the opportunity to participate in seminars in which I have met and learned from faculty from a wide variety of disciplines. This kind of support has made it much easier to take risks, although I have to say that risk-taking is also one of the great advantages of seniority. Some of the most important lessons I've learned about how to assign work and assess learning have come from my secondary-school colleagues, who on average spend much more time than university faculty in the trenches trying to figure out how to reach students with widely different cultural and linguistic back-grounds, academic preparation, motivation, and learning styles. During the past decade, I have worked to develop networks and resources for secondary-school teachers who teach and are interested in interdisciplinary studies. Part of my agenda has been to break down the often artificial barrier that exists between high-school and university teachers' curriculums in order to have us work more productively in the areas where we have the most to teach one another.[3]

These influences, combined with the dreams of my students to succeed and the difficult realities of their lives, have encouraged me to go beyond the standard essay paper and exam as classroom assignments. I offer students a variety of venues through which to demonstrate how they make sense of the course and make meaning of history: field trips, dramatic performances, role-playing, self-improvement exercises, citizenship and work polls, and small group work. Even my standard essay assignments have undergone changes over the years to meet the challenges my students pose. Because I want students to wrestle on their own with the primary sources they use to write their papers, I prepare them ahead of each paper with relevant readings and discussions of the kinds of materials they will be writing about, but I leave them to write their essays on readings we have not yet discussed.

In their first two papers, students are asked to wrestle with variant interpretations of a single historical event, and I provide them with topics that are structured to match different ability levels. In each case, the most challenging version of the assignment requires students to work with more versions of the same event and thus with more points of view. Usually, though not always, the minority of students that chooses the more difficult assignment handles it well. In order to encourage students to consider the more challenging assignment, I explain that I give credit for risk-taking by grading more leniently than I would if this were their only option for the assignment.

Building on what I hope are the lessons they have already learned from classroom lectures and discussions of preconception and point of view, the first paper asks them to examine the confrontation between Thomas Morton and the Puritans. Morton, an Anglican lawyer and speculator who set up a trading post about twenty miles from Plimoth colony, carried on a very lucrative trade with the Indians, with whom he also "consorted" in festivities that took place around a maypole he erected. He was seen as both a pagan infidel and an economic threat to the Plimoth colony, as noted in a section of William Bradford's *History of Plimoth Plantation* (1650; first published in 1856). Morton offered his own version of the events that led to his arrest and deportation to England for trial in his *New English Canaan* (1637), in which he describes the Algonkian Indians much more favorably than he does the English settlers. After reading the two polemical versions of this confrontation, the class holds a mock trial, which is more of a hearing, since the London court judged the charge against Morton—selling firearms to the Indians to enhance his fur trade—as too feeble to lead to trial. Morton's Anglicanism, of course, was an enormous advantage for him in an English court with no fondness for Puritan heretics. With those activities as background, students are asked to write an essay on Nathaniel Hawthorne's fictionalized reinterpretation of the conflict, "The Maypole of Merrymount" (1836). One of New England's greatest historical chroniclers, Hawthorne takes a minor historic event and turns it into a major cultural commentary on the future of New England, including its cultural hegemony over the rest of the country.[4]

The last essay for the course also plays with point of view, but offers a creative writing option that has proved to be an excellent vehicle for students' self-expressiveness. Students are asked to read four nineteenth-century women reformers (Elizabeth Cady Stanton, Angelina Grimké, Fanny Fern, and Catherine Beecher) who write from different perspectives on the issue of women's nature, rights, and roles. They choose one of these reformers and explain how she might have commented on one of four short stories by four other women writers that represent differing perspectives on women. Students can choose to write the essay in the form of a short story review, using the persona of their woman reformer. Typically, more than half the students choose this option. They almost invariably write papers that are right on target in terms of understanding the reformer's and the short story writer's points of view about the nature of women's "nature" and sphere. Moreover, these creative papers often demonstrate an impressive appropriation of the women reformers' voices and styles. I can't stress enough how liberating these role-playing exercises are for students. Students come alive in unexpected ways when they think they aren't writing an "academic" paper. By speaking in the voice of an authoritative historical figure, they themselves gain the "right" to speak powerfully. What is particularly interesting is that the male students who take on the woman reformer's persona write as convincingly as the female students in the class.[5]

While I and most of my students are relatively pleased with these essay assignments, some students do their best and most engaged work in nongraded and extra-credit assignments. These include small group workshops in which students work collaboratively to answer specific text-related questions, with roles assigned for the leader (responsible for reporting on the group's work), the facilitator (responsible for encouraging all members of the group to participate), and the scribe (responsible for writing up the group's worksheet). Class discussions improve dramatically after these workshops, in which, to be frank, some students are confronting the readings for the first time. Although not all students appreciate this format, I explain (at the beginning of the course) that different class formats serve different student learning styles and that I don't expect them to necessarily like them all.

As my extra-credit assignments expand, I have begun to offer some of them as alternatives to one of the required essays. I have built a series of field trips into the class—formal trips that I lead to Plimoth Plantation, the Freedom Trail, Concord, and the Lowell Mills, along with other sites students can visit on their own and write about. The students who take trips with me or on their own clearly get more out of the texts we read that are associated with these sites than when reading the texts alone. Thus I decided to allow a detailed field-trip report to substitute for one of the formal essays. One student who took advantage of this wrote a superb critique of a history museum that (mis)displayed Native American artifacts. Because this site-based learning is so powerful, I now require one field trip (and brief write-up) for all my students. Despite their heavy workloads, as my students admitted at the end of one class, when required by professors to take field trips, they find the time to go.

A number of the extra-credit assignments for this course have grown out of one of the best pieces of advice I received from a student. The student said that the course would be more interesting if we made more connections between the early history we studied and the contemporary world in which we live. So when we study the American Revolution, the students fill out an extensive questionnaire on their political activities, or lack of them, and their ideas about democracy and citizenship. A student collates the responses and presents them to the class. (This exercise is partly intended to encourage them to think about their civic activities and responsibilities beyond the periodic voting that seems to be their main involvement.)

When they read Emerson's "American Scholar" (1837), I ask them to write not only about why the essay is called America's "Intellectual Declaration of Independence," but also about how much of their own education has been "original" in Emerson's sense of the word. Here are some of their responses, written before we have had any discussion of the essay in class. Most of the students like the essay, and some are even inspired by it, at least in part because Emerson respects the kind of "real world" education that many of them have had outside of the classroom. Just as the men in the class seem to enjoy "cross-dressing" in the third essay assignment on women reformers, the women in the class figure out how to read Emerson's "Man Thinking" more inclusively. Here are what I consider some fine examples of men and women thinking:

> Emerson's idea of education seems to me to have no boundaries. He tells us "it resembles his own spirit, whose beginning, whose ending, he never can find—so entire, so boundless." Here Emerson demonstrates through not only his argument but also his language and imagery that man need not be tied to traditional limitations of education. . . . He also calls for an educated person to be not only scholarly but assume the work of a laborer, to be in the world with others and not isolated.

> Like our Declaration of Independence, Emerson's speech to the scholars of 1837 serves as a wake-up call; a call to arms, but the arsenal here is in the mind. As Emerson says, man "in the right state" is man thinking, but in the "degenerate state" he is the product of other men's thinking.

> Emerson would construe a "booksmart" graduate of Harvard as a "mere thinker" if he held restricted views in accordance with experience. . . . I think he would be more inclined to respect the UMass student working full-time, raising a family, and trying to experience all life has to offer.

> I think college has brought out the Woman thinking in me. Instead of simple facts I can use book knowledge to better understand and delve into the events of the day. It is always a good feeling to understand rather than just to know. My knowledge relates to the world around me as well as the classroom.

Earlier in the course, students are offered as an out-of-class, extra-credit assignment the "The 'Be All That You Can Be' Benjamin Franklin Challenge," which invites them to follow a modified version of Franklin's moral perfection program by choosing one or two virtues to improve while keeping a twenty-four-hour diary of their living habits. The students who do this learn more about themselves than they expect, as well as having the experience of testing empirically Franklin's "enlightened" (if somewhat tongue-in-cheek) theory of human self-improvement. Last time I taught the course, I tried to counteract the obsessive self-discipline of the Franklin exercise with "The Henry David Thoreau 'Be Here Now!' Challenge," which invited students to simplify their lives by giving up three items for a week that are not necessities, spending eight hours of that week "in nature" (according to one environmentalist, we average five minutes a day outdoors), and keeping a journal of their observations.

My last in-class role-play assignment (though not the least in terms of the power of dramatic play) is a student performance of Hawthorne's short story "Rappacinni's Daughter"(1844), which comes before our unit on the women's rights movement. Students who volunteer to play the characters receive extra credit: the evil doctor who turns his beautiful daughter Beatrice into a poisoned flower for the advancement of science; her callow boyfriend, Giovanni; the doctor's academic rival; and the landlady who lures Giovanni into the doctor's garden, where he meets and falls in love with Beatrice. The class "interviews" the characters and then interviews me (I play the author). This turns out to be one of the best "discussions" we have during the term, because the class is fully responsible for it, though I manage to direct some of their questions to contemporary issues related to the improprieties of certain kinds of scientific and academic pursuits.

The course ends with what I call (to myself) my "impossible dream" final take-home essay, in which students have a week to trace the evolution of one theme of the American dreams/realities they defined at the beginning, while accounting for its continuities and changes over the historic periods we cover in the course. Seven years ago, I added a bonus option to the exam, a brief but "thoughtful reflection" on how they would now define the American Dream. This exit question, which about half the class answers, is an important reminder to me that how I teach and what I assign is only a small component of what influences my students' thinking about themselves as learners and citizens.

While most of those who choose to answer the bonus question seem to be students who have come to some new idea or awareness of the meaning of the American Dream, there is a wide range of thinking and feeling about the topic. In general, students tend to be more reflective about their answers than they were at the beginning of the semester. Some refuse to admit the possibility of impediments standing in their way. Others hold to their personal dreams of success while acknowledging the constraints on personal freedom that affected the lives of their forbears. Some feel more ambitious about their dreams, others less so. Some have broadened their dreams to encompass a larger human community, while others embraced that community to begin with. I asked students, "What's happened, if anything, to your ideas about the American dream over the course?" Here are some of their responses:

> By studying the American history, and the autobiographies of some authors, I find myself that I have more than I expected that I could have the life that I always wanted, . . . but, on the other hand, I feel that I am paying a big price, which is to either let go of my own culture, or have to live a double-cultured life that I find hard to pursue. I think I am setting my roots in the American land just like the first Pilgrims. Will I ever be the ancestor of a countless number of Americans?

> My opinion of the American dream is to have a family, live in a house with a white picket fence. This dream is my dream and I haven't changed my mind about it. . . . Hopefully my reality will turn out to be my dream which I feel I deserve. I have worked very hard in and out of school for the past ten years. I have paid for my tuition and have worked very long hours while in high school and college. I am a very good worker and I can see myself having a pretty good well-paying job as I feel I deserve it.

> Personally, I feel that after studying the people and attitudes which make up these four historical periods my own idea of the American Dream has been deflated a bit. It isn't that my goals or desires have been changed, but that I have realized that people have had, or have been fighting for, such dreams and desires since the history of this country began. . . . I learned that my dreams of the kind of life and country that I want are not all that different from the dreams and desires of those who came before me. Studying American history, and the origins of the American Dream, have allowed me to see my own dreams and my contemporary America from a new perspective. It is a perspective in which I no longer feel so original, but I also do not feel so alone.

The final exam is very demanding but also rewarding for students, who have to make their own sense of the course while demonstrating their knowledge of the peoples and movements we have studied. Most of them succeed. Working at a university that is consistently underfunded by the state and undervalued by its citizens, it is sometimes difficult to remember the extraordinary pride we should take in ourselves and our students for these kinds of accomplishments. In her answer to my exit question for the American Dreams course, a returning woman student who was studying for certification as a social studies teacher reminded me of why I wanted to come to UMass/Boston and why I want to stay:[6]

My American Dream is to live equally with all peoples. I want to have autonomy, respect, and consideration from all of those around me as well as from our government. I want to live in a space where I can look around and see black, white, women, men, Asians, Europeans, Latinos, people overcoming or living with their handicaps, older people, and young children. I want education, for myself, and for the people of this country that are overlooked or cast aside for their differences. For me, the experience at UMass has proved to be just that. My idea of a great country is right here. For the most part all of us at UMass survive together. We work hard, we respect each other for our accomplishments, and we empathize with each other's hardships. We are living my American Dream.

Notes

1. For discussion of the "contact zone," see Mary Louise Pratt, Chapter 1 of *Imperial Eyes: Travel Writing and Transculturation* (New York: Routledge, 1992).

2. Ronald Takaki talks about the importance of "connecting the differences" in "Teaching American History Through a Different Mirror," *Perspectives* [newsletter of the American Historical Association], October 1994. See also David Roediger, *The Wages of Whiteness: Race and the Making of the American Working Class* (London: Verso, 1991), and Nancy Cott, *The Bonds of Womanhood: 'Woman's Sphere' in New England, 1780–1835* (New Haven: Yale University Press, 1977).

3. These activities have included working with the American Studies Association to develop a position on its national council for a secondary-school teacher, to start helping to establish a committee on secondary education within the association, and developing a "Focus on Teaching Day" for our annual conferences, with sessions on collaborative secondary-school–university endeavors. I have edited the "National Resource Guide to American Studies in the Secondary Schools," which contains essays on model secondary-school programs and courses in American studies and integrated humanities, as well as listing schools throughout the country that offer such programs and courses. The guide can be purchased for ten dollars from the American Studies Association, 1120 19th St., NW, Suite 301, Washington, D.C. 20036; it is also available at no charge on the ASA Crossroads Web site: <http://www.georgetown.edu/crossroads/highroads/>. The ASA maintains a listserv for secondary-school teachers interested in sharing ideas about pedagogy and curriculum. Contact listserv@listerv.georgetown.edu. Those interested in seeing some of the innovative work that has been developed in interdisciplinary teaching by high-school teachers should look at the winter 1999 issue of the *Magazine of History*, published by the Organization of American Historians, which I edited under the theme "Using Literature to Teach History."

4. Most of the primary texts for the course can be found in Paul Lauter, ed., *The Heath Anthology of American Literature*, vol. 1, 3d ed. (Boston: Houghton Mifflin, 1998). I supplement the anthology with a substantial reading packet that includes secondary sources, as well as primary sources related to the three essays

assigned in the course that are not found in the anthology. These include the readings for the second assigned essay, on different versions of the Indian captivity of Hannah Dustin. A useful supplementary source for teachers of American literature and American studies can be found on the Web site that was designed to accompany the Heath anthology. "Syllabus Builder" offers numerous suggestions for course design and pedagogy, using the anthology as a base but going beyond it to other sources as well: <http://www.hmco.com/college/english/heath/index.html>.

5. A student from this class won the 1992 D. C. Heath Student Essay Contest. The student's essay was printed in the spring 1992 *D. C. Heath Anthology of American Literature Newsletter*, Vol. 7.

6. I would be happy to share my syllabus and assignments for the course with interested readers. You can reach me at the American Studies Program, University of Massachusetts Boston, 100 Morrissey Blvd., Boston, MA 02125.

WINSTON E. LANGLEY

9   Teaching, Learning, and Judging

Some Reflections on the University and Political Legitimacy

THE OBJECTIVE of this chapter is to show some relationships between teaching, learning, and judging, on the one hand, and political legitimacy and the role of the university, on the other. It does so by (1) looking at the backgrounds of the author and some students he has taught and from whom he has learned, (2) defining "the political," (3) reviewing some problems of teaching and learning, (4) examining the nature of political legitimacy and its relationship to the "self" that judges, and (5) analyzing the role of the university in the construction of that self. The courses I teach are in the area of international relations, with an emphasis on international law, international organizations (particularly the United Nations), international political economy, and world order. On occasion, I teach other courses in political theory, twentieth-century political ideas, and foreign policy (United States and Japan). While from time to time I teach other courses to help meet unexpected student demands, the courses specifically named above have formed the core of my teaching responsibilities and have generated the experiences I will discuss below.

Related to the courses I teach is the backgrounds of the students. As has been mentioned in other essays in this volume, most of the students are the first in their families to pursue a college education. So the culture of university life is new for them. For my students, that general newness is usually compounded by the absence of much, if any, knowledge about the world outside the United States. An appreciable number of younger students have never physically left the community in which they were born and went to high school. Even the capital of the state (Boston) seems somewhat alien to a few. Older members of my classes generally possess a greater awareness; but with the exception of students whose parents have recently come from other countries or who are themselves recent immigrants, that awareness rarely extends beyond U.S. borders. In gen-

160

eral, student awareness is not usually associated with any sense of coherence about the events that shape that awareness. Teaching international relations at the University of Massachusetts Boston, therefore, contradicts many of the assumptions that might be generally made about college students.

One of the assumptions I have been unable to make, for example, is that my students understand what is meant by the political. As a consequence, I have been forced to reflect more seriously on my conception of the nature of the political, as well as on what I understand the university to be and the character of the education with which it should be concerned. In short, instead of assuming that my students and I share certain taken-for-granted views about the discipline and about university education, I have consistently been obliged to reflect on and redefine them for my students. And because I have had to define them for my students, I have been obliged to reflect on and define them for myself. I will give a partial definition of each, in this essay, because they bear significantly on what I have to say.

By the political I mean the area of human activity that is concerned with the process and the general arrangements (as well as rearrangements) through which a group of people, brought together by chance or informed choice, pursues jointly shared ends. In the identification and pursuit of those ends, especially in their nuanced forms, not all members of the group are conscious actors; but they are presumed to be. In the sense of this definition, one may think of the politics of universities, labor unions, families, professional societies, and, of course, student associations. But politics and the political are more: they are constituted also by the ideological and normative statements that justify and delimit the ends to be pursued as well as the means by which that pursuit is to be effected; likewise, they are by nature empirical activities from which the previously mentioned general arrangements and normative contents are deduced, formulated, and supported.

The university I understand to be not so much a place as an environment within which the practice of thinking is taught. Although there are many such environments, what distinguishes the university is its claim to represent the universe of modes of such thinking, the varieties of articulations, the pluralities of forms that people's voices have assumed in the conversation of humankind (what we call human civilization). The university not only represents those modes of thinking, but also prepares students to become parts of, to extend, and hopefully, to add to that conversation. Education in political science and international relations, therefore, is concerned with the practice of thinking about the political, as defined above.

Since political science is empirical in character (and by empirical, I mean that it originates in or is based on observation and experience), it follows that its conclusions are provisional, probationary, and tentative. That is, they are capable of being disproved through further observation, as well as through the evolution of human experience. And since human observations and experiences are bound by many contexts, including social, moral, psychological, historical, and economical contexts, one should properly study political activities from the standpoint of those contexts. This approach to the study of political science is one that I have consistently followed, sometimes criticizing my professional colleagues whose approaches I have viewed as methodologically wanting, because they have been concerned with prescriptive modes of governing. (Generally, those approaches either disregard considerations of contexts or offer some contexts but limit them to political institutions and ideologies.) In short, I have been what is generally described as "certain of himself."

Given this approach and a classroom environment that encouraged and urged active student participation, I found students attentive, eager to learn, and, in general, engaged in the subject areas in which I taught. Although often burdened with academic uncertainties and problems of writing, I also found them on the whole intellectually able. In cases of academic uncertainty, I have counseled students that the classroom is, perhaps, the one place where they have "a right to be wrong," and I invite them to play some role in the subject matter under discussion that would give them a sense of partnership in the process of teaching and learning. For example, one person may be designated from a preceding class to be the leader of discussions for the succeeding class, and all questions from me will be directed at that student, who is required to explain issues directed at her or him to the class. Her or his classmates also turn to her or him for clarifications, before turning to me. Two or three others are identified as "back-up leaders," in case the designated leader is absent or has difficulties responding to questions. Dates for examinations (I generally determine the number of examinations) are agreed on by students, and I schedule conferences with each student I have not previously taught so that I can, through a friendly chat (usually dealing with students' backgrounds, career interests, and assurances of my readiness to help, if help is needed), reduce some of the often-perceived social and academic distance between student and professor.

The good grades students were getting, the excellent students' evaluations I was receiving (my department conducts a course evaluation each semester), and the comments from my colleagues who had either visited my classes or heard "good things about (my) teaching" reinforced my previously mentioned confidence in what I saw as my superior approach to teaching. But then something unexpectedly happened to challenge my confidence.

In the mid 1980s, I decided that I would change the format of my examinations in my class on international law in order to help students gain greater mastery in the application of concepts. The format I chose was one that presented problems to students and invited them to play the roles of decision-makers—presidents, prime ministers, economic advisers, teachers, judges, moral philosophers, diplomats, cultural critics, law-makers, and political theorists, among others. They were furnished, as parts of the context of the problem presented, with all the historical, social, economic, moral, and other data deemed necessary to support an informed decision and required to justify the elimination of several reasonably acceptable alternatives in the *process* of decision-making. (Adopting and eliminating alternatives in this manner would require the type of conceptual refinement I sought.) Examinations of this kind were long (some turned out to be ten or more single-spaced, typed pages, in the case of final exams), but such lengths seemed necessary to provide students with as many "real life situations" as possible—the conflict in former Yugoslavia, age levels in Germany and the United States, or adjustment programs of the International Monetary Fund in Ghana and Pakistan, for example.

Throughout the first examination, students were nervous—something I expected. But the number of questions they asked, and especially those questions to which there were self-evident answers, surprised me. I could see uncertainties and frowns on their faces as some submitted their examination books to me; others tried not to make eye contact at all as they hastily left the examination room. The seminal surprise for me, however, came from student performances on the examination. Unlike previous tests, on which most students had done well (meaning they earned a B minus or better), only about 5 percent of them did well on this occasion. And this was not an introductory course in international relations, in which I knew little of the student quality of academic performance. It was a senior-level course with students who had taken other courses with me and had performed very well. Some were known "academic stars" within the department. A crisis had developed.

I spent most of the weekend reflecting on the results of the examination (the examination was given on Thursday, and I would not meet the class again until the following Tuesday). If—as I thought—the new format was important in helping students develop a more refined grasp of concepts, then perhaps I was not as effective a teacher as I had supposed myself to be. Perhaps I had been giving students grades that did not truly reflect a developed capacity to think. Indeed, perhaps many of the complaints I had heard from some professors about the limited intellectual abilities of our students were true. Was the test too long (I had allowed eighty minutes to take the examination)? Perhaps I had failed to prepare students properly for the new format; or could it be that the test was unfair? The results may even have been an anomaly, most likely the product of inadequate student preparation. These were some of the speculations in which I engaged, but they gave me little or no comfort.

In the matter of the possible inadequate preparation on the part of the students, for example, I could not explain why *all* the students would be unprepared, absent some common problem before the examination that prevented them from preparing. But I could think of nothing of this sort. To calm my anxiety, I vowed to have a follow-up examination soon, to expand my efforts to help students prepare for the examination, and to tell students, upon returning their papers, that they should not trouble themselves unduly, although I would seek to ascertain their interpretations of the results.

On the reconvening of class, some of the explanations offered by the students paralleled my own speculations: time limitation, novelty of format, inadequate preparation. I felt better. I had been partially restored to a sense of teaching effectiveness. There was one group of responses for which I was not prepared, however, and it came from about two-fifths of the class. I had asked students who were uncomfortable about discussing in an open class the reasons they saw as the causes for the poor performance on the test to communicate their views in writing to me. Their responses indicated that students had prepared diligently and felt they knew the information. "I just could not answer the questions," one wrote. "Something prevented me from answering the questions," said another.

"I can't explain it, but I sat there with all my information in my head, I felt prepared. I was prepared and yet I was unprepared," said a third.

Such were some of the written explanations I read, and they immediately invited me to think that scheduling the make-up examination in ten days, as we had, might have been a mistake. The reasons advanced for the poor performance were, I intuitively felt, far more complex than I had thought. It might be better, therefore, to postpone the scheduled test and discuss further the problems we were having as a class. But I was dissuaded from this course of action by four seniors who visited my office later that day to say that their performance on the new format had made them anxious about their academic averages and their prospects of getting into graduate school. When I tried to assure them by indicating I was thinking of postponing the scheduled make-up in order to review more effectively the problems we were having in class, they pointed out that we did not have many more opportunities for testing before the final examination. So the test was given as scheduled, after what I thought was a successful review of the course material and some approaches to a more effective encounter with the new format.

The results were only marginally better. And, despite concerted efforts by myself and the class as a whole, the results of the final examination four weeks later were somewhat better for only one-third of the class. For the rest, the improvements were so slight that they could be properly called negligible.

The following summer, I spent most of my time reviewing my teaching strategy, reading some material on teaching, and generally reflecting on the problems I'd had the preceding semester. I came to a few conclusions: I would not change the format—students would have to learn to deal with the concrete in all its nuanced complexities. More hypothetical problems, which students in their course evaluations found helpful, would be used, and students would be encouraged to construct their own hypotheticals. Further, to involve students more in the instructional portion of the classroom experience, I would divide one of my classes into groups, with students more successful in grasping concepts taking turns to lead the groups. A final approach would be to spend some time examining, in class, a few past examination questions, so that the format would not be a surprise to students.

The results of the first examination in the course I taught after a summer's reflection were somewhat better than those in international law the previous semester. Students (based on their comments during a midterm course evaluation I conducted to help me in my experiment) seemed to have benefited from the extensive use of hypotheticals and from the division of the class into subgroups. But I was still baffled by the limited number of students who were doing well. I therefore sought to interview as many of those who had done poorly as would accept my invitation to visit my office for a conference. Through the process of these interviews, I discovered that almost everyone knew the material on the examination. Indeed, their knowledge sometimes surprised me. They understood the concepts but had difficulties applying them because they had problems judging. At least, that was my tentative conclusion.

Before the last-mentioned examination, two events took place that helped me, and both—one involving an American student and the other a Japanese student—took place in the course on political economy. In discussing the international monetary order, I had begun by noting the mystery that has often surrounded money and how its functions frequently confuse people. Then, in discussing one of those functions—that of money serving as a medium of exchange—I sought to have members of the class think of some other entity that, in part, had for them served as a medium of exchange. In doing so, I thought I could use their examples to further elaborate the function under discussion. For a few seconds, no one responded. Then a woman who always sat in the back of the classroom and had never uttered a word in the course said, "Food stamps; that's my money!" (It turned out that she was on welfare.) A few of her fellow students laughed, but I immediately took the opportunity to use her example to make the point I wanted to: that, although food stamps served as a means of exchange, their exchange function was limited. They could only purchase food, not unlike a theater ticket, which can only be used in exchange for a scheduled performance. Money, on the other hand, represents the one commodity in any given society that is universally acceptable for all other commodities. Had she dollars rather than food stamps, she could exchange those dollars for anything she desired; she would not be limited to food. In addition, I went on, although states are said to be equal and, as such, can create their own money, in international society not all monies are equal. Some, like food stamps, can only be exchanged for limited purposes—to purchase goods *within* the societies of their origin; others, like the U.S. dollar, are internationally acceptable and can be used as a means of exchange everywhere.

The countries collectively called the Third World, I informed the class, have currencies that are generally spendable (exchangeable) in those countries only. And before I could proceed to say that those countries, like food-stamp recipients in the United States, are unfree to use their currencies to purchase international goods and services they desire, the same student, whom I will call Yvonne, said, "Women are the Third World." While pausing to disguise my pleasant surprise at what I considered, among other things, a rather apt metaphor, I asked her what she meant. She said that most of the people with whom she associated were women on welfare. And she thought they were as unfree, or as limited in relationship to what they could exchange their food stamps for, as people in the Third World.

Yvonne had set the stage for my discussion of the political economy of freedom, equality, social class, and, indeed, gender. Besides, given my own conception of the Third World as less of a place than a condition—a condition of relative powerlessness, vulnerability, inequality, and limited freedom—I could and did readily use her metaphor to discuss both the officially designated Third World and the condition of "third worldization" within and between countries. And Yvonne helped me much more. She pointed me in the direction to understanding, at least in part, the previously mentioned relationship between knowing and judging.

I had been very surprised that Yvonne, who had done so poorly on the midterm test, was able to grasp the concept of money as a means of exchange (she also successfully grappled with the other two major functions of money) so well that she could anticipate the direction of my lecture and, most impressively, construct a brilliant metaphor out of it. So pleasantly surprised was I that, following two more lectures on the global monetary order in which her performance in class discussions was nothing short of spectacular, I asked her to visit me in my office. She made the visit; and when I asked her to explain the difference between her recent performance in class and the results of the midterm test, she told me that once she saw the link between the means of exchange and food stamps, she felt she was "on safe grounds." And she was able to "see and evaluate" immediately the exchange relationships. She assured me that she knew the answers to the questions I gave on the test—the very answers we had reasoned through in the class discussions following the return of the corrected exam. But she could not "appreciate" the facts and the issues well enough to answer them. When I asked her what she meant by "appreciate," I found that she meant assess, evaluate, affix value, order, decide, judge. Because she was on "safe grounds," because she could "appreciate" the issues of food stamps and the exchange function of money, she could judge.

The insight she gave me resonated with what a Japanese student, who was also having problems with the examination's format, had told me. He indicated that, to make refined evaluations, he had to compare most English words with their Japanese counterparts, just as he had had to do in assessing the prices of goods in dollars. (He first had to appraise the price in yen.) He also said that, in the case of English words for which there were no Japanese counterparts, he could not assess well, although I know his knowledge and academic use of English were superior to that of most students in the course. When I compared what other students had said from the previous semester (such as "I was prepared, but unprepared" or "I can't explain it, but I sat there with all the answers in my head"), the information from the Japanese student, and the insight from Yvonne, I found support for the tentative conclusion about the difference between knowing and judging. Perhaps the difference, I told myself, had to do with "being on safe grounds." In short, using information with which students feel "safe" may be the key to their comfort with judging, and that safety may be found in using materials from the students' own life experiences—not by way of an occasional *factual example,* which everyone does, but as a central part on the *process* of reasoning through the elaboration of *concepts.*

My own schooling experience also furnished some support for my thinking. I was born in the former British colony of Jamaica and was regarded as sufficiently "clever" to have been selected for special classes and scholarships. Because the British had no interest in my maintaining links with the immediate environment within which I was born or with my early life (one of relative poverty), schooling meant not only physical but also cultural separation from that early life. I came to know the world—the world of ancient Greece and Rome, the world of Europe (their history, music, literature, philosophy, and science), and the world of the British Empire, in all the details of its geography, its history, its government, its "learning and honor," and its enemies—Russia, Germany, Japan, China, and, on occasions, France and even the United States. But I knew nothing about Jamaica; I was not exposed to even a single

Caribbean writer. Thus I have always felt I had little basis (I have felt unsafe) to compare and make judgements about the country of my birth.

Armed with this new thinking, I began to consider ways to demonstrate how students' everyday experiences are parts of the wider world of international relations, instead of being preoccupied with "bringing the world" to them. The results from tests constructed on this basis have been outstanding, and some of my class discussions have been electric. Instead of beginning (in the case of a study of the United Nations, for instance) with a history of the principal organs of that international organization, I begin with the weather, newsprints, or water. In international political economy, I may begin with a movie, a paper bag, a sandwich, or an alarm clock. In the case of the latter, for example, it could have been made by Sony, a Japanese transnational business corporation; if so, it would have been most likely assembled in the company's plant in Brazil from component parts produced in Japan, Germany, the United Kingdom, and Mexico. And it could have been shipped to the United States aboard a Greek-owned ship, a ship made in South Korea, licensed in Liberia or Panama, with a Latvian and Portuguese crew. The student immediately becomes aware that s/he is enmeshed in international relations, and the class can return to this example again and again to discuss foreign investment, the nature of multinational corporations and their impact on the lives of people and countries, and the reticulated world of licensing, taxation, and international liability. The same might be done with a sandwich—perhaps even by introducing the history of wheat and how it got to the Americas.

One area in tests administered so far has continued to be a problem. That area involves questioning the decisions or conclusions of government, including supreme courts or respected persons in known positions of authority, such as the pope. My interviews with students and my discussions with teaching colleagues suggest that the problem may have its seat in a lack of self-esteem. But, in my judgement and as we will see below, it is a type of self-esteem that is related to the need for unity.

Students have consistently (a fairly large percentage of test-takers, about 20 percent) found it difficult to engage in evaluations leading to conclusions that differ from those of certain governments, for instance. Even when they have conducted the appropriate systematic analysis and the overwhelming weight of evidence urges a conclusion contrary to that for which the government stands, many students will invariably find themselves unable to take the next step and draw the factually and conceptually supportable conclusion. Why? For most the answer is, I think, that they doubt the validity of their own analysis; they doubt themselves and, therefore, give the benefit of the doubt to the government's position—usually their own government's position, not so much that of foreign governments, with which there is no felt identity. The following example may illustrate a typical response to a government's position as well as the difference between knowing and judging.

Let us suppose that, while in the port of Boston and still aboard the vessel, crew members of the ship that carried the previously mentioned alarm clocks to the United States had used a drug. Let us further suppose that this drug is of a type whose use carries a criminal penalty in the United States; that the United States has been informed of its use, and that the government has arrested a Portuguese and a Latvian, charging each with illegal use of drugs, although neither Portugal nor Latvia considers the use of this drug a criminal act. Portugal and Latvia have lodged strong diplomatic protest with Washington, contesting the U.S. claim that the very nature of the crewmen's conduct within its territorial waters allowed it no alternative but to arrest them. Panama is not only protesting diplomatically, but has instituted a suit in the U.S. District Court of Boston, claiming exclusive legal and political jurisdiction over the ship's crew. Each student is to play the role of an arbitrator in the case.

Typically, the most able students would correctly deduce from the facts given that the ship involved in this case is a *commercial* vessel— s/he would be expected to advance reasons (nature of the goods carried and licensing arrangements, for example). Those students would also recognize and present the applicable general principles of law governing commercial vessels, one of which is that the flag state (Panama) has exclusive jurisdiction over the crew of a vessel, even when that vessel is in the territorial waters of another country (the United States). The students would then indicate exceptions to the general principle, one of which is that, if conduct aboard the vessel within those territorial waters disturbs the public order (peace) of the port, then jurisdiction shifts from the flag state, Panama, to that within whose territorial waters the ship is located, the United States. The important issue at this point would, therefore, become, Was the conduct of the crew (using drugs) such as would disturb the public order of the port? Despite all the admirable preceding display of knowledge of the law, modes of reasoning, and general analytical skills, students would suddenly become unable to do the appraisal required to make a decision. They invariably would turn to the position of the government with which they identify, often repeating that government's position, or would resort to ideological and other clichés to justify their conclusions.

The issue of knowing and judging is clearly implicated here. Knowing entails having information, knowledge, and insights—all of which the students would have displayed in the above example. Judging, however, involves evaluating and deciding (fixing, determining) disputed or conflicting claims to values, whether those values be principles, positions, freedoms, or powers. To decide between and among such claims is to place oneself in a position of authority and power in relationship to those claims and their claimants. In the example given above, students would have to decide the conflicting claims of the United States and Panama (among others) to the legal value of jurisdiction. To do so, they would have to reflectively determine whether the conduct of the crew disturbed the public order of the port of Boston, with public order defined by international custom and treaty. (That definition, incidentally, has seven components to it, and the student would have to use his or her discretion to evaluate and interpret the facts—according to the applicable component or components of the definition—and then decide.) Many have not been able to make determinations of this sort, because they have felt unable to assume the authority involved. They have been unable to judge.

Students have not only instructed me concerning the difference between knowing and judging, but in reflecting on that instruction, I have come to believe that the capacity to judge may also be connected to identity, to one's sense of self (a self having the authority mentioned above); and that this sense of self has a bearing on our need for unity and on matters of political legitimacy.

POLITICAL LEGITIMACY AND THE "SELF"

The term political legitimacy I understand to mean the quality or condition of political life, which defines the conduct of the state (or the government which acts on its behalf) as one that is in conformity with the common good. In societies that claim to be democratic, that common good is determined, in large measure, by what is authorized by the general body of citizens. What is deemed legitimate in a democracy, therefore, is presumed to be that which is authorized by citizens (through legislative enactments, constitutional orders, electoral choices, and even public opinion). To the extent that the state's conduct expresses that which is authorized by its citizens, it gains their allegiance and loyalty and is said to have political legitimacy. What I will call the "surface theory" of political legitimacy[1]—that which largely dominates contemporary political discourse and practice—takes the position that in societies identified as democratic, the state or its government is legitimate unless there is wholesale, overt opposition to it or to its policies. The theory assumes that when citizens "freely" elect a government, that government, in turn, is reciprocally free to act in accordance with shared common ends. When those ends are not served, citizens become disaffected and not only confront the government, but also forswear allegiance to it.

In modern, complex societies, the pursuit of certain ends, by definition, creates inconvenience, social injury, and disaffection. Sometimes the common good cannot be pursued at all, because powerful interests limit the freedom of the government to advance commonly desired ends. And at other times, a governmentally imposed limit or sponsored injury should be accepted, because it comports with ends people seek in common. To grapple effectively with the often complicated and sometimes confusingly interlacing features of contemporary political life, citizens must have not only a developed intellectual capacity to understand, but, as well, a self that is confidently (authoritatively) able to engage in informed discrimination and reflective judgement.

Such a self is not produced automatically. It is the product of social consistency and continuity, a certain sameness of experience. It grows from the "recognition that there is an inner population of remembered and anticipated sensations and images which are firmly correlated with the outer population of familiar and predictable things and people."[2] In short, it is developed from the correspondence between an inner core of sensations and images (of oneself, other persons and things) and the experiences generated by the many roles, institutional and other, one assumes in social and political life. When that life and the experiences it offers do not minister to the concerns, the deeper longings, or "the most painful grievances" that one has, when life's sociopolitical conditions bear little relationship to what has been internalized as the common good, there is alienation and disaffection, because one cannot identify with or endorse those conditions of life. And if one cannot endorse the conditions of one's life, one cannot approve what one has become. The disjunction between one's "inner population of remembered and anticipated sensations and images" and the outer population of encountered things becomes the source of a fragmented self—a self that, from the standpoint of the state, must be "reconnected" if alienation is not to rise to the sociopolitical rejection (delegitimization) of the established public order.[3]

Instead of repairing that fractured self by reordering political life so that there can be an actual recoupling of the outer experiences with the inner population, there is generally a substitution of an artificial (rhetorical) connectedness. This rhetorical coupling does not provide an authentic fit, and it would be quickly rejected, but for the need human beings have for social unity and community. Modern political systems manipulate this basic need for social unity as an aid to rhetorical connectedness. These systems do more: they socialize members of the general population not to trust, not to believe in the reality of their own experiences, because on that socialization depends the success of rhetorical connectedness. And where there are efforts to give those experiences validity, every effort (usually through the process of defining what is real, normal, sane, proper, patriotic, important, etc.) is made by the established order to discredit them.

For instance, one whose children are malnourished and who is homeless may question the government's commitment to certain human rights—the rights to food and to shelter. Instead of dealing with the reality of that person's experience and the issues of human social and economic rights, the government and its defenders would most likely say this mother or father lacks a "proper understanding of how the free market system works." The person is left to doubt the validity of his or her understanding of human rights, as well as the government's responsibilities in relationship to those rights. And what of someone, outraged and ashamed that one's "democratic government" has been part of a system of torture sponsored by close allies, confronts one's government about its conduct? Instead of discussing the issue or changing its conduct, modern governments will claim that the issue concerns matters that are linked to "national security," too "sensitive to be discussed," or that are part of some unspecified "danger" or "evil" of "some delicacy" (meaning it cannot be discussed). And if one insists on having a say on the issue, one will be accused of being "improperly or inadequately informed" or of being "unpatriotic." The issue of a democracy involved in torture will not be discussed; and the questioning of one's patriotism is designed to isolate, to disconnect one from the community—something that no one wants to experience, especially when that community contains many whom one has been taught to respect. The questioning of one's patriotism is also directed at offering a basis for connectedness, which will exist if one forswears one's own view and feeling about patriotism based on values of human rights and accepts the implied rhetorical definition. Of course, one is also left to question the adequacy of one's information (and one is unlikely to have adequate information, because the government will not share it). The rhetoric of "free market," "patriotism," and "proper understanding," among others, has "won," although the persons involved in each of the examples given is left with a self or a circumstance that s/he will find difficult to approve.

Hence, members of the general population—especially the least socially favored—are induced to escape from the actual world in which they live into one (the rhetorical) in which they cannot exist and over which they have no control. Further, with the circumstances of their lives often defined by constant shifts, sometimes even chaotic changes, the artificial conjunctions afforded by rhetorical connectedness is many times "welcomed." The disenchantment and actual alienation caused by the disengagement between people's inner population of remembered images (of what democratic societies or human rights are) and the outer lived experience is thus, from what we have said above, contained by the state. And that containment produces two major results. One is related to our original definition of the political, and the other concerns the personal condition of the "citizen."

As regards the first result, the agent of the state, the government, can deal with the general public arrangements—including the setting of political priorities—without having to account for the inconsistencies or incompatibilities of those arrangements with the actual experiences of large numbers of nationals. Linked to the state's ability to act without having to account to many of its citizens (because their disenchantment has been contained by rhetorical unity) is its nurturing of an antidemocratic form of allegiance, an allegiance that is unreflective.

An underlying assumption of liberal democracy is, of course, that citizens have the capacity for reflection, and that it is through such reflection that they determine and pursue their individual as well as joint interests and authorize government to act. But since reflection entails a marriage between the inner and outer populations of experiences we have been discussing, and, in addition, entails trusting and believing the reality as well as the validity of one's own experiences—things modern "democratic" states do not urge or allow—unreflective allegiance must be encouraged and normalized. And this brings us to the second major consequence of containment, which is the personal condition of the citizen in general.

That condition is one of a fractured self. This is not a self in the tradition of Whitman and Wordsworth—one that, though composed of many experiences, feelings, insights, inclinations, and intuitions, is woven into "some loose but clear unity" and that, though pragmatically linked to a core, ventures to new encounters, always returning to that core for confirmation, reaffirmation, and passion to venture still farther. Neither is it the self of a Proust, Confucius, or Isaiah—one that, despite its supposed and traceable empirical identity, operates as a double through art, social relations, and dreams to recreate itself. And it is decidedly not the self of Marxism, which finds its true identity as an emerged historical expression, or of Rousseau, in which affirming the events of the inner life as constituting sovereign importance becomes the public expression of the private inner voice and inner face.[4] The fractured self of which we speak is so weak, disjointed, and lacking in self-esteem from having to lead a life the condition of which it cannot approve, that it is anxious and demoralized. And yet, in the midst of this disaffection, this alienation, and this anxiety, the self must "choose" politically, and, in choosing, must "decide." Since one's own experiences (with one's Jewish, Black, Muslim, gay, or Chinese friends, or one's homelessness or job insecurity, for example) are not grounds on which decisions can be properly made, one must rely on the rhetorical presentations that, within themselves, contain the proper decisions. Decisions, therefore, are not one's own; they belong to others. And so one becomes unpracticed in deciding, in judging, in appraising public life, absent formulations from others. This brings us back to the surface theory of legitimacy, as well as to the issues of learning and judging.

The absence of open challenge to what we have come to call democratic government and the modern state on whose behalf that government acts is not because "citizens" consider those actions expressive of their experiences or as ministering to their paramount concerns. Nor is the absence of overt challenge the offspring of a felt authorship (from which the authority of government comes) of what that government does. The practice of overt challenging is really the product of a careful "political" cultivation, on the part of the state, of a divided self, an anxious self, a self that gives unreflective allegiance, because it cannot appraise and judge. In the absence of the capacity to judge, that self acquiesces in the conduct of government and in "doing one's patriotic duty," including even becoming a part of a "shared innocence about the historical course a people is on." Citizenship, as seen by the surface theory of legitimacy, is but an extended apprenticeship in a process of being separated from one's experience and taught to have an inner face that will have no public representation.

The students about whom we began this discussion in this essay were and are often the children of parents who have rarely developed the capacity to evaluate and judge the relationship between their personal experiences and what purports to be the pursuit of the common good. And the capacity of the students, far from transcending the capacities of their parents, are also shaped by a socialization process that leads them to view personal experience as false, unworthy, or, at best, suspect. Concomitantly, the experiences and judgements of "significant others" (priests, professors, presidents, authors) are important. Further, since the self possessed by many of these students is fragmented, they are less comfortable with an empirical approach to academic subjects that views all conclusions as probationary, tentative, and subject to the disconfirming experiences of others than they are with nonempirical certainties. Most important, they do not feel ready to judge and are anxious when required to do so.

My students have taught me that the inability to judge on their examinations bears some relationship to the inability of citizens to evaluate and decide in political life. The uneasiness (sometimes panic) students feel in making judgements on an examination is what citizens feel in having to evaluate and decide complex issues in politics. What is common to both cases is the apprenticeship students and "citizens" undergo that teaches them to deny the validity and doubt the reality of their own experiences. So the explorations outside one's immediate experiences— a major part of that with which education should be concerned—cannot be brought home, brought to a center (a self) from which they may be evaluated, judged and affirmed; they must be assessed and decided on, if decided on at all, by reference to authority.

Teaching that begins with experiences distant from those of students devalues the personal experiences of students, contributes to an uncertain self, and academically constructs a person who cannot reflectively judge. This is particularly easy in international relations, which has had a tradition that says efforts to make the general public understand it is a waste of time. To teach students effectively, however, one must begin with some of their personal experiences so that they can have the sense that it is "safe" to use those experiences as a basis for judgement in things considered important by persons (like professors) who are viewed as significant. By teaching students in this fashion, the professor simultaneously does a number of things. She helps the student to link the personal with other experiences that are not personal; she helps the student to see and hear his or her own voice in distant persons and things; and she helps the student understand that it is out of the aggregate of specific experiences that general conceptions are constructed and to which those conceptions must return to ensure their continuing validity. Further, she will help students understand that their own reflections (which they author and for which they can safely claim authority) can become part of the modes of thinking that characterize the university—as earlier defined. Residing in those reflections on their experiences, there may be something new in nature—something to be added to the human conversation. An example may be helpful here.

One of the ways of thinking characteristic of the university is the effort to recognize, classify, and develop configurations of relationships or of properties between and among "things." These things include one's experiences and the experiences of "others," including their academic classifications, which may be in the form of concepts, theories, models, and even worldviews (paradigms), among others. Yvonne, who we earlier met in this essay, recognized a relationship between the relative powerlessness of women and the Third World—a relationship she expressed in the form of a metaphor.[5] This recognition sprang from her own experiences as a person on welfare, one using food stamps, and her understanding of the concept of money and some of its functions in national and international societies. Recognitions of this kind are, however, but the beginning of the process of the thinking that defines the university. The uniting or conjunctive relationship that Yvonne identified has to be further classified (conceptually refined) and then developed. That refinement and development may come about through systematic research that can, at least potentially, lead to important findings that confirm or refute the relationship she initially saw. She may even, in the process of that refinement, develop new insights into power, money, women, and the Third World, among other things, and begin adding to the human conversation. She will certainly have developed new insights into herself and the relationship of that self to the thing refuted, as well as to the process of confirmation or refutation. This is what the professor can do by helping students to link the personal with other experiences that are not personal.

Yet the professor does more. In linking the personal experience to other experiences, she helps to construct or reconstruct the fractured self, to lend some coherence to an incoherent self that, by virtue of that reconstruction, can afford to engage in the risk of dealing with probationary conclusions, can begin to feel "safe" enough not to sacrifice the inner face in favor of social unity, and with some self-esteem and authority, can begin the process of judging. She also begins thereby to become the true citizen—one who now trusts his or her own experiences and forces political leaders and the state to devise policies that bear concretely on those experiences. To the extent that the citizens believe in the reality and validity of their own experiences, they will proportionately question and reject the false claims made by those who rule and who build their supposed legitimacy on rhetorical unity. Such citizens will also insist that their deeper concerns be appropriately addressed. Finally, among other things, they will help to make the political, as we have defined it, more of a reality, as the personal experiences of the general citizenry actually become part of jointly pursued ends. And since it is the general concept or body of concepts—with all its cultural and other nuanced enmeshings that, finding correspondence in the experience of a particular person, makes it intelligible, exciting, and truly credible—a healthier social passion will begin to inhabit public life. A passion that is not brought into being by the political rhetoric of the demagogue, but one that emanates freely from citizens. Indeed, political legitimacy will reacquire its true definition. And governmental authority—the right to rule—will become coextensive with the joint authorship of free citizens. Perhaps one could then begin to speak of democracy.

On the other hand, to engage a teaching approach that excludes or makes light of the personal experiences of the general citizenry, as many of us inadvertently or intentionally collude in doing, is to degrade the persons whose experiences are being excluded and to cleave society, socially, in favor of those limited few whose experiences are considered and used as the basis (usually, the standard) for the ends said to be jointly pursued. It is also to make a mockery of the political, since public life cannot be grounded on the impersonal, at least to those whose experiences are excluded. It undermines the true tradition of the university by suggesting that the unexamined life is one that people should live. Finally, it abdicates its role in helping to develop the citizen and reinforces the surface theory of political legitimacy.[6]

NOTES

1. See William E. Connolly, "The Dilemma of Legitimacy," in John S. Nelson, ed., *What Should Political Theory Be Now?* (Albany: State University of New York Press, 1983), pp. 308–37. He refers to a "thin theory" of legitimacy, and his analysis has, in part, informed some of my views.

2. Erik H. Erikson, *Childhood and Society* (New York: W. W. Norton, 1963), p. 247.

3. Connolly, "The Dilemma of Legitimacy."

4. Irving Howe, "The Self and the State," in G. B. Peterson, ed., *The Tanner Lectures on Human Values* (Salt Lake City: University of Utah Press, 1991), pp. 203–51. Though I have strong disagreements with some of Howe's position, his general appreciation of the role of the self in helping to define the nature of public life is admirable.

5. It is the contention of this writer that all concepts or theories are essentially metaphors.

6. My views on political legitimacy have been generously informed by Connolly's "The Dilemma of Legitimacy."

ESTELLE DISCH

10   Gender Trouble in the Gender Course

Managing and Mismanaging Conflict in the Classroom

1991: "We were raised never to hit girls but now with the women's movement we want to know whether or not that's OK."

—a male student

1995: "I'm against rape, but what if her tongue is halfway down your throat?"

—a male student

1996: During an entire class period in about the tenth week of the gender course, not one woman says a word. Two-thirds of the people in the class are women.

—author's observation

I WRITE this essay situated in a number of identities and experiences. As a fifty-six-year-old, able-bodied, white, Anglo-Saxon, ex-Protestant woman who has been economically comfortable for most of my life, I frequently have very little in common with my mostly urban, mostly young, mostly working-class, racially and ethnically diverse students. As a woman in a long-term relationship with a woman, my choice of a life partner also sets me apart from most of my students. Like most teachers, I am challenged to become multiculturally literate as I attempt to establish rapport with my students across differences of race, class, gender, ethnicity, national origin, age, ability, and sexual orientation. Among all these differences, however, the one that has emerged as most challenging in my course the Sociology of Gender is gender. Among the women and men who take the course, it is white heterosexual men who seem to have the greatest difficulty with me and/or the subject matter. Colleagues of color, in contrast, have told me that white students generally—both women and men—provide the greatest source of resistance in their classes. Thus, although my whiteness probably eliminates one source of resistance from white men, easing my way to some extent, the realities of gender often provide a major source of trouble.

I believe that there are several reasons for my difficulty with white heterosexual men in this course, given that I do not routinely have difficulty establishing rapport with white heterosexual men who take my other classes. One is the constancy with which we examine gender—it is the lens through which everything in the course is viewed, and there is no break from that focus. Another is the necessity to examine the close relationship between sexism and homophobia, which many people, especially some heterosexual men, find difficult to deal with. Related to this, although I do not explicitly come out to classes, I attempt to establish a gay-friendly atmosphere that appears to threaten heterosexual men who were raised to define as a "sissy" or a "faggot" any man who is not adequately masculine.[1]

A third possible explanation of white heterosexual men's discomfort is the fact that I present material that is critical of the gender system and the position of privileged men. I imagine that some of them think that, in doing so, I am in some way protecting my own interests rather than protecting theirs when presenting course material in this way. Thus, some assume that there is nothing in the course for them. Finally, men are always outnumbered in the class, which probably contributes to the defensiveness of some of them, and in a typical gender course at UMass/ Boston, there might be only three or four white heterosexual men out of forty in the class.

My experience as a white feminist teacher links to that of other women faculty and to observations by researchers who have addressed male resistance.[2] Crawford and Suckle summarize the problem of feminist classrooms thusly: "The likelihood that a woman (and perhaps one who is not straight and not white) is in charge, the unconventional teaching methods, and the woman-centered curriculum of the feminist classroom all provide potential challenges to men steeped in conventional masculinity and gender relations."[3] Orr develops this point more fully, discussing how feminist content and pedagogy threaten men in two major ways.[4] First, courses like this threaten the *promise* of white heterosexual male power held out to them in the wider social order. Men who expect to claim that power once they establish themselves in the workforce do not want to address the reality that power is frequently elusive for men. Secondly, these courses ask men to take responsibility for the *real* power that many of them do have, particularly in intimate relationships, and to examine the impact of the misuse of that power on its victims—especially women, children, men of color, and gay men. Most heterosexual men have called other men sissies or have been called sissies; the course helps everyone look at the costs of that practice, among others.

Thus, the sociology of gender is a perfect course in which to deliver a piece of bad news to those white heterosexual men who hope someday to achieve the elusive power they think is owed them as males. In the context of this course, men in the class have an opportunity to read about the experiences of a wide range of men, many of whom are deeply troubled by the gender system. Men are helped, too, to examine their own sense of real powerlessness as they compete with other men, feel cut off from the more nurturing aspects of themselves, and face the pain they have encountered in their relationships with women and with other men—especially bullies on the playing field, braggarts in the locker room, obnoxious bosses, abusive men (and sometimes women) in their families, and violent people they encounter in the street. Working-class men in particular can usually identify with the class-related aspects of male powerlessness.

The sociology of gender is a standard course offering in most sociology departments. At the University of Massachusetts Boston, it is a junior/senior level course capped at thirty-five to forty-five that primarily attracts upper division majors in sociology, social psychology, and women's studies. This course is optional for majors and minors in women's studies and is also one of many courses that meet the diversity requirement in the College of Arts and Sciences. It therefore usually attracts a few majors from other departments, who take it in order to meet the diversity requirement. White women usually constitute the largest group in the class. About a third of the students are men and about a third are people of color. I have been teaching one or two sections of this course each year since 1990–1991. Before teaching the course, I had for a long time been interested in women's issues, had taught courses in women's studies, had done my doctoral research on gender, and had taught courses on men's and women's adult development. Although I gladly took on this course when the colleague who regularly taught it left my department, I did not anticipate the level of volatility that would accompany it.

Apart from the kinds of difficulties described at the opening of this essay, which I will address in some depth below, the gender course has routinely been problematic for me in other, less troublesome ways. For example, there are frequently some women's studies students in the class who expect the course to focus entirely on women and who resent both the presence of men in the room and the coverage of men's experiences. ("I thought this course was going to be about women. I don't want to read about men.") Some are lesbians living relatively separatist lives, working and living in mostly female contexts. Some are out lesbians who pressure me to announce publicly that my life partner is a woman.

Another difficulty I have frequently faced stems from the fact that many of the women and some of the men who choose this course have had major problems related to gender. On the one hand, this provides part of their motivation to take the course. On the other hand, it makes them vulnerable to reliving painful experiences when topics such as physical violence, incest, rape, pornography, and male-female communication are addressed. For example, in one of the classes to be discussed in this essay, at least a third of the women in the room had been raped. In another class, a third of the students reported growing up in families in which a parent had terrorized the household.

Also, among the people who take this course, a few do so because they need an upper-level course in sociology or social psychology and this is the only one that fits their schedule. Thus there are inevitably a few people in each class who bring little or no enthusiasm to it. Among these, I can usually get through to the women but have a more difficult time reaching the men. Some of them reluctantly tolerate the subject matter and act like they are "doing time" in the course. Occasionally, someone mounts active resistance.

Finally, I have had a lot of difficulty in the past related to the course readings. For several years I used a text that I think is the best in the field and that compares the experiences of women and men while foregrounding women (Margaret Andersen's *Thinking about Women*, in various editions).[5] Finding the right balance of inclusive supplemental readings that would accompany this particular text was an ongoing struggle. Since the study of women is much more developed than is the study of men, it is easier to find gender-focused writings by and about women of various races, ethnicities, classes, ages, abilities, and sexual orientations. The challenge of managing a large reading packet was also a problem. I resolved this dilemma by digging more deeply into the men's studies literature (which is, luckily, growing rapidly now) and editing a reader that I am currently using as a stand-alone text with a few supplemental readings. In the text I have edited, nearly half the readings are focused on men and a wide range of other identities is represented.[6] Since using this text I have received none of the standard complaints, which included comments like, "I have no use for this reading packet, you can have it back"; "Will you buy back my textbook? I don't want it"; and "There is nothing in this course about men." The latter comment was made at a point when 40 percent of the readings addressed men's experiences.

A primary goal in my teaching is to establish a safe and productive learning environment in the classroom in which students can explore what they are learning, freely question new ideas, and communicate with me and with each other about how they are reacting to what they are learning. For me this means a context in which we set the conditions for respectful conversations so that people can listen to each other with some degree of openness and, hopefully, understanding; a context in which the teacher builds relationships with students and helps them to do so with each other to whatever extent possible, given the size of the class; a context in which differences of power and privilege can be named and owned; a context in which people can begin to respect each other genuinely, care about each other, work cooperatively as they learn, and minimize competition; a context in which people can feel less alone, less to blame and less crazy in response to difficulties created by oppressive social structures; and a context in which difference as well as commonality can be acknowledged and respected. I hope that in such a learning environment students can practice communicating across differences and become more proficient at living and working in multicultural contexts—in their communities and families and in collaborative efforts to create a more humane world. Since every human being is confronted with the realities of gender differences and many have experienced intense pain as a result of gender-related conflict and violence, I hope that students will gain a better understanding of the causes of difficulties between women and men and will know better how to relate to people of all genders[7] by the time the course is over.

In order to establish this kind of environment, I routinely do several things. First, I present ground rules for respectful discourse at the start of the semester and ask students to either accept them or adapt them. These are incorporated into a statement of student/teacher rights and obligations that I ask people to read in the first week. In discussing the ground rules, I emphasize the importance of sharing only what feels safe to share in this context and acknowledge that the subject matter is likely to be difficult for many people in the class. I have received no objections to the ground rules in the eight years since I began using them. I usually ask people to think about them and propose additions at the next class meeting, and occasionally students have things to add.

Second, for many years I have opened my courses with some kind of icebreaking exercise. More recently I have focused this exercise on diversity, helping people to look at how and where they learned various attitudes about differences as children. My goals here are to acknowledge differences, to encourage students to begin listening to each other, and to discuss how attitudes are learned. Third, I ask the class to do introductions—either asking each person to introduce him- or herself, or asking each person to interview and then introduce one other person. Fourth, I routinely ask the class to practice saying one another's names. Fifth, I assemble a list of everyone in the class who is willing to be contacted by others in the class, including whatever information each individual is willing to have circulated.[8] Thus, by the end of the first week, students have met several other students, have heard something about everyone in the room, have learned the names of many students, have received the names and phone numbers of most people in the class, have looked at the syllabus, and have reviewed a set of rights, obligations, and ground rules for discussion.

During the first several weeks of the course, I routinely put students in small, task-oriented groups so that they can talk more freely, get to know more people, and begin to have a better sense of their colleagues in the class. While I find that these techniques are frequently successful at helping to establish the sort of learning environment I aim for, I have had several very difficult experiences when attempting to do so in the gender course and have not experienced such consistent difficulty in any other course during my thirty-two years of teaching. The difficulties have centered on classroom dynamics leading to either explosions or women's silence. Other authors have also addressed these sorts of dynamics.

Klein identified three types of troublesome men in women's studies courses.[9] The "expert" is someone who claims to know more than other students, sometimes acts like he knows more than the teacher, and attempts to save the world from "reverse sexism" or "male bashing."

The "ignoramus" presents himself as ignorant of what feminism and women's studies are all about and asks to be educated. The "poor dear" aligns with how difficult it is to be part of the dominant group, soliciting attention on that basis.

Another dynamic addressed in the literature is the tendency for women to be less verbal than men in classrooms.[10] Couched in the language of resistance, some analysts of classroom dynamics interpret women's silence as their inability to embrace equality, find their voices, take on difficult men, and face whatever consequences follow from challenging the expectations that they will be silent. Thus, a resistance to embracing feminism is sometimes equated with an inability or a refusal to find and use one's voice. This might stem from either the powerlessness inherent in women's position in the social order[11] or the tendency of women to want to take care of men in the classroom, especially in situations where men are in the minority, even when men have said things that are offensive to some women.[12] Finally, silence might result from the sexual dynamics in the classroom, particularly men's tendency to sexualize the atmosphere and objectify women. Thus, Lewis argues, "the antagonistic relationship drawn between women's desire for knowledge and our embodiment as sexually desirable human beings is an issue that lies always just below the surface in the classroom."[13]

Women's studies classrooms have been designed to help women find and use their voices to whatever extent they are able and ready to do so, and to use their voices on their own behalf. A participatory atmosphere and a discussion-based classroom structure are designed to encourage a wide range of participation, with the goals of challenging women's traditional silence in gender-mixed settings and supporting women to speak in their own interests, rather than simply in the interest of protecting or impressing the men who happen to be present. I have in many ways designed my own courses with these goals in mind.

The incidents from my classes referred to at the opening of this paper reflect aspects of these typical classroom dynamics found in other feminist classrooms to varying degrees. I will address each incident in turn and will discuss how I handled or mishandled the situation at the time. I will also describe what I wish I had done and hope I would have the wisdom to do differently should similar events or dynamics repeat themselves. I will put these incidents in the context of other teachers' experiences and conclude with my current strategies for dealing with volatility in this course. Although these events occurred in courses that were evaluated very positively by students overall, I still feel haunted by what occurred in each of them.

"WE WERE RAISED NEVER TO HIT GIRLS, BUT NOW WITH THE WOMEN'S MOVEMENT, WE WANT TO KNOW WHETHER OR NOT THAT'S OK."

Shortly after the beginning of the semester several years ago, I asked students to sit in same-gender groups and to identify a gender-related problem that they were willing to share with the class. The class had read an excerpt from C. Wright Mills's *The Sociological Imagination* in which Mills makes a distinction between personal troubles—those difficulties specific to an individual or a family—and public issues—those difficulties that are reflective of problems in the social order that affect many people.[14] I had asked the small groups to assess whether their gender-related problems were private troubles or public issues. By this point the class had received my ground rules for interaction, had practiced each other's names, had heard people introduce themselves, and had done some sort of icebreaking exercise. When a group of two white men reported their concern regarding whether or not it was OK to hit "girls," the room exploded with rage. About eight women in this class of about forty started yelling at the men, incensed that they would even *consider* hitting a woman. They shouted things like, "How can you even think about hitting a woman?" "Don't you know how much violence there is against women?" "Don't you know many women are battered and raped?" "It's men like you that make this world such an awful place for women."

While the yelling was going on, I lost control of the situation. I was shocked by what the men had asked and, rather than coolly asking them what had triggered their question, I sat back, kind of stunned, while the more verbal women students launched and maintained their attack for perhaps ten minutes. I was unable to establish a respectful level of discourse and instead let the students run the discussion, with no effective leadership from me. I did monitor somewhat who spoke next but did not set any limits on the kind of discussion that could occur. Finally, when the screaming was over, a woman defended the men's right to say what concerned them, which provoked a few groans from several women. Although I felt relieved when the class ended that day, I remained troubled by what had happened for most of the semester.

As soon as I could, I met with the two men involved to find out what had provoked their question. It turned out that this issue belonged to just one of them, but in reporting it, they had made it sound like a concern of both. (In fact, the other man was much more concerned about the reactions he provoked by wearing an earring.) Apparently, the man with the question about hitting women had been punched at a bar by a man he didn't even know. He figured out that a woman with whom he had had a conflict had convinced the man to hit him. Based on his analysis of the situation, he believed that the attacker was innocent of any real motivation to hit him, so he wanted to get back at the woman involved. Hence, a reasonable question: "If I am going to hit back, is it OK to hit the person who provoked the attack on me, even if she is female, rather than to return the hit to the person who happened to deliver the punch?"

In the office, this student and I were able to address his question as a reasonable one and then to put it in the broader context of male violence in the social order and the absence of alternative dispute resolution. I pointed out how men are frequently socialized to resolve disputes by physically fighting rather than talking things over. I suggested that the high rates of violence against women—especially rape, incest, and battering—were a likely explanation for the women's angry responses in class. We discussed the importance of learning and utilizing methods of conflict resolution other than physical violence. He understood, seemed to agree, and said that he had not meant to provoke so much turmoil.

Although I felt better after talking with the men who had been in that subgroup, I did not find a way to constructively process this event with the class. By then the event was two or three weeks old, and I think I feared recreating it by opening the discussion again. We proceeded with the topics that followed, and I hoped that that level of volatility would not emerge again. After talking with the men involved in that particular incident, I believed that a statement that provocative would not emerge from those same students, but other dynamics in the class kept me both on my toes and quite anxious. For example, a black woman had confronted a white woman about what the black woman believed were racist assumptions, and the white woman became very defensive. This same black woman had been confronted by others about her antichoice position. A lesbian had complained that there was not enough material about lesbians in the course. And I later learned that at least a third of the women in the class had been raped and that many were hurting badly over their experiences. The women who were rape survivors had come out to each other in a break-out group, and one of them reported this to me.

This was the first time I had taught the Sociology of Gender, and the syllabus was inadequate in many ways. I had failed to address the causes and possible prevention of violence in enough depth. In spite of what I defined as a gay-friendly atmosphere, I did not have enough material about lesbians and gay men in the course. And I had assumed that gender meant "primarily women," and thus had too little information about men in the readings. Ironically, the men in this particular class didn't complain about that, although most of them probably felt that they had better not complain about anything, given how the course had begun.

The dynamics represented in this incident only partially fit the descriptions of dynamics in gender-mixed feminist classrooms named above. There was certainly an aspect of the "ignoramus" in the men's comment, and perhaps an edge of hostility in the way it was phrased—especially using the term girls in a situation in which they were talking about adult women. But after speaking with the men, I thought that their question could have been a very productive one, had I figured out how to handle it. There was some caretaking done on the part of a couple of women in the class who tried to protect the men, but that position was openly criticized and was certainly a minority response. In fact, rather than being silenced, a large group of women found their voices and let them out, loudly and clearly. They had had it with men's violence and were not about to address the men's question as having any possible legitimacy. Ironically, one of the silenced voices was mine, as I processed my shock and then addressed the issue privately with the men, rather than taking it back to the whole class. Of course, it would have been very interesting to do so, had I not been so caught up in my own discomfort at what occurred. We could have addressed the tendency for men to be ready for violence and to protect women when it serves their interest. We could also have addressed men's victimization by other men.

Based on this experience, I tried to address these shortcomings by adding more articles about men and readings that addressed violence more directly. I also learned to monitor the level of discussion better by interrupting and calling for order when people started raising their voices. I practiced monitoring who spoke next, keeping track of the queue but committing myself to call first on people who had not yet spoken. I paid more attention to the rules of discourse in the ground rules. I learned to refer more effectively back to this document when the atmosphere in a class became tense or aggressive and found that students were usually willing to adjust their interaction style to respect the ground rules. Things went well in this course for two consecutive years, until I was caught off guard again.

"I'm Against Rape, But What If Her Tongue Is Halfway down Your Throat?"

By the spring of 1995, I had resolved my content concerns by assembling a group of readings to accompany *Thinking about Women*. The readings included seventy-one items combining sociological theory, personal narratives, essays, and research. Half of these were by or about men. The text also paid substantial attention to men via many comparisons to women. Taking the text's comparative nature into account, the overall ratio of attention in the readings was about 60 percent attention to women, 40 percent attention to men. The articles and the text represented other groups as well. For example, about 30 percent of the articles were by or about people of color in the United States, about 15 percent were by or about lesbians or gay men, and two articles addressed disability among women. Issues of social class, of course, intersected these categories in various ways.

From the beginning of the course, a white heterosexual man who might be defined as one of Klein's "experts" continually challenged both the text and me. He would frequently disagree with data in the text when it contradicted his own experience, but he was not able to pose his comment in an intellectually mature way. Given that he was a senior majoring in a social science and had already completed many upper-level courses, his entrenched refusal to consider facts that contradicted his experience was quite disturbing, both to the class and to me. His way of "disagreeing" was aggressive, and I found him personally annoying for the first month or so of the course. A few students, both women and men, attempted to talk or argue with him politely, but most of the class did not. I sensed that he was reacting to several of the issues that typically trouble white heterosexual men in this course: the fact that the teacher was a woman, the challenge the course posed to traditional models of heterosexist masculinity, the fact that men were in the minority, and the presence of only a few straight white men in the class. I reached out to him here and there via conversations before or after class, and he seemed to me finally to settle down a bit. The women in the class were mostly silent at first in response to his behavior, leaving me to manage the situation. His way of interacting seemed to have the effect of silencing women from within;[15] they were not about to offer themselves as targets for his aggression.

About five weeks before the end of the course, a white woman in the class called me to express her discomfort with this man. She was critical of my failure to set stronger limits on his way of interacting, which she believed was at best annoying and at worst overtly offensive or dangerous to other members of the class as well. I took her concerns seriously and consulted with two colleagues regarding what, if anything, I could or should do in response to her request. Both thought that I could not do anything of a formal nature since the issue seemed related to free speech. I considered talking with the man but decided against it, given his generally defensive and aggressive attitude toward me. Given her level of fear, it didn't even occur to me to encourage her to address him herself.

I had conducted a midsemester evaluation in this course and had processed it briefly with the class. We had acknowledged the judgmental atmosphere that several students identified but left it at that. I see now, looking back over those evaluations, that I should have paid closer attention to that issue. Because half the class reported that they felt quite comfortable speaking in class, I did not worry as much about the fear of being judged negatively as I might have.

Two weeks later as a white woman student began her report on date rape, this same male student interrupted her and said things that many of us found very offensive. He started out by asserting that Mike Tyson, a famous boxer found guilty of date rape, had been framed, and then used the language cited above in trying to open a discussion of how to handle a sexually charged social situation in which a woman "comes on" to a man and then doesn't choose to have intercourse. Almost everyone in the class thought that he seemed very insensitive to the issue of rape. As men and women in the class confronted him about how he was coming across, some of them raising their voices, some of them coming out as date rape survivors, he got very defensive. Finally, to prove that he was sensitive, he reported that someone very close to him had been raped and that the consequences to her had been horrendous. He claimed that the class was all about "male-bashing" and that he was tired of that and glad he didn't have to take any more courses like this one. To that a woman asserted, "Good!"

From this male student's standpoint, he had a legitimate question. But the way he asked it—interrupting, using crude language, being aggressive and defensive—left the class unwilling to address his concern because they didn't believe his question was serious. Rather, they seemed to think that he was purposefully trying to offend women. I failed to intervene soon enough to prevent a very volatile and painful exchange. Before the class was over, about six people had left the room, some of them crying. A group of several women and a couple of men from the class spent the next several hours in the cafeteria, supporting each other and processing what had happened. Periodically one of them would come to my office to let me know they were still there, and a couple of times I checked in with them. Several of the women in this group had been sexually traumatized in various ways. The men were allies, there to lend support. Several other students checked in with me during the afternoon. I was so upset about what had happened that I spent many hours during the following few days phoning everyone in the class whom I could reach. I asked each student how she or he was doing with what had transpired, briefed those who had missed the class, and offered support, especially to several women in the class who had let me know that they were survivors of rape or incest.

The student who had made the offensive comments was also upset. He said he was sorry that he had expressed his concern in a way that upset people and asked me especially to apologize to the women who had shared with the class that they were rape survivors. He offered to stop coming class if I wanted him to. When I said that that decision was up to him, he said he would continue coming to class but suggested that it would be better if he stopped talking in class. I supported that idea and tried to help him understand why his comments were so provocative and hurtful. He said that his way of expressing his concerns often offended people; he seemed to accept my feedback and seemed glad that I had called. For the remaining five classes (yes, I was counting them), he remained almost entirely silent, and when he did speak, he did so respectfully and unaggressively.

At the end of the semester, he and the woman who had phoned me wrote assessments of the course that reflected the opposing views of free speech and danger that had emerged in the class:

> The class has been a learning and growing experience for me. . . . It has made me think about some issues that I need to resolve. . . . You did an

excellent job of protecting everyone's feelings and rights in the class and did a good job of allowing both sides of issues to be discussed.

—male student

The instructor must recognize that in her efforts to be fair to men in this largely female class, she herself was not protecting (fostering) women's rights. I felt very unsupported in that environment.

—female student

Looking back, I wish I had figured out what to do when the woman in the class called me to ask me to do something about a classroom dynamic that was very troubling to her. I also wish that, when the male student involved began to use crude language on the day of the blow-up, I had forcefully intervened by asserting that he was using sexually harassing language that was not acceptable in the class. I also wish that I had found a way of restating his question so that we could have tried to address it more calmly. In fact, his issue never got addressed because a semester's worth of the women's anger got unleashed. Following his comments, many students who had left it to me and a few others to deal with him now joined the fray, having sat on their frustrations too long. As with the first incident described, the male student believed that he had a legitimate question that needed attention. Unfortunately, I was unable to translate his way of asking it into something acceptable for the class. Instead, a battle ensued that left a lot of casualties.

On the positive side, many women students found their voices that day. And there are clusters of students from that class who have remained bonded as a result of this experience. Occasionally I still encounter one of them and almost inevitably learn something about someone else in the class because they have been in touch with each other. In that sense, my work to establish a sense of community in the classroom succeeded for at least a part of the class. I would have preferred, of course, that the students had bonded through some other type of experience.

For Seventy-Five Minutes, Not One Woman Spoke

In 1996, an extreme version of male dominance developed in one section of this course. During an entire seventy-five-minute class, not one woman spoke. This dynamic was particularly distressing given that women constituted two-thirds of the class. I had observed the tendency of men to dominate the discussion and tried to address the phenomenon of "those who don't talk in class" during the midsemester course evaluation by encouraging the quiet students to participate. I did not, however, press the gender issue per se. There were a couple of men who said very little, and some of the more vocal men were consistently prepared for class and contributing thoughtful responses to the readings. I didn't want to appear to be critical of the input of those men who were participating in a constructive way.

There was, however, one very verbal, white heterosexual man in the class who annoyed me and most of the class—another "expert."[16] He kept asserting that there was bias against men in the court system and that women exaggerated and lied about the issue of domestic violence. Apart from correcting misinformation and trying to keep this man centered on the topic at hand when he digressed, I did not intervene in any other way because I sensed that most members of the class were not taking him seriously. Although he was annoying, he didn't present his opinions as aggressively as did the man in the previous incident, and I didn't find him as difficult to deal with. He constantly repeated the same points, and it seemed that no matter what the topic was, he found a way to make his usual plea. He would make unsupported comments like "Rapists get treated badly in the criminal justice system" and "Most restraining orders are filed as revenge, rather than related to male violence." Although many people in the class really didn't take him seriously, I think now that his constant refrain had a demoralizing effect on many women in the class because some did, in fact, take him seriously enough to allow him to silence them.

At the time of the midsemester evaluation, about a third of those responding (eight out of twenty-two) reported that they did not feel comfortable talking in the whole class (they had checked the three numbers at the "very uncomfortable" end of the ten-point scale). This is an unusually high level of discomfort for my classes. However, since their most frequent explanation was "I'm shy in groups this large," I was not particularly alarmed and did not make a big deal of the discomfort; I didn't want to seem critical of people who were afraid to speak.

Around this same time, the man who complained about women and the criminal justice system stated in class that men could not feel safe expressing themselves in the class since they were outnumbered. In response to this comment, a black man with a good grasp of gender issues cleared his throat very loudly, as if to say, "You've got to be kidding!" and the room broke into roaring laughter. The group seemed to understand the irony of the situation: a man who had been assertively insulting women all semester said he felt unsafe to express his opinions. Frankly, I did not attempt to process this. Everyone was laughing so hard (including me) that there seemed to be nothing to say. Even the man who complained about feeling outnumbered was laughing, and it is hard for me to know to this day how serious his comment about feeling outnumbered really was. The fact that the class was able to laugh so freely led me to assume a level of safety that was not really there.

In reality, although the men were technically outnumbered, their dominance of the classroom discourse was unwavering. On close examination of the midsemester evaluation forms, I found that at least one woman who reported feeling comfortable speaking did observe that the men dominated the conversation. Unfortunately, that response was not read aloud in class, and I didn't address the issue. About three or four weeks later, however, the session occurred in which no women spoke.

Not really understanding what was wrong, I decided on impulse to telephone as many of the women in the class as I could reach during my office hour and ask them to participate more. I reached about ten of the twenty women in the class. I assured them that I would call on them as soon as they raised their hands rather than making them wait. I asserted that, having read their papers, I knew that they had thoughtful, important things to say. I gave them some information about male and female participation in college classes, and I supported them to take charge of the discourse in proportion to their numbers. This pep talk/explanation strategy worked to some extent. The proportion of participation women provided got close to 50 percent during some of the remaining class sessions. But there was something sluggish about the process. It felt a bit forced at times, and the spontaneity and humor that had characterized the group early in the semester was gone. Although most of the women in the class were animated and enthusiastic in small groups, once back in the large group they were hesitant to speak. Unfortunately, it didn't occur to me at the time to ask the women why they were so quiet in class. I had accepted the "shyness" explanation at face value and had not looked for other explanations.

Shortly after the class in which no women spoke, I met with the man who continually repeated his complaints about women and the court system. Since he asserted that he was in favor of women's rights and was planning to volunteer in a shelter for battered women, I thought that I had some leverage for asking him to change his approach. In response to my asking him about his comment about rapists' alleged bad treatment in the criminal justice system, he admitted that he didn't know anything about rape and didn't know why he had said that. I encouraged him to think before he spoke, to address the readings more closely, and to address a variety of themes. I encouraged him to talk about justice for everyone in court—not just men—so that he could gain some allies for his cause. He seemed to understand my point and said he was sorry if he had offended anyone. On the last day he apologized to the class for any hurt he might have caused.

Although I can't prove this, on the last day of the course, I got the sense that his constant harping on a pro-male, anti-female theme had affected several women in a negative way. While some of the men and a few of the women had actively argued with him at times, many of the women had verbally disappeared. In the last class of each semester, after students fill out course evaluation forms, I ask the class to sit in a circle and name appreciations, regrets, and resentments related to any aspects of the course. This is a chance for people to name things they haven't said and want to say before the class is over, to appreciate each other and/or the course, and to flag unresolved issues. This is the context in which the man who was troublesome delivered his apology. Although I stay in the room for this and students can obviously fear that what they say might affect their grades, some surprisingly honest things are frequently stated in this process. In the go-round, several women said that they felt too intimidated to talk in the class because of things that had been said that they chose not to describe.

In this class, I wish I had done several things differently. For one, I wish I had spoken alone sooner to the man who had felt so hurt in the court system. He was not entrenched in an immovable position and didn't want to be hurtful; yet his style was intimidating to some people. Most of the men in the class didn't take him seriously, and he ended up being laughed at at times, which was not an acceptable dynamic either. Rather than intervene earlier, from the beginning I left things alone, which I now understand to have been a mistake. I also wish I had tried to address the gender imbalance in talking. I think I allowed the fact that the whole class seemed to function well in small groups to convince me that the large-group dynamic was somehow acceptable. And I think I was fooled by the willingness of the class to laugh together. I interpreted that as a sense of comfort and safety, when instead it was probably serving as a release of tension in response to a stressful situation. I especially wish that I had asked people to explain their silence. I could have asked for that anonymously and would have probably learned something useful, especially about why the women were silencing themselves.

Managing the classroom conversation can be a daunting task. Helping silenced students find their voices, whether in response to aggressive men or for whatever reason, is for me the central task of classroom process. I know colleagues who enjoy a fast, loud argument in the classroom, but I personally find that mode of communication upsetting, and I know from talking with students that many of them do as well. This is especially true for ESL students and others who, for whatever reasons, entered college with a fear (or even a terror) of speaking in groups. The gender dynamics in the above examples illustrate a point argued by Amy H. Shapiro: when men are present in a feminist classroom, the reality of male power is everpresent.[17] In my experience, when the men present are aggressive, there is likely to be trouble.

LESSONS

These three incidents illustrate the complexity of silence and voice—how voice is expressed, how it has power to silence some people and not others, how it can sexualize the atmosphere in uncomfortable ways, and how central the teacher's role is in attempting to establish a setting in which a maximum of voices can be heard in a respectful context. The learning that I am most struck by as I write about these three incidents is the need for frequent reassessment of what is going on in class—not just in terms of learning, but in terms of individual experience and classroom process. I realize that the midsemester evaluation, while always very helpful, is not always adequate to allow you to figure out what is happening on a day-to-day basis, especially when there is a potentially volatile topic and when there are passionate opinions. I have recently tried two new strategies that seem promising, and I think that one of them has helped a lot in the last few gender courses I have taught. These strategies include the use of reading responses and the practice of collecting brief, in-class feedback.

In the spring of 1997, I began assigning weekly reading responses in the gender course that I grade pass/fail. I design them to be short (one page per week), convenient (they can be handwritten if the writing is legible), frequent (they are assigned almost every week), and current (they have to be handed in the day the reading is assigned or I won't accept them). I read and return them every week, responding at length to individual students who pose questions or share personal experience. Typically I write short comments. I pose questions each week to be addressed in the responses.

These sorts of reading responses serve many purposes. First, students read prior to class. Second, they arrive in class with some thoughts already formulated about the readings. Third, they can lean on their writing during class discussions—in fact, they frequently refer to their papers—and I think that the number of people who participate in class discussions is larger as a result. Fourth, I can get to know each student and respond as I feel is appropriate. As a result of these writing assignments I have been able to address conflicts that might otherwise have blown up in class. Finally, I frankly enjoy getting to know the students.

Since the reading responses open a direct line of communication between me and each student, I learn what the students find interesting, what they seem to understand (or not), and how they relate the course material to their lives. For example, in one class I discovered that three white, working-class men were very angry about affirmative action. Each had hoped to become either a police officer or a firefighter. In each case, a white woman or a person of color with a lower score on the exam had gotten the job, presumably because they were not white men. Reading about these men's experiences gave me the opportunity to empathize with their thwarted career goals, to offer academic and career counseling, and to attempt to help them understand more about affirmative action and workplace discrimination. I also learned that one of these men had felt put off by the attitudes of some of the women in the class and felt effectively silenced. Through my responses to his writing I was able to offer empathy for his experience in the classroom and could offer to help him address the issue. Although he never took me up on this, I was glad to be able at least to offer to try to help him resolve the conflict he had experienced (I never did learn the details, so I don't know what exactly was so hurtful to him and therefore could not address it myself).

In another example of how student reading responses have helped me to understand better the people in the gender course, I learned one semester that at least a third of the class had grown up with an emotionally abusive parent. Among the six readings to which students could have responded when we read about families, twelve of the twenty-five people who handed in reading responses that week chose to respond to a piece by Christopher Scanlan entitled, "It's Late at Night and I'm Screaming at My Kids Again: A Father Confronts His Rage."[18] The first student whose response I read asked me please to not return his paper in class because he was embarrassed that another student might see it and discover that his father was like Scanlan. As I proceeded through the pile of responses, I found eleven others similar to his. One student had had a screaming, threatening mother; the other ten had had fathers like that. By the time I read the responses, we had already discussed the readings on families and no one had raised what I've come to call the "Scanlan issue." It was apparently too embarrassing for each individual to mention. At our next meeting I was able to tell the class what I learned in their responses, was able to set what they believed were personal troubles in the context of a public issue, and was able to let those students who felt embarrassed know that they were not alone.

In a third example, a white heterosexual man had expressed outrage at many of the articles in the text, especially those critical of male abuse of women. He interpreted the writers to be overgeneralizing and labeling all white men as rapists. In my responses to him I could appreciate his assertion that he would never abuse a women, tell him I wished there were more men like him, and urge him to begin to question why there was so much documented violence by other men. He seemed to begin to believe that I was not a man-hater and began to open up a bit. Near the end of the semester he shared with the class a very personal and embarrassing story about a fight he had been provoked into by a man he didn't even know. The stranger had attacked him out of the blue—a perfect illustration of what I had been helping him to examine. I believe that the one-to-one, ongoing conversation we had via the reading responses allowed him to become a part of the classroom community in a way that was productive for all of us. He had begun as a Klein "expert" and later joined the community in the classroom as much more of an equal participant.

The second strategy I've used occasionally is a variation on the one-minute paper described by Tom Angelo and Patricia Cross in *Classroom Assessment Techniques*.[19] To do this, I stop the class a minute or two early and ask students to write anonymously for a minute about how they are reacting to the material or to the process in the classroom. In one section of the gender course, for example, I had shown a film about pornography that included some violent excerpts from pornographic movies, and I wanted to know how the class reacted. I learned through the short papers that a few people had felt upset at the film and wished I had not shown it. This taught me that if I were to show it again, I should prepare the class more carefully and allow anyone who might be offended or traumatized to skip the class. Based on the students' feedback, I have not used that film again (in spite of the fact that many found it incredibly informative) and have instead encouraged students interested in learning more about pornography to make a visit to a pornography store to meet the field visit requirement for the course.

In another example of the use of brief feedback, I conducted a short survey of opinion on different types of pornography. Our discussion of pornography in class had been dominated by a few articulate and assertive people who supported the First Amendment unconditionally. Examination of the harm done by pornography had been skirted each time the topic came up. Two white women students complained to me privately about this but said they were afraid to speak up for fear of being criticized. Through the survey I discovered that nearly everyone in the class was highly critical of portrayals of sex with violence and that most of the class thought that that sort of pornography should be illegal. Without that survey, which took about a minute or two to fill out, the free speech contingent would have effectively silenced the discussion of the harm done by pornography. The survey showed the class that there was widespread agreement about the existence of a problem, and that the disagreement lay in what to do about it. The students who had been troubled by and effectively silenced by the previous discussion were greatly relieved, and the conversation about this topic was able to move in a new direction; common ground had been found where it seemed not to exist.

Since incorporating weekly writing into the course and requesting occasional brief, anonymous feedback from everyone, I have not encountered any of the extreme difficulties described above. I think that the weekly writing is especially effective, since I can get to know each student and respond as I feel is appropriate. My one-to-one, written interactions with students who are troubled by the course material have enabled me to engage individually with each student around what they find difficult, painful, or enraging. This has especially given me an opportunity to empathize with men's experiences and to help them see the downside of masculinity and therefore the downside of the gender system. Orr argues that helping men to see masculinity in both its empowered and disempowered aspects is one of the most important pieces of learning that can occur in courses like these.[20] My experience supports her position. And, as is clear from the above incidents, each time I was able to speak with a troublesome white heterosexual man in an open way, the man responded in an open way himself. This gives me hope and inspires me to continue with both the reading journals and the brief feedback. It also inspires me to attempt to have more conversations in my office when I feel trouble brewing.

The ideal of knowing what is going on for every student all the time is, of course, impossible. My concern here is not to gather a complete reporting of everyone's experience in the course. Rather, I am concerned about what gets in the way of learning and verbal communication in class. I assume that learning is greatly enhanced when people are asked to effectively communicate their learning to others. This opportunity is lost when students feel silenced in a classroom. What I feel able to do, having reflected upon these incidents, is to check in periodically with people in each class regarding both learning and classroom process, and to be more assertive about any dynamics I learn about that are getting in the way of people's learning, freedom of expression, and ability to communicate.

The probability of any of my students seeing a world in which there is true gender equality is slim. I hope that in the meantime they will be able to make better intellectual sense of the gender system in which they live, to make better choices in their relationships, and to raise their children in more egalitarian ways. We are all working against the odds in this course, grappling with painful aspects of life that often seem highly resistant to change. My hope is that, as students are better able to conceptualize aspects of their everyday realities and are better able to understand why things are as they are, they will be better able to act as ethical human beings, freer from the bonds of gender. Students bring their gender socialization into the classroom, including the real and potential conflicts that being women or men entail. The conflicts described in this essay are the conflicts of the wider social order expressed in the classroom context. I do not expect these conflicts to disappear. I hope, however, that I will become increasingly proficient at identifying and managing them and, in so doing, will help my students to do the same.

Notes

Acknowledgments: Parts of this essay were presented in a plenary session at the meetings of the National Women's Studies Association, St. Louis, MO, June 1997. I would like to thank Pam Annas, Rita Arditti, Esther Kingston-Mann, and Tim Sieber for thoughtful feedback on an earlier draft.

1. M. Kimmel, "Masculinity as Homophobia," in Estelle Disch, ed., *Reconstructing Gender: A Multicultural Anthology*, 2d ed. (Mountain View, Calif.: Mayfield, 2000), pp. 132–39.

2. See D. M. Bauer, "The Other 'F' Word: The Feminist in the Classroom," *College English* 52 (4): 385–96 (1990); S. Bernstein, "Feminist Intentions: Race, Gender, and Power in a High School Classroom," *NWSA Journal* 7 (2): 18–34 (1995); M. Crawford and J. A. Suckle, "Overcoming Resistance to Feminism in the Classroom," in S. N. Davis, M. Crawford, and J. Sebrechts, eds., *Coming into Her Own: Educational Success in Girls and Women* (San Francisco: Jossey-Bass, 1999), pp. 155–70; R. D. Klein, "The 'Men-Problem' in Women's Studies: The Expert, the Ignoramus, and the Poor Dear," *Women's Studies International Forum* 6 (4): 413–21 (1983); M. Lewis, "Interrupting Patriarchy: Politics, Resistance, and Transformation in the Feminist Classroom," *Harvard Educational Review* 60 (4): 467–88 (1990); and, D. J. Orr, "Toward a Critical Rethinking of Feminist Pedagogical Praxis and Resistant Male Students," *Canadian Journal of Education* 18 (3): 239–54 (1993).

3. M. Crawford and J. A. Suckle, "Overcoming Resistance," p. 161.

4. D. J. Orr, "Toward a Critical Rethinking."

5. M. L. Andersen, *Thinking about Women: Sociological Perspectives on Sex and Gender*, 3d ed. (New York: Macmillan, 1993).

6. Estelle Disch, *Reconstructing Gender: A Multicultural Anthology*, 2d ed. (Mountain View, Calif.: Mayfield, 2000).

7. I say "all" genders here to include people who are transgendered in various ways (androgynous, transsexual, living as the other gender, intersexual, transvestite, etc.).

8. Lately I've been providing an information sheet for each student to fill out (name, address, phone numbers, email address, and any other information I might need relevant to the course). On the sheet I ask whether it is all right to circulate any of the information to others in the class for the purposes of networking, finding resources, working on group projects when relevant, etcetera. Usually about 95 percent of the class agrees to have at least a phone number or an email address on the list.

9. R. D. Klein, "The 'Men-Problem' in Women's Studies."

10. American Association of University Women Educational Foundation, *How Schools Shortchange Girls: The AAUW Report* (New York: Marlowe, 1992);

Estelle Disch, "Encouraging Participation in the Classroom," in S. N. Davis, M. Crawford, and J. Sebrechts, eds., *Coming into Her Own: Educational Success in Girls and Women* (San Francisco: Jossey-Bass, 1999), pp. 139–54; P. Orenstein, *School Girls: Young Women, Self-Esteem, and the Confidence Gap* (New York: Anchor Books, 1994); M. Sadker and D. Sadker, *Failing at Fairness: How Our Schools Cheat Girls* (New York: Simon and Schuster, 1994); B. R. Sandler, "The Classroom Climate: Still a Chilly One for Women," in C. Lasser, ed., *Educating Men and Women Together: Coeducation in a Changing World* (Urbana: University of Illinois Press, in conjunction with Oberlin College, 1987); S. Vandrick, "Feminist Teaching in the Mixed Classroom," *Peace Review* 9 (1) 133–38 (1997); M. Lewis, "Interrupting Patriarchy".; S. Bernstein, "Feminist Intentions."

11. M. Lewis, "Interrupting Patriarchy"; S. Vandrick, "Feminist Teaching in the Mixed Classroom."

12. M. Lewis, "Interrupting Patriarchy."

13. Ibid., p. 481.

14. C. Wright Mills, *The Sociological Imagination* (New York: Oxford, 1959).

15. M. Lewis, "Interrupting Patriarchy."

16. R. D. Klein, "The 'Men-Problem' in Women's Studies."

17. Amy H. Shapiro, "Creating a Conversation: Teaching All Women in the Feminist Classroom," *NWSA Journal* 3 (1): 70–80 (1991).

18. C. Scanlan, "It's Late at Night and I'm Screaming at My Kids Again: A Father Confronts His Rage," *Boston Globe Magazine,* March 5, 1995, pp. 14ff.

19. Tom Angelo and Patricia Cross, *Classroom Assessment Techniques* (San Francisco: Jossey-Bass, 1993).

20. D. J. Orr, "Toward a Critical Rethinking."

11 Odd Man Out

IN THE summer of 1995, my family and I packed up and moved across the country, leaving UMass/Boston after fifteen years of teaching. I left because I had been called by Reed College and asked if I were interested in a job. Reed made me feel wanted. The teaching load was lighter. The pay was more. I was immediately promoted to full professor. I was also ready for a change from UMass/Boston.

When I first went to UMass in 1980, it was an incredibly exciting place to be. The average age of the students was almost twenty-seven, and the faculty was excited about working in an institution committed to the education of the working class. Having grown up in New York City, I thought UMass was the next best thing to City College. Of course, working at UMass had its difficulties. Students entered with serious writing problems that needed to be worked on, and they often had to miss class because of real-life difficulties with jobs or family, or had to bring their children to class with them. While this created difficulties at times, it was also what made UMass so exciting. There was no ivory tower divorce between the real world and the academic world. Students had done more than go to school for their entire lives, and their real-life experiences gave them a perspective that enriched classroom discussion. It was also exciting being at a place with such a wide age range. Not only did I have traditional eighteen-year-olds who were the first people in their families ever to go to college, but many who had worked for years after high school were deciding to go to college in their late twenties or thirties, or forties, or fifties. I even had students in their eighties.

During these years, I never had an interest in being anyplace else. Seeing students who started with marginal skills and who worked hard to improve, students who were paying their own way and so really cared about education, and students who were taking their hard-won knowledge and education and immediately putting it to use in their community made teaching at UMass not only fun, but rewarding. During this time I taught a wide variety of courses, including African American literature, modern and contemporary American and European drama, modern British fiction, creative writing, contemporary American Indian fiction, nineteenth-century American literature, freshman English, the literature of the 1950s, and two of the English Department's three required sophomore introductions to the major. Virtually every semester I taught a new course and included books I had never read before. I believed that this put me on the same level as the students. We were all reading a text together for the first time in our lives. I also made students write papers before we had discussed the book in class so that they would have to function independently, without the benefit of class discussion. This, I believed, helped them develop confidence in their own abilities, a tool they would need when they graduated.

By the fall of 1994, however, things had deteriorated. Budget cuts brought many changes. We had not had a pay raise in five years, and there were no funds for travel. Faculty who had left for other institutions, died, or retired had not been replaced. Class sizes increased. There were no funds for building repairs. The main entrance to the library was blocked due to fear of falling bricks. I had my office garbage can in the middle of the floor to collect rain from the leaking roof. Because of the lack of new hires, the percentage of tenured faculty approached 80 percent. After fifteen years at UMass, I was still one of the younger faculty members in the English Department. Because it is a state institution, the operating budget of UMass comes from the state legislature. Additionally, and unfortunately, UMass is in a geographical area filled with more prestigious private institutions: Harvard, Radcliffe, MIT, Wellesley, Tufts, Brandeis, Boston University, Boston College, and so on. Anyone who has it together academically goes to one of these institutions, so the theory goes, and only the dregs who can't get in anywhere else go to UMass. Operating under this mindset, the legislature cut the budget by seventeen million dollars between 1988 and 1995. In 1993–94, Massachusetts ranked forty-third in the nation in dollars spent per student on public higher education. Between 1980 and 1995, "the state's inflation-adjusted appropriations per student . . . dropped 26 percent, compared to a national average of 11 percent."[1]

To cover the budget deficit, tuition was continually increased. Between 1988 and 1995, tuition tripled. This resulted in pricing out of the market many of the working-class students UMass was designed to serve. The student body changed. There were many more middle-class students, more eighteen-year-olds right out of high school, and fewer minority students in the English Department, and the average age of students plunged. Faculty morale, to put it kindly, suffered. With the faculty morale change came a change in teaching. Many of the English Department faculty became less accessible, there were more complaints about the students, and the number of papers assigned decreased, while the number of exams increased. A number of faculty wanted to come in, do their thing, and get out as quickly as possible.

The two CIT Ford seminars I was in were particularly helpful during this period. Finding other faculty from a wide variety of departments who were still incredibly dedicated to their students and willing to struggle to make themselves better teachers helped make the tough times easier. I have to say, however, that the CIT seminars seemed to me an anomaly. Although most of our students were not destined for Ph.D. programs, we were in the same "publish or perish" bind that constrain faculty everywhere else. My first Ford seminar was before I got tenure, and so there seemed to be this double message about what was really important. Fortunately for me, I found sufficient support for my belief that teaching was what was most important, and this was very gratifying.

One afternoon, I received a call in my office asking me if I would be interested in a job at Reed. Quite frankly, I leaped at the opportunity. I had always had an interest in being on the West Coast, and Reed had a reputation as a college that truly cared about teaching. The thought of smaller classes and a more supportive environment made the choice pretty easy.

This is not to say there weren't drawbacks to consider. After fifteen years at UMass/Boston, I was apprehensive about going to a traditional institution filled with eighteen-year-olds, most of whom had no idea what the working class was. Unlike UMass students, Reed students had parents who were paying for their education ($25,000 per year), often without the need for financial aid; and most of these parents had attended college. They were the exact opposite of the students I had been dealing with at UMass. Although my teaching load was going to be lighter, one of my two courses was going to be on Ancient Greece and Rome, something I knew nothing about; in addition, I found out that I was going to be one of only two African American faculty members in the college and that I would be the first African American full professor in the history of Reed. Despite these potential drawbacks, the challenge seemed worth it. I believed that in hiring me, Reed was signaling that it was changing the way it had done business.

At the beginning, Reed seemed ideal. The college had provided us a nice house to live in, directly across the street from the campus. The president appeared on our doorstep our first night in town with a bottle of champagne, and later he gave me basketball tickets for the Portland Trailblazers. This sense of community was appealing.

Reed makes it clear that being a good teacher is the most important thing. You are expected to be available to students. A directory is published with all the faculty's photos, home addresses, and phone numbers. Students demand your time. The freshman humanities course (Greece and Rome) *requires* a half-hour conference with each student for each paper. I had seven thesis students (the average is three) and met each one for an hour a week for the entire school year. Reed also has a weeklong orientation program for new faculty. This is a community that cares about good teaching. There is, however, nothing at Reed comparable to the semester-long Ford seminar on teaching at UMass. Being a good teacher, of course, not only means that one is extremely accessible to students, but also that one has reflected deeply on pedagogical issues.

Reed is also run differently from most institutions. The faculty has real power here, unlike at most institutions, where the faculty makes recommendations to administrators, who then do what they want. Because of this, meetings are much more important than normal and can't be missed. Tenure and hiring decisions are made by faculty rather than administrators, and departmental chairs and even the dean (there is no provost) have relatively little power. But at the same time, some things were less than ideal.

The students at Reed were clearly hungry. My courses on the literature of slavery, Ralph Ellison, and the African American novel were all over-enrolled; 50 percent of the senior English majors asked me to be their thesis advisor (all seniors must write a thesis); and most of the African American students make it to my office at one point or another to talk about life at Reed. On the one hand, I felt gratified by the attention. I felt wanted and appreciated, and that was nice, but I was also overwhelmed. With seven thesis students, normal office hours, and required conferences for humanities, there were many weeks when I ended up with twenty or more office hours. There were also department meetings, division meetings (literature and language departments), faculty meetings (all faculty and administrators), humanities staff meetings, and various committee meetings. Too often, one could get the feeling that Reed owned your life.

There is also what I call the "Reed Bubble." It is as if there's a giant plastic bubble dome covering the campus that no one acknowledges or perhaps is even aware of. Despite being in the middle of a major city—Portland, Oregon—there's an air of unreality about Reed. People act as if Reed is the essence of the real world. I think this is particularly true of the faculty, who are, by and large, much more conservative than I expected them to be, certainly much more politically conservative than the faculty at UMass, and much more conservative than the students. I believe this stems, in large part, from the Humanities Program, the cornerstone of which is the first year course on Greece and Rome. The course has an implicit assumption that everything "we" are derives from Greece and Rome, and this notion is seldom challenged or problematized by the faculty. My lecture this past year on Herodotus and Martin Bernal's *Black Athena* was the first time at Reed that Bernal has been the subject of a lecture, even though *Black Athena* is more than ten years old. At UMass, it's inconceivable that such a monocultural course would be required of all students. The faculty as well as the students would never go for it.

It is on the issues of race and diversity where, perhaps, the most significant differences can be seen between UMass/Boston and Reed. Diversity at Reed is a major institutional problem. I have already pointed out that I am one of only two African American members of a faculty of 105 (the other is in physics) and the first full professor. For the freshman class of 1996–97, there were no African American students. That is zero. Reed accepted fewer than twenty African American students of the fewer than thirty who applied. In contrast, Swarthmore, a school the same size as Reed, had 276 African American applicants; 137 were accepted, and forty-two enrolled.[2] When I left UMass, the African American student population was 13 percent. Being in an environment as undiverse as that at Reed is exceedingly unpleasant.

What happens in the classroom at Reed with African American students is also very different from what happens at UMass. The African American students at Reed are in an isolated environment. They are also less likely to have come from a predominantly Black environment before Reed. The classroom thus becomes a much more significant source of identity. African American students at UMass have their Black lives outside of the university. At Reed, the classroom becomes a major source of their Black lives. In a course with African American subject matter, Black students at Reed have a great need and desire to talk. They are on a campus that, to a large extent, ignores them. They can't wait to talk in my courses because it gives them an outlet for talking and thinking about their lives that they are denied in most of their other activities. This is not only because the subject matter of the course is Black. I have heard from many Reed students that too often, when white professors have taught courses in African American subject matter, the courses have not been successful because the white professor has not been sufficiently in touch with the emotional needs of the African American students. I want to make it clear that I am not arguing that courses in African American Studies can only be taught by Black people. It is a legitimate academic field of study like any other, and anyone who is qualified to teach it can and should. It is also true, however, that Black students at a place like Reed are looking for something emotional as well as something intellectual. They are looking for a role model as well as a teacher, and a white professor is much less likely to be able to fill both roles. This results in a kind of passion in the classroom that is usually missing at UMass. While I get a great deal of pleasure out of this and the African American students clearly do also, it is not always the case with white students.

Last semester, about midway through my course on Ralph Ellison, I noticed that the level of class participation had mysteriously decreased. I came into class and put the issue on the table for discussion. We had been reading Ellison's *Shadow and Act* and discussing questions of democracy, race, and America, past and present. I had noticed that the more African American students talked, and the more passionately they got involved with the implications of the text, the more silent the white students became. In the discussion, it became clear that many white students felt both intimidated and angry. They couldn't or wouldn't talk in class because of feeling intimidated, but they had no problem expressing anger at the students who made them feel that way.

When I began teaching, I had always feared this situation, but it had never materialized. I have to admit I was really caught off guard. Several white students spoke, and all expressed the same feeling. When they were done, the woman who was the focus of the comments spoke, and she both defended herself and apologized. She eloquently explained how isolating and lonely a place Reed is for nonwhite students and how courses such as this one provide an anchor and help keep sanity and a sense of definition and identity alive. She also apologized for her passion and remarked that it wasn't good if it was preventing others from talking. After all, the more people who talk, the better the classroom situation. The class then ended, and I asked everyone to think about all that had been said and to come back next time prepared to continue.

My initial response was to be somewhat angry at the white students. I didn't feel an apology was necessary. To me, the white students were uncomfortable, and they were locating the source of their discomfort in other students in the room. To me, the source of the discomfort should have been located internally rather than externally. They were being forced both to think about new things and to think about things differently, and they didn't like it. As a result, they resisted. I wondered why these students had chosen to take a course in African American literature. What did they expect to find? Was this merely a fad? Or, more likely, did they assume this would be like most other Reed courses, unemotional and overly intellectual?

You can't teach at UMass without bringing the real world into the classroom. What I mean by this is that the classroom is always an extension of one's experiences in the real world. The middle and upper classes have layers between themselves and the world that insulate and protect. The working class has no such layers. One of these layers is intellectual discourse that is divorced from politics. My classroom situation suggested that, despite its reputation as a radically untraditional institution and often associated wrongly in many minds with John Reed, Reed was not that different from other places and was not at all interested in shaking the world.

I received many phone calls before the next class, most from white students, and most opposed to the view of the white students who had spoken. At the next class, the student who had apologized spoke first and recanted her apology. She read aloud the opening paragraphs from *Invisible Man* and talked about how she had been made to feel invisible both at Reed in general and by the response of her classmates the previous day. She had realized that she had allowed herself to be intimidated, and she said that she felt white students needed to hear what she had to say.

At this point, I jumped in and said there were too many white students who hadn't commented at all, that the original problem was white students' not speaking, and that this was still the case. Every student who had not spoken then spoke, saying on the one hand that they hadn't spoken out of fear of "saying the wrong thing"; but, on the other hand, they rejected the condemnation the other white students had made of the students of color, and they too rejected the idea that an apology was necessary. At this point, the white student who had first raised the issue of intimidation also apologized and suggested that she had been too harsh. I closed by speaking on the necessity of open dialogue, saying that knowledge has to be used in real ways, that trying to separate the real world from the classroom world is a mistake that leads to disaster.

Back at UMass, when I taught African American students, it was usually in the context of courses on African American literature. Despite over seven hundred English majors, hardly any were African American. My African American students at UMass thus tended to be social science majors, with little experience discussing and analyzing literature. I think this is one major reason that they tend not to talk in class. (Although there is also a gender difference; African American women are always much more vocal than men.) It didn't matter whether there were two out of thirty in the sophomore-level course Six American Writers or twelve out of thirty in The Harlem Renaissance, an upper-level course intended primarily for English majors.

In the lower level class, in addition to the non-major issue, there is an intimidation factor. One or two African American students out of thirty tend to feel somewhat intimated and surrounded. They are also wary of being spokespeople for all African Americans.

In the upper level course, I think something different is going on. It isn't any longer the intimidation factor. African American students don't feel surrounded. Nevertheless, the result is the same; many African American students at UMass don't talk in upper-level English courses either. In this case, I've been told privately by students that the reason is because they don't think they need to. They are sitting back, waiting to hear what the white students will say. At UMass, there is a significant African American population, and that population comes from a predominantly African American environment. They don't feel the need to share their insights or to seem to be teachers for white students. I know that if the course were all Black, things would be different, and Black students would talk. I'm not saying this is good. I want every student to speak in every class meeting. And in fact, both in comments on papers and in my required paper conferences, I spoke with African American students at UMass about talking more in class. The results, however, were mixed at best.

It is interesting to note some of the differences between these situations. African American students at UMass come from a primarily Black, working-class background; don't see the classroom as a major source of identity; don't have a need to be heard by whites; and tend not to talk as much in class. African American students at Reed come from an integrated, upper middle-class background, see the classroom as a major source of identity (especially because there is no critical mass of Black students), have a need to be heard both by themselves and by whites, and talk a lot. Four African American students in a class of twenty-six at UMass will, for the most part, remain silent, either because they are intimidated into silence by being in the unfamiliar environment of a literature class, or because they refuse to be educators for whites. Four African American students in a class of twenty-six at Reed dominate the conversation and intimidate some whites into silence.

What this makes clear is that nothing is totally clear. Neither side is internally consistent, and it is seldom if ever clear that one side is clearly better than the other. From the UMass perspective, I wished my African American students spoke more. From the Reed perspective, I wish the African American students had to speak less. Each situation causes its own stress. What I am arguing is simply the existence of difference. The context determines the response.

When I lived in Massachusetts, I always thought Boston was the most racist place I had ever been. There seemed to be an open hostility toward all people of color. I hated living in an environment in which there were places I did not feel comfortable going, whether it was to the Italian North End, to Irish South Boston, to Fenway Park to see the Red Sox, or to Foxboro Stadium to see the Patriots. Living in "The People's Republic of Cambridge" made things much easier to bear, but not totally. At UMass, I felt marginalized and to a large extent ignored. I was the dangerous radical people had to be wary of. In fifteen years, I was never elected to my department's personnel committee, never chosen to serve on an administrative search committee, and never even asked to give any kind of presentation during Black History Month. This, in addition to the financial problems at UMass, made me eager to leave.

On the other hand, my children went to schools that were very ethnically diverse, approaching 50 percent nonwhite. In Oregon, my older children attend a middle school where there are not more than ten